D1084108

Wanton Eyes and
Chaste Desires

WANTON EYES
AND
CHASTE DESIRES

Female Sexuality in
The Faerie Queene

Sheila T. Cavanagh

Indiana University Press

Bloomington & Indianapolis

The paper used in this publication meets the minimum
requirements of American National Standard for Information
Sciences—Permanence of Paper for Printed
Library Materials, ANSI Z39.48-1984.

Manufactured in the United States of America

Library of Congress Cataloging-in-Publication Data

Cavanagh, Sheila T.
Wanton eyes and chaste desires : female sexuality in the
Faerie queene / Sheila T. Cavanagh.
p. cm.
Includes bibliographical references and index.
ISBN 0–253–31367–8. — ISBN 0–253–20889–0 (paper)
1. Spenser, Edmund, 1552?–1599. Faerie
queene. 2. Feminism and
literature—England—History—16th century. 3. Women and
literature—England—History—16th century. 4. Women in
literature. 5. Sex in literature. I. Title.
PR2358.C37 1994
821'.3—dc20   93–40515
1 2 3 4 5 99 98 97 96 95 94

For S. E., with much love

Contents

Acknowledgments

IT GIVES ME great pleasure to thank some of those individuals and institutions who helped make this work possible. First, I am grateful to the American Association of University Women; the National Endowment for the Humanities; the Emory University Research Committee; and the Emory College Faculty Development Fund for grants in support of the research and writing of this book.

I have been exceptionally fortunate in those who have read parts of the manuscript and/or provided timely advice and I am very thankful for their insightful comments. Any errors remaining are, of course, my own. Harry Rusche, Anne Lake Prescott, and Leeds Barroll each provided very welcome good counsel and good humor. I appreciate their patience. Maureen Quilligan offered invaluable suggestions. David Lee Miller, Lena Cowen Orlin, S. K. Heninger Jr., John Sitter, Gail Kern Paster, Barbara Mowat, Heather Dubrow, Mihoko Suzuki, Barbara Freedman, Karen Cunningham, and Peter Stallybrass graciously offered pertinent comments and/or vital encouragement at key moments. Susanne Woods was ever patient and supportive while I did my initial research and early writing. Catherine Belsey helped stimulate my thinking during my final revisions. Susanne Wofford, Lauren Silberman, Dorothy Stephens, Susan Frye, and Clare A. Lees kindly made portions of their work available to me prior to publication.

I am also grateful to session leaders and audiences at the Modern Language Association; the Shakespeare Association of America; the Sixteenth-Century Studies Conference; Spenser at Kalamazoo; and the Society for Values in Higher Education, who provided significant feedback and a welcome sense of community. I am particularly thankful for the many members of the Spenser Society and the Shakespeare Association of America who have been wonderfully supportive.

I did most of my research for this book at the Folger Shakespeare Library and offer warm thanks to the reading room staff for their assistance. Betsy Walsh, Rosalind Larry, LuEllen deHaven, Harold Batie, Kathleen Stewart, and Camille Seerattan have helped make the process of research and writing much more pleasurable for many years. Thanks also to Jean Miller and Georgianna Ziegler.

Michael Bellesiles, Kate Dornhuber, and Lilith offered me welcome respite—and sustenance—on countless occasions. Bill Lioni kept me thinking. Cris Levenduski, Priscilla Echols, Tom Bertrand, and Bill Fox are among those who make me glad I came to Emory. My mother, Eileen Cavanagh, Lisa Gim, Kenny Fain, May Lee Eckley, Patricia O'Connor, Leona Fisher, Teri Matthiesen, and Deborah Middleton provided much needed encouragement from afar. My colleagues and students at Emory kept Atlanta a comfortable place to write, while Nancy Cooley, Brad Brown, Maya Smith, and Michael Campion helped me keep body and soul together. I am very grateful to all of my friends for their continuing support.

My deepest gratitude goes to my husband, Chris Davis. Not only did he endeavor to keep me reasonably sane and cheerful throughout this process, he also spent long hours sharing his computer expertise. His partnership makes everything more joyful.

Wanton Eyes and
Chaste Desires

Introduction
The Manliness of Virtue

"LO I THE man" (Proem 1. 1).[1] A reader first opening *The Faerie Queene* immediately confronts the importance of gender identification through these Virgilian introductory words to Book One.[2] By announcing gender here, at the start of his epic, the narrator signals the primacy with which *The Faerie Queene* constructs and evaluates gender. The narrator is first man, then poet. He fixes his identity as male within a landscape which continually demands, judges, and explores such positionings.[3] Within the same stanza, the narrator predictably identifies his Muse as "her" (Proem 1. 2) and emphasizes her sex throughout the Proem. The gendered foundation of these opening conventions, emphasizing the relationship between a male poet and a female Muse, exemplifies the gendering which helps shape numerous facets of the epic—an important feature which structures the poem in a dramatic, but often unnoticed fashion.[4]

In fact, a muted but powerful ideological thread runs throughout *The Faerie Queene* which designates gender as the most salient distinguishing quality in the epic.[5] In Faeryland, anatomy is clearly destiny; gender is repeatedly more important than deeds.[6] The problematic choice of Britomart—an anatomical female, whose "gender" typically is determined by her apparel rather than her genitals—as exemplar of the only "female" virtue posited and the awarding of "the fayrest Dame" title to a male spright in drag at Satyrane's tourney (IV. v: 16), characterize the largely unspoken but central subversion of women which infiltrates the epic.[7] In Spenser's epic, women, however virtuous, generally evoke suspicion. Female sexuality remains intertwined with images of danger, actual or potential. Women and wickedness often seem synonymous, resembling Hercule Tasso's misogynistic pronouncement in 1599 which equates women with "a foule fault, a wicked vice or a hatefull monster" (sig. C3v) and Alexander Niccholes's warning in

1615 that "good wiues are many times so like unto bad, that they are hardly discerned betwixt" (sig. B4v). Despite the many "good" women presented in the epic, this thread of suspicion winds through the entire poem.[8]

The Faerie Queene, of course, presents a richness of ambiguity. Neither plot details, characterizations, nor interpretations can be fixed definitively. Both surface and allegorical meanings often elude even the most persistent reader. Nevertheless, the epic offers representational patterns which contribute to the portraits of women described. Although there are occasional exceptions, most of the poem's depictions of female characters raise significant questions concerning female sexuality, while undercutting the possibility of female virtue. By focusing on the narrative and juxtaposing widely disparate scenes, we can begin to recognize the often subtle, but consistent means by which the poem encourages suspicion about women's sexuality and character.

Furthermore, many critical readings of the epic reinforce such interpretations. "Blaming the victim" is a particularly standard occurrence, especially where Amoret and Florimell are concerned. Camille Paglia recently pronounced, for example, that "In *The Faerie Queene*, the ability to fend off rape is a prerequisite of the ideal female psyche" (186). Under this rubric, Paglia is able to find both characters seriously wanting: "Amoret's inability to defend herself shows she is incomplete. . . . It is her [Florimell's] impoverished lack of sexual complexity which allows a knock-off copy of her to be so easily fabricated" (186–87).[9] Paglia's scapegoating of the two besieged damsels is part of a long critical tradition. Thomas Roche, Jr., for instance, contends that Busyrane's house "is the objectification of Amoret's fears of marriage" (1964: 83); Alastair Fowler proclaims that Amoret's terror "is occasioned by sexual penetration" (53); Pamela J. Benson announces that the fisherman's attempted rape of Florimell "is delightful for the reader" (1986: 89); Kathleen Williams tells us that Florimell gets chased primarily because she is always in flight (113); and Helen Cheney Gilde dismisses Amoret's fear of the disguised Britomart as "charming and humorously pathetic" (71). Even more striking is Stevie Davies's remark in her discussion of Chrysogone's impregnation with Amoret and Belphoebe: "though this is technically a rape, it is never other than benign" (83).[10]

So long as critics use terms such as rape which they then describe as "delightful" and "benign," the ideological implications of such scenes are not being addressed adequately.[11] There are undoubtedly allegorical and metaphorical—even comic—aspects to many of these and similar characters and incidents, but those do not erase the metacommunications about women being presented simultaneously in the text. Rape, kidnapping, and torture are still being enacted upon the bodies of women in this poem with astonishing frequency. Regardless of a few pivotal moments of gender consciousness, however, such as Rosamund Tuve's now legendary rejoinder to Thomas Roche: "Hon, women do not fear sex!" (Roche 1983: 129), *The Faerie Queene* has traditionally been read without much overt recognition of the poem's repeated displacement, subversion, and abuse of female characters.[12]

In her fascinating account, *Milton's Spenser: The Politics of Reading*, Maureen Quilligan asserts that "*The Faerie Queene* is aimed at a distinctly double-gendered readership . . . [Spenser's] genius is to call each gender to experience the heroism of the other" (1983: 181).[13] While much of her argument in this book is convincing, Quilligan is overly generous here. Women can certainly read *The Faerie Queene* with pleasure and appreciation, but Spenser's awareness of a "double-gendered readership" seems to be fundamentally restricted. Although the poem is presented in honor of a queen,[14] and acknowledges that both men and women will read the epic, it shows little recognition that male and female readers might bring different perspectives and presuppositions to the text.[15] To borrow Kate Soper's phrasing, *The Faerie Queene*—and much of its criticism—is presented "as if one were male" (256). Female readers can certainly relish and learn from the poem, which many of us do, but historically we have done so only by positioning ourselves in alignment with what Laura Mulvey famously described as "the male gaze."[16]

In her recent book *Troubled Pleasures*, Soper describes her vexed experience of reading the works of James Joyce. Her account parallels the double bind facing many feminist readers of Spenser:

> I am without gender as a reader until some image, or association of images, intrudes too grossly for me to continue in this ignorance, and I am suddenly brought up against the fact that it does after all matter somewhat that I happen in the real world to be a woman. Within the same moment, I am made aware that I cannot really share the textual world. . . . I am enfolded within a perspective on women from which I sense my own exile. (248–49)

In light of the often conflicted portrayal of female characters in the poem, the disjunctive experience Soper describes is likely to arise for Spenser's gender-conscious readers. *The Faerie Queene* can become a "troubled pleasure" indeed.

The modern feminist reader, for example, may well be struck by similarities between the many acts of violence against women depicted in *The Faerie Queene* and incidents discussed in current analyses of pornography. Busyrane's torture of Amoret, for example, closely resembles what Linda Williams has termed "aesthetic sadomasochism" or "violence as art" (198–99). Although Williams is describing cinema, her observations easily apply to the actions of Spenser's enchanter and possibly to the responses of his readers:

> The "look" that governs cinematic narrative is founded on voyeuristic and sadistic male desires that, at best, treat women as exhibitionist objects, fetishizing their difference, or, at worst, aggressively master their threat of difference through various forms of sadistic punishment. (204)

The complex interplay in this scene between the reader's, the narrator's, and both Busyrane's and Britomart's "looks" clearly keeps Amoret classified as an "exhibitionist object" "mastered" through sadistic punishment.[17] Since the tortured figure is represented as silent, except when she pleads for the evil magician's life, she largely remains a site for narratorial and critical projections. As Roger Sale comments, "There is no woman here, only a breast" (141).

In a similar vein, Margaret Intons-Peterson and Beverly Roskos-Ewoldson describe violent pornography in terms which could also apply to incidents such as Busyrane's capture of Amoret and to the response of many readers: "The danger here is that its sexual themes may lull us into a sense of contented complacency" (218). Their additional remarks resonate through much of the Spenserian commentary cited above, especially when they note the ease with which pornography becomes "increasingly violent and more likely to portray female acceptance and enjoyment of male sexual aggression. . . . Violent pornography frequently portrays the victim as secretly desiring or seeking the assault and as deriving sexual pleasure from it" (219; 227).

These descriptions come perilously close to comments such as A. C. Hamilton's announcement of Amoret's "inner compulsion" toward rape (1977: 473), and indeed, to Spenser's own account of Leda's coyly smiling capitulation to Jove's sexual conquest:

> Whiles the proud Bird ruffing his fethers wyde,
> And brushing his faire brest, did her inuade;
> She slept, yet twixt her eyelids closely spyde,
> How towards her he rusht, and smiled at his pryde.
>
> (III. xi: 32. 6–9)

While the parallels between *The Faerie Queene* and pornography occasionally have been noted critically,[18] they are far more commonly explained away with allusions to Spenser's poetic purposes—or else the implications for women remain unspoken. The significance of these analogies for Spenser's poem, however, needs further exploration. Such scenes confirm Susanne Wofford's contention that the epic's allegory is dependent upon "violence and domination . . . to establish the empire of its meanings" (1992: 371).

As noted, it traditionally has been easy to dismiss such presentations of female characters by deferring to allegory or other poetic conventions, but as Quilligan reminds us, it is important to remember that "Allegory has always named a special kind of pleading for texts. If they appear to be immoral, outmoded, insipid, or wrong, allegory licenses the reader to correct them by saying that all the meanings he prefers to find there are 'hidden' within" (1979: 30). By ignoring or dismissing disturbing incidents in the name of allegory, Petrarchism, or Neoplatonism, we not only silence a central element both of the epic's structure and of the gender-conscious reader's experience, we also risk becoming complicit with the ideology which produced it.[19] Angus Fletcher astutely remarks in his study of allegory that "Allegories are the natural mirrors of ideology" (368).[20] Although allegory's mystifications often mask this ideological bias, in *The Faerie Queene* this underpinning subtly helps perpetuate images of female weakness, fearsomeness, and unreliability.[21] As Ann Rosalind Jones has observed, in early modern Europe "The extreme codification of Neoplatonism and Petrarchism establishes a common linguistic ground against which gender-differentiated writing practices come into high relief" (7). One of these "writing practices" is the structuring of allegory wherein conceptualizations of virtue shift according to the gender of the individual figures in it.

Significantly, allegory frequently appears to glorify and expand the fetishization of female bodies expressed by knights and others.[22] Just as the term "allegory" conveys from the Greek the sense of "speaking otherwise than one seems to speak" (OED), female figures regularly seem to *become* the allegory. Notably distinct from most dissembling male characters,[23] female characters repeatedly signify something other than they seem. Duessa and the False Florimell, for instance, present deceptive facades, while even Una possesses a shadow alter who makes the pure virgin appear unfaithful. Britomart, of course, looks like a man most of the time, while the dazzling False Florimell is a male spright in disguise. Knights and readers are forever cautioned to read between the lines or beneath the surface where women are involved, since neither appearance nor behavior can be trusted. In many cases, the poem is also bringing other values into question, such as the knights' repeated susceptibility to female beauty, but in the process, attitudes about female duplicity receive reinforcement.

Throughout Spenser's epic, female characters regularly serve as tropes, their meanings tentative and deferred, with their bodies seemingly reflected through fragmented "mirrours more then one" (III. Proem: 5. 6). Under provocation, Duessa's body reveals the loathsomeness hiding behind her beauty, and the Snowy Florimell evaporates in front of the assembled company. Even Gloriana's body epitomizes deferral by its continual absence and single uncertain moment of possible presence, helping focus our attention on the insubstantiability associated with women's physicality in the poem.

Female bodies remain open to endless interpretation. Luce Irigaray's formulation of "this sex which is not one" aptly describes many female figures in *The Faerie Queene*, whose sexual identities defy neat categorization.[24]

In response, where gender is concerned, allegory in *The Faerie Queene* is most fruitfully approached initially through its literal level, an aspect often belittled or ignored.[25] Attending to the narrative details first provides an invaluable insight into the gendered infrastructure of the poem. Critics understandably often jump quickly into complex readings of the poem informed by theology, archetypal theories, typology, or other important scholarly concerns. Nevertheless, by suppressing the surface meaning of the poem and leaping immediately to its allegorical intricacies, readers occlude the gender-bias such interpretations rest upon, thereby creating a reading environment for women resembling one which Claudine Herrmann describes in her recently translated *The Tongue Snatchers*:

> The woman who seeks to understand her condition immediately finds herself struggling with a cohesive group of concepts that are both suspect and well organized, a complicated network that crisscrosses all the givens of culture, whose every link interconnects and whose entirety unerringly reflects a man-observer. (5)

We can substitute various literary conventions for "culture" in the passage just cited in order to categorize the ideological nature of *The Faerie Queene*.[26]

Since traditional approaches to the poem have helped camouflage the gendered metacommentary which pervades the epic, it has not often been noted that, far from being gender-neutral, the poem employs representational strategies which undermine efforts of readers to approach the text from female perspectives. The narratorial manipulations of Mirabella's story, for instance, which I discuss at length in chapter four, keep us from hearing the captive woman's version of her adventures until after she has capitulated to "male" standards. We never hear the independent woman speak, but we hear several versions of her downfall addressed from a "male" perspective. In addition, the narrative often abandons Florimell and other women during their moments of greatest peril, a tactic whose frequency belies narratorial claims of remorse: "It yrkes me, [to] leaue thee in this wofull state" (III. viii: 43. 8). The narrator commonly employs similar tactics which encourage readers to adopt a "masculine" stance for addressing the epic.

One important step toward redressing such gendered misprisions is to return to those aspects of the text which have been suppressed, including the literal level of the allegory. As Herrmann reminds us, reclaiming or fashioning a female subject position demands that we set aside many of the presumptions we hold about language and literature: "If we do not want to be devoured by language, we must look directly at it, point-blank, as at a stranger with whom we share no prior understanding, no commonality of ideas to refer to tacitly" (12). Here again, we can add or substitute "allegory" for one of the central terms she presents; namely, "language." Traditionally, as readers of this text, we have done a disservice to ourselves and to the poem by relying too heavily upon tacit "prior understanding[s]" about allegory and other conventional elements of the epic—a process which has helped "devour" both female characters and readers. To adopt a phrase from Trinh T. Minh-ha, it is time for us to disrupt this "reign of worn codes" (47).

The dilemma about the gendered role of women in Spenser's *Faerie Queene* is most broadly illustrated by Spenser's approach to the concept of "virtue," which is the allegorical subject of his poem. For, of course, the word "virtue" derives from the Latin term for "manliness" or "valour" (OED).[27] Common usage of the word has expanded its meaning to include references to concepts such as good behavior, purity of thought, and spiritual transcendence, but this initial signification bears witness to the largely unacknowledged, though pervasive use of the word in Spenser's *Faerie Queene*.[28] Not surprisingly, "virtue" is generally assigned from the narrator's male subject position. In the very familiar words of the Letter to Raleigh, Spenser speaks of his desire to "fashion a gentleman or noble person in vertuous and gentle discipline." Such a "noble person" in theory could be female, but *The Faerie Queene* is more directly designed to teach *gentlemen* the kind of virtue drawn from "manliness."[29] Despite the poem's surface and stated emphasis upon the "virtue" inherent in the triumph of good versus evil, the epic's presentation of virtue actually foregrounds gender rather than behavior.

This conceptual model remains particularly relevant for female characters. "Virtue's" root in "manliness" is apparent throughout *The Faerie Queene*. With few exceptions in the poem or in the life many writers in this period portray, since women cannot achieve "manliness," they aspire instead to "their" virtue—chastity—thereby opening up a new realm of contradictions and problems. Many writers during this period, for example, present views of women from which the possibility of virtue seems excluded. "Good" women, it is frequently asserted, are actually treacherous or unreliable women in disguise or in remission, as William Whately maintains:

> Good bringing vp may conceale them [women's faults]; good instructions may diminish; and good nature for a while, may keep them vnder, and keepe them secret: yea the worke of grace may mortifie, quell and ouer-master them; but nothing can al-together root them out, so long as flesh and spirit doe strive together in one soule; that is, so long as soule and bodie liue together in this life. (1624: sig. D6v-D7)

Similarly, the anonymous *Discourse of the Married and Single Life* asserts that women's desires can neither be satisfied nor repressed successfully—a status not conducive to virtue: "If thou fulfillest all her desires, thou makest her vnbridled and licentious. / If thou doest not fulfill them, shee will then alwayes be melancholy and wrathfull" (1621: sig. E1v-E2). The misogynistic *Discourse* presents such opinions particularly forcefully, but the long, contentious debate about women which occurred during this period indicates that similar views attracted a significant audience.[30]

Spenserian "virtue" may seem to be comprised of more general attributes toward which all humankind should aspire. Indeed, it is often presented as though it means more or less the same thing for everyone. But *The Faerie Queene* did not stand apart from its cultural context in the promulgation of these confusions regarding female virtue. In the poem, female virtue is regularly subverted. It is often conflated with beauty, which is then shown to be illusory. At other times, it is subjected to incessant scrutiny or suspicion.

As I discuss in subsequent chapters, the representation of female virtue is almost always qualified in ways not replicated for male figures.

Spenser's presentation of "virtue" resonates with an effect astutely described by Jessica Benjamin in her discussion of unspoken gender influences in public institutions:

> The public institutions and the relations of production display an apparent genderlessness, so impersonal do they seem. . . . The apparent gender neutrality is a kind of mystification, like the mystification that Marx identified as commodity fetishism—an illusion created by the social relations themselves. (187)

Nothing in the epic openly acknowledges that seemingly immutable "virtues" shift in accordance with the gender of individual characters, but as the etymology for "virtue" suggests, women in the poem are excluded from being "virtuous" and the term's root in "manliness" closely characterizes the tenor of virtue promoted and valued in the text. Women in the epic tend to be judged by their beauty, not their behavior, for instance, while male behavior and attitudes consistently undermine female efforts toward virtue. Descriptions of figures such as Mirabella highlight unacknowledged connections between gender, economics, and constructions of virtue. In addition, the inordinate emphasis upon the gendered bodies of "evil" women, which I discuss in chapter 2, can be contrasted with the relative absence of such emphases when the subject is an evil male. Despite the exception of Britomart, whose ambiguous gender often displaces the misfortunes associated with her sex, repeated gaps in the poem between stated or assumed values and narratorial judgments are manifest, which often can be classified by the gender of the characters involved. The Squire of Dames' disparagement of the possibility of female chastity, for example, receives subtle reinforcement by the narratively adjacent display of "chastity" offered by the *male* Snowy Florimell (III. viii: 10), which the Ladies at the tourney do not emulate. Though the narrator claims that the Squire's story "The which himselfe, then Ladies more defames" (III. viii: 44. 3), repeated assaults in the text on the concept of female chastity imply a degree of disingenuousness in such assertions.

Spenser's epic is entitled *The Faerie Queene*, thereby accurately but silently marking the text as one emanating from the body and aura of a woman. Like the elusive Gloriana, female sexuality in the poem is fundamental to its structure and message but impossible to situate and define with precision. Also recalling Gloriana, however, female sexuality leaves many traces through the epic, which help elucidate the ideology even while resisting strict categorization. The tumult of meaning evoked through the "wanton eyes" and "chaste desires" of my title only hints at how richly available *The Faerie Queene* is for feminist and postmodern explorations. The poem repeatedly relies upon hints, clues, and deferral; disjunctures abound, and the narrative often shifts dramatically when stories are retold by various characters. Incidents and happenings can never finally be situated with authority in this text. Concurrently, struggles with many of the same issues involving gender to which we are now attending recur in *The Faerie Queene*, even though the vastness of Spenser's poem and the abundance of apparently contradictory messages make it a particularly challenging text. The poem itself encourages us to raise some of these questions, just as it brings many of its own conventions under scrutiny.[31] In other cases, the complexities of female representation seem less deliberate.

It is important, therefore, that we reconsider our ways of reading characters and incidents in *The Faerie Queene*. In particular, readers need to fantasize the possibility of female subject positions in relation to the poem. From such vantage points, we can reassess the role of Petrarchism and other conventional constructs in the poem; we can more readily recognize the interrelatedness of gender and status with formulations of "virtue"; and we can generally bring closer to the surface the mode in which narratorial maneuvers and characterological choices contribute to a poetic fabric which often disqualifies women from manifesting the virtues it exalts.

It is, of course, impossible to theorize a monolithic or universal female subject position. As Lorraine Gamman and Margaret Marshment rightly note in the introduction to their recent collection *The Female Gaze: Women as Viewers of Popular Culture*, many questions arise when we consider possibilities such as the formulation of a female gaze: "So how do women look at women? Are female looks at other women always about identification or (by analogy with male looking) objectification? Or do the dynamics of fascination and difference have other, more progressive resonances?" (4). Additionally, as Diana Fuss among others reminds us (35), the controversy over what constitutes "reading as a woman" and how or whether such a construct is available to members of what gender(s) is far from resolved. In reading Spenser's text, we confront further interpretive dilemmas, such as whether we can identify an Elizabethan woman's perspective. Despite these difficulties, it is possible to gain a clearer perspective on the "masculinist" shaping of *The Faerie Queene*, even though such a positioning necessarily only partially addresses female and/or gender-conscious experience(s) in approaching the poem.

Throughout the chapters which follow, therefore, I explore in detail the narrative strategies and maneuvers in *The Faerie Queene* which comprise the epic's gendered infrastructure. Simultaneously, in accord with Herrmann's pronouncement, I urge us to face the ideological implications of Spenser's language head-on, exploring, for example, the poem's many gendered manipulations of terms such as "worth" and "fairest."

In chapters 1 and 2, I discuss the epic's vexed representations of adult female sexuality. Chapter 1 focuses upon the prevalence of dream visions in female-male encounters and the tendency for suspicious sexual activities to vanish into the margins. I also highlight the emblematic and erotic aspects of "good" females, such as Alma and Mercilla. In contrast, chapter 2 focuses upon the frequency of witches, hags, and succubi in the epic and their shared etymology as nightmares. In this section, I introduce relevant material from early modern witchcraft treatises and from modern feminist theory in order to explore the ramifications of these demonic females' dominant presence in the poem.

In chapters 3 and 4, I emphasize the subtle importance of beauty and birth in designations of virtue. Patrilineal ties, for example, often quietly influence the fates of women caught in Faeryland's patterns of kidnapping and courtship, while designations of material or social "worth" contribute substantially to narratorial— and critical—judgments about characters. Gayle Rubin's classic formulation of "the traffic in women" finds many parallels in the structures of Faeryland.[32] Finally, in chapter 5, I maintain that

Britomart represents the only kind of female character capable of fulfilling the culture's and the epic's conflicting expectations of women; namely, one who generally acts and dresses like a man and who expresses little overt knowledge of her virtue or her sexuality. Like the male knights associated with the other titular virtues, Britomart displays an uneasy relationship with her "virtue"; in this chapter, I explore the role of gender in this complex configuration.

Since *The Faerie Queene* is a multivalent text, the task of teasing out its gendered foundation invites a breadth of reading strategies. Accordingly, I draw upon varied modern theoretical writings in order to elucidate the poem's polysemous patterning of virtue with gender. Feminist film theory, for example, helps us to theorize the positioning of female figures with regard to "male" observers, while the work of other current theorists helps illuminate the array of gendered structures within the epic.[33] My main objective is to bring to the surface elements of the epic's gendering which have remained hidden or ignored through "masculinist" readings of the poem. Just as feminism has rightly become "feminisms" due to its diversity, Spenser's multifaceted poem could be called *The Faerie Queene*[s]. In response to its multiplicity, I employ a range of linguistic and cultural perspectives to help situate possible "female" reading positions for the poem.

The Faerie Queene is a provocative text. It has inspired countless scholars to illuminate much about its historical, philosophical, literary, and theological foundations. Presently, however, we also need to explore the gendered assumptions which concurrently imbue this epic. For *The Faerie Queene*, it is time to reclaim "the woman's part."[34]

1

'Beauties Chace'

Male Responses to Women in Faeryland[1]

... by my side a royall Mayd
Her daintie limbes full softly down did lay

(I. ix: 13. 7–8)

Was neuer hart so rauisht with delight,
Ne liuing man like words did euer heare,
As she to me deliuered all that night

(I. ix: 14. 6–8)

When I awoke, and found her place deuoyd,
And nought but pressed gras, where she had lyen,
I sorrowed all so much, as earst I ioyd.

(I. ix: 15. 1–3)

ARTHUR'S ACCOUNT OF his first encounter with the Faerie Queene who then becomes the focal point of his quest can leave many unresolved questions in the mind of the reader.[2] If the meeting actually took place outside of the Prince's dreams, one is left to wonder, as A. C. Hamilton notes: "either the fairy rose with her virginity intact or she did not" (1977: 121).[3] Even if the pair came together only in Arthur's imagination, one might remain puzzled about the moral implications of such an erotic dream, since lustful thoughts can be as morally suspect as illicit actions. As the figure in Faeryland who generally rescues the other knights from their battles with temptation, Arthur's actions are normally exemplary, but the epic's portrayal of his responses to women greatly problematize his status as a superior knight and can unsettle the reader's understanding of the modes of behavior toward women seemingly offered as appropriate. As one progresses through the text, this discomfiture increases. Although the virtue receiving primary attention changes in each book, with the respective temptations shifting accordingly, disturbing sexual encounters seem to remain a constant. Women, especially beautiful ones, continue to provoke suspicious responses from Faeryland's heroes, no matter which virtue is the nominal focus of the legend under scrutiny and no matter how praiseworthy individual men might seem under other circumstances.

The question of Arthur's sexual behavior, for example, arises again in Book Three, where the passage providing the title for this chapter occurs. At the opening of the legend, Arthur, Guyon, and Britomart are riding together through the forest, exchanging stories about their quests and adventures. Their calm is soon interrupted by the appearance of the ever-fleeing Florimell, maniacally pursued by the evil foster:

> Lo where a griesly Foster forth did rush,
> Breathing out beastly lust her to defile:
> His tyreling iade he fiercely forth did push,
> Through thicke and thin, both ouer banke and bush
> In hope her to attaine by hooke or crooke,
> That from his gorie sides the bloud did gush:
> Large were his limbes, and terrible his looke,
> And in his clownish hand a sharp bore speare he shooke.
>
> (III. i: 17)

Arthur and Guyon immediately join in the chase, but there is a disturbing suggestion that their motives might not be in the best interest of Florimell's virtue: "The Prince and *Guyon* equally byliue / Her selfe pursewd, in hope to win thereby / Most goodly meede, the fairest Dame aliue" (III. i: 18. 6–8).[4] This impression persists when Britomart's response indicates that she assumes they are acting in lust: "The whiles faire *Britomart*, whose constant mind, / Would not so lightly follow beauties chace, / Ne reckt of Ladies Loue, did stay behind" (III. i: 19: 1–3).

Arthur's and Guyon's intentions remain enclosed in mystery and Florimell eventually escapes all the men who are following her,

but the perplexing implications of Arthur's participation never fully
dissipate, particularly since the incident occurs in the only book of
The Faerie Queene—the Legend of Chastity—in which Arthur does
not rescue the titular knight. His failure to intervene in the book
could be interpreted as one result of Britomart's inability to fall
and need rescue if she is to remain chaste, but the two episodes
considered here suggest that Arthur's own relationship with the
virtue of chastity is too dubious for him credibly to educate others
in its essential properties.[5] Despite the lack of conclusive evidence
against the Prince, the hints of something amiss are too strong to
be repressed, though the reader may understandably hesitate before
directing accusations of concupiscence at the ostensible representative of Magnificence in the epic.[6] Nevertheless, Arthur's relationship with the women in *The Faerie Queene* demands more attention
than it is normally given. The questions it raises help illuminate
the difficulties attendant upon portraying women in the epic generally and emphasize the problems of reconciling chastity with sexual desire.

Reading the episode in conjunction with modern theories of
gender helps reveal the vexed issues concealed in the epic when
women disappear into the forest or out of the text. In *Dissemination*
and *Spurs*, for instance, Jacques Derrida discusses gender and texual-
ity from a perspective which can help the confused reader understand the possible sexual and textual strategies explored in these
episodes with Arthur.[7] One of the most notable—and puzzling—
aspects of the Prince's sexual adventures is their repeated tendency
to occur somehow off the page. Guyon and Arthur disappear into
the folds of the text when they pursue Florimell, just as Gloriana
appears only in the shadows where her presence as well as her
behavior is suspect. The reader never gets a good view of the
proceedings and must surmise what happened from the most tan-
gential evidence.

Derrida's description of the text and its parallels with virginity
resonates with echoes of the questions surrounding Arthur and
suggests an explanation for the amount of activity which occurs
in obscure spaces: "The fold is simultaneously virginity, what vio-
lates virginity, and the fold which, being neither one nor the other
and both at once, undecidable, *remains* as a text, irreducible to

either of its two senses" (1981: 258–59). Here, the fold of the text becomes the space representative of the hymen, the membrane whose contradictory connotations surpass even the questions enveloping Arthur. Symbolizing both marriage and virginity, the hymen is the physical manifestation of the virtue the Faerie Queene and Florimell presumably seek to preserve. Allied closely with the text, "the closed, feminine form of the book" (1981: 259), the hymen becomes incorporated with what cannot be known; hence, characters such as Arthur manifest unclassifiable responses to its simultaneous presence and non-presence. The hymen presents a challenge to masculinity, but demands protection at the same time. Thus, male knights face an apparently irreconcilable dilemma. As Derrida notes: "The hymen 'takes place' in the 'inter' in the spacing between desire and fufillment, between perpetration and its recollection" (1981: 212). Arthur's relationship with Gloriana seems perpetually situated in just this space; he forever desires her, but the quest which would enable him to return to Faery Court and potential fulfillment is never complete. Similarly, he inhabits the area bound by real or imagined penetration and by his inability to recreate the moment except through recollecting it for the knights he meets on his journey. There can be no present moment for the hymen or for Arthur and his Queen; therefore, the frustration engendered for the reader by her entrapment in the margins of the text replicates the role of woman within the epic. As Derrida suggests: "The interim of the hymen differs (defers) from the present, or from a present that is past, future, or eternal . . . [it] belongs neither to reality nor to the imaginary" (1981: 231).

Applying Derrida's analysis of the hymen is less anachronistic than it may seem, since it considers concepts of virginity which confused writers long before *The Faerie Queene* was being composed and because it offers a useful vocabulary for discussing the prevalent distancing in the text of issues concerning licit adult female sexuality. Derrida confronts a recurrent theoretical inability to reconcile ideas of virtue with active sexual involvement, consonant with that which pervades Spenser's epic. In *The Faerie Queene*, the disparity between the governing presumptions of knightly conduct and the demands of physical desire remains largely unarticulated though dominant. Within the epic, the physical expression of sexual attraction is repeatedly withheld from virtuous couples, suggesting an insuperable discomfort with the potential spiritual and psychic ramifications of sex with honorable women.[8]

A similar question concerning the status of sexual intercourse in Eden stymied church leaders for centuries. Numerous disputes raged over the moment of Adam and Eve's first sexual engagement.[9] Some thinkers, such as Jerome, contend that sexuality belongs solely to postlapsarian humanity, with such physicality as one mark of the Fall. Others, such as Augustine, assert that the first couple had physical intimacy in Eden also, but that its form differed from that which evolved after original sin. According to this theory, had Adam and Eve remained in Paradise, Eve would have been able to conceive and give birth without the rupture of her hymen. In Eden, therefore, "virgin" births would have been the norm and the apparent contradiction which demands that chastity be both innocent and fecund would simply mirror the physical reality of female physiology.

There is a suggestion that the confusing encounter between Arthur and the Faerie Queene enacts a return to this prelapsarian sexuality. Since the pair apparently represent the highest fulfillment of virtue possible for humanity, their access to a form of sexuality available only to those of the purest chastity could be a further manifestation of their human perfection. Their union would thus always be deferred because such perfection must be impeded on earth, but the intimation that it is attainable could stand as an additional whisper, however soft and indistinct, of the ecstacy which could be achieved if Gloriana and the Prince were ever actually joined. Since such transcendent sex cannot even be imagined by the "unworthy," nor recaptured once past, Arthur can only try to refashion it fleetingly through further dreams or retellings of his tale. At the same time, since it remains forever unclear whether the tryst ever took place, neither Arthur, his auditors, nor the reader are forced in this instance to contend with those aspects of sexuality which disturbed the church patriarchs. Erotic thoughts may prompt censure, but they are not as compromising for virtuous knights as erotic actions would be.[10]

When the Faerie Queene is absent, Arthur consoles himself by recreating for his companions, through narrative, the nocturnal

scene of passion, real or imagined.[11] Such storytelling evolves into
an act of verbal masturbation, in part since the sexual encounter
being described derived much of its intensity from the Faerie
Queene's words: "Was neuer hart so rauisht with delight, / Ne liuing man like *words* did euer heare, / As she to me deliuered all that
night" (I. ix: 14. 6–8; emphasis added). This emphasis upon aural
sex may make Gloriana's existence merely as a phantasm somewhat
suspect, since, as Freud reminds us, most dreams are dominantly
visual, not auditory (1965b: 82).[12] At the same time, it increases our
awareness of a close interweaving of sexuality and textuality and
of a further distancing of physical union from sexual fulfillment.
Arthur's powerfully erotic engagement with his beloved seems remarkably unconcerned with the body. As befits a love organized
around a monumental separation, orgasm here emanates from
words, not deeds.

Arthur attempts to resuscitate this verbally induced ecstacy
through his storytelling in Book One and by encouraging Guyon
to recount tales of Gloriana's beauty in Book Two. Resembling
Britomart, who regularly seeks news of Artegall through disingen-
uous means, Arthur here feigns non-recognition of the portrait
decorating Guyon's shield, and urges his companion to reveal the
woman's significance: "why on your shield so goodly scord / Beare
ye the picture of that Ladies head?" (II. ix: 2. 7–8). When he admits
his prior affiliation with the Queen, he reveals his sexual longing
for his imaged love: "sufficient were that hire / For losse of thousand liues, to dye at her desire" (II. ix: 5. 8–9). Denied the physical
union he yearns for—"such happinesse / Heauen doth to me enuy,
and fortune fauorlesse" (II. ix: 7. 8–9)—he counters the barrenness
of his quest with long discussions about his beloved: "So talked
they, the whiles / They wasted had much way, and measurd many
miles" (II. ix: 9. 8–9).

Arthur's conversation with Guyon also introduces another dis-
concerting element of the Prince's deferred reunion with the source
of his desire. His questions about the shield recall his description
of the dream in Book One, where an unexplained pallor of death
hovers over the proceedings, "Ne *liuing* man like words did euer
heare" (I. ix: 14. 7; emphasis added). Although death and sex are
commonly connected linguistically in the sixteenth century, this

departure from the normal pun on "to die" increases the uneasiness associated with this scene. The emphasis rests upon the already dead, not upon an analogy between death and orgasm or upon what might occur in the ecstacy of heaven. Similarly, Arthur focuses upon the deathly manifestation of Guyon's shield—"in that picture dead"—rather than upon either the insufficiency or success of the portrait's depiction of a living beauty: "Full liuely is the semblaunt, though the substance dead" (II. ix: 2. 9).[13]

These instances of equating Gloriana with death suggest one possible reason for Arthur's perpetual sublimation of his sexual desire for the Queen. In each case, the representation of the beloved distances the knight from the danger implicitly allied with the actual woman. The protection of the dream, for instance, prevents Arthur from becoming the actual embodiment of "no liuing man"; instead, he is cast as a dreamer, caught in the limbo between conscious life and the abyss of death. In *Spurs*, Derrida traces a similar pattern connecting women, dreams, and death, which highlights the fear often portrayed as commingling with male desire: " 'When we love a woman' describes a simultaneous movement of the somnambulistic risk of death, death's dream, sublimation and the dissimulation of nature" (1978: 45; 47); and, "The dream of death begins. It is woman" (1978: 89). The ambiguity of the dream's essence seems to protect Arthur, despite the deathly aura of the encounter, but the implied equation between women and lifelessness continues to exert a powerful influence.

Similarly, the image on Guyon's shield paradoxically lives, even though the narrative intimates that its original "substance" may not. The "living" portrait can therefore be honored without fear of engulfment by the deathly environment of its model. The verbal and pictorial representations of the idealized woman seem to guard against the possible sinister aspects of Gloriana's female power; hence, although Arthur repeatedly proclaims regret for their separation, there are numerous indications that imagined consummations are preferable to actual encounters. Directing his praise and sensual response toward an absent, unattainable Gloriana separates the Prince from the close contact with death which threatens to accompany her actual manifestation.

Even though Arthur's adulation and demonstrated passion for his faery love suggest that he desires her presence greatly, these repeated allusions to death indicate the "dread," as Freud terms it, which a man may feel in the presence of a woman, whose "eternally inexplicable, mysterious and strange nature . . . seems hostile" (1947: 228). The poem here, as with other knights, elects to stage Arthur's "experience" of sex in narrative terms, rather than risk an immediate physical union. Since numerous early modern tracts describe the purported dangers associated with sexual intercourse— "For in some Women the wombe is so greedy and lickerish that it doeth euen come down to meet nature" (Guillemeau, sig. o2–o2v)—while discussing the multiple problems acccompanying any interaction with women, it seems entirely conceivable that Arthur would choose narrative sex rather than risk physical union with even a majestic member of the gender so closely affiliated with the end as well as the beginning of life. Verbal intercourse about one's beloved can be infinitely safer than sexual intercourse with her.[14] When Lacan speaks of the "castrating and devouring, dislocating and astounding effects of female activity" (92), he is merely reiterating what Arthur is being shown to sense and what numerous writers in this period insisted upon.

Hélène Cixous's discussions of masculine dreams and the so-called "enigma of woman" help illuminate this reading of the dream sequence. The incident, whether real or imagined, could be transformed into a dream in order to keep Gloriana in a more empowering position than as the threat her presence would provide. In Cixous's terms: "Man's dream: I love her—absent, hence desirable . . . Because she isn't there when she is . . . Where is she, where is woman in all the scenes he stages within the literary enclosure? . . . she is in the shadow. In the shadow he throws on her; the shadow she is" (67). Gloriana's image on a shield and the pressed grass where she lay keep her embodied solely as image or shadow. Knights work hard to preserve virtuous women in *The Faerie Queene* as objects for quests or inhabitants of domestic spheres of learning rather than as daily companions; therefore, encapsulating Gloriana in a dream or in an emblem ensures that love will remain, as Cixous calls it, a "threshold business" (67) which will not interfere with male domains or adventures. Woman thus occupies the place of the trace,[15] forever deferred and yet endlessly sought, even though she is neither truly obtainable nor often sought directly. When he enlists his dreams for "wish-fulfillment" (Freud 1965b: 155), Arthur is shown situating himself within a sexual milieu which facilitates all the pleasures of genital contact without any potential concurrent threats.

Unfortunately, however, Arthur's pursuit of the regrettably magnetic Florimell, which pointedly constitutes his only activity in Book Three, can be readily perceived as one repercussion emanating from suppressed erotic feelings. In a dramatic departure from the pattern followed in the other books, Arthur does not arrive to rescue the titular knight in the eighth canto of the Legend of Chastity. Instead, he is already present when the tale begins and he devotes all of his energy to this fervent chase after the woman whose haste "scarse them leasure gaue, her passing to behold" (III. i: 15. 9). The narrative attempts to deflect accusations of unseemly Princely ardor, claiming, for instance, that Arthur's praiseworthy motive is "To reskew her from shamefull villany" (III. i: 18. 5). But such assertions lose credence when Timias is left alone to pursue the source of Florimell's distress, while Arthur and Guyon "Her selfe pursewd, in hope to win thereby / Most goodly meede" (III. i: 18. 7–8). The emphasis throughout this interlude remains on male "leasure" and desire, with Florimell's fate left fixed within its usual perilous space. The definition of "meede" as "reward" may dominate, but its secondary sense, that of "unlawful gain" (OED), cannot be completely suppressed and the "reward" need not be virtuous.

As Arthur approaches Florimell, the erotic nature of his quest comes into sharper focus—"Then gan he freshly pricke his fomy steed" (III. iv: 48. 2)—and she renews her efforts to escape, "With no lesse haste, and eke with no lesse dreed, / That fearefull Ladie fled from him" (III. iv: 50. 1–2). Hamilton's gloss on the passage suggests that her continued flight emanates from "the apprehension of women in love" (1977: 344), but the pitch of Arthur's sexual frenzy and his method of reassuring her of his honorable intent rightly fail to calm this perpetual prey. While there are regular

indications that Florimell is presumed to possess limited powers of
discernment which impede her ability to distinguish between worthy and suspect offers of assistance or sanctuary, her refusal to
tarry here seems warranted, despite the narrator's assertions to the
contrary.[16]

Not only does his lustful chase introduce ample cause for caution, but the Prince's "Many meeke wordes" (III. iv: 48.
9) do little
to assuage the atmosphere of erotic intent when the reader recalls
the meaningful collaboration between words and sexual intimacy
discussed above.[17] Since the potential rescuer has already helped
establish a sensual association between language and sex, his unavoidable panting here—from his sustained haste, if not completely
from sexual arousal—merely increases the suspicion he incurs when
"Aloud to her he oftentimes did call" (III. iv: 48. 6). With the
foster long gone, Florimell has no immediate need of Arthur's aid,
but she receives ample warning to fear the kind of assistance he
might be offering. Proteus's parallel "speeches milde" (III. viii:
34.1) later prove to be the prelude to an attempted "bold assault"
(III. viii: 36.1), thereby justifying this tremulous maiden's caution
in this episode.

When Florimell's phenomenal riding ability and the onset of
night allow her finally to lose her pursuer, the lustful origin of the
Prince's chase becomes even more apparent. As soon as she eludes
him, he falls to the ground, clearly hoping to induce a dream such
as the one he experienced earlier in the poem: "Downe himselfe
he layd / Vpon the grassie ground, to sleepe a throw" (III. iv: 53.
7–8). The scene contrasts harshly with the previous situation, however. Instead of the rapturous words and embraces of his faerie
lover, "The cold earth was his couch, the hard steele his pillow"
(III. iv: 53. 9). The knight displays an overwhelming interest in his
own erotic loss, rather than Florimell's safety, as he tosses and
turns, bemoaning his hard fate. It seems unlikely that he would be
presented in such a distraught state if a pleasant chat or comfort
for the frightened lady were the goal. The substance of his anguished thoughts indicates how completely, though unsuccessfully,
the two women were conflated through desire: "Oft did he wish,
that Lady faire mote bee / His Faery Queene, for whom he did

complaine: / Or that his Faery Queene were such, as shee" (III. iv: 54. 5–7). The vehemence of the aubade which replaces his slumber and his "heauvie looke and lumpish pace" (III. iv: 61. 7) the next morning reinforce the suggestion that Arthur is evincing strongly disappointed sexual desire for a lost lady.

The Prince's lament renews questions about the mode of male sexual behavior apparently being sanctioned. There is no tangible evidence that Florimell has aroused Arthur's desire purposefully; hence, she cannot be held responsible for the heat of his pursuit.[18] On the other hand, since the Prince is supposed to be an exemplary figure, his actions may prompt doubts about the virtue he represents.

The disturbing nature of Arthur's response to Florimell suggests that the pleasure derived from serving the image of an absent love does not suppress all erotic impulses, especially because Arthur's knighthood precludes a sexual relationship with Gloriana outside marriage. Although Florimell should also be protected by this precept, her victimization here indicates that the Prince transfers to her the weight of his sensual desires, which he cannot rightly direct toward Gloriana. The chaste, iconic lover can only be guarded successfully, the text implies, if physical demands can be diverted elsewhere.

Although Florimell safely eludes her eager pursuer, she remains the target of Arthur's deflected lust for Gloriana. The fetishistic quality of the portrait on Guyon's shield, combined with the Prince's profound interest in the image, further illustrates Arthur's displaced desire, which helps preserve Gloriana's position as the unsullied site of future consummation. His residual sexual energy needs to be diverted, (seven years of celibacy is apparently seen as a bleak prospect for a young knight, no matter how august he might be) and Florimell's renowned beauty becomes the object of his quest to satisfy excess libido.

Subsequently, in the Legend of Friendship, Arthur is also shown attempting to channel some of his passion toward Belphoebe, but his efforts here do not succeed. Nonetheless, before rescuing them, he presses Æmylia and Amoret for information regarding the sylvan virgin,[19] who bears a close resemblance to his absent Queen:

And euermore he greatly did desire
  To know, what Virgin did them thence vnbind;
  And oft of them did earnestly inquire,
  Where was her won, and how he mote her find.
                                    (IV. viii: 22. 1–4)

The women would not tell him anything—"when as nought according to his mind / He could outlearne" (IV. viii: 22. 5–6)—so he continues on his way with the pair, but his insistent interrogation seems too emphatic for a mere casual interest in an unknown person. Belphoebe, like Florimell, offers the possibility of communion with an image of Gloriana.

The narrator again tries to deactivate any suspicion that the women's sexual integrity enters into jeopardy, but his reassurances lose their effectiveness in light of Arthur's other encounters with women, particularly since this journey includes substantial "conuersation." The readers are told that the meeting took place in a time of "simple truth and blamelesse chastitie" (IV. viii: 30. 3), when "The Lyon there did with the Lambe consort" (IV. viii: 31. 1). Nevertheless, in typical Spenserian fashion, we are also reminded of the obstacles impeding chastity which assail young, lustful knights: "And hard to finde, that heat of youthfull spright / For ought will from his greedie pleasure spare, / More hard for hungry steed t'abstaine from pleasant lare" (IV. viii: 29. 7–9). The potential danger represented by Arthur should not be minimized, particularly since the narrator frequently reminds us that the epic takes place after the Golden Age has ended, not during the halcyon era invoked. When one notes further that the narrator hopes that none of "These gentle Ladies will misdeeme too light" (IV. viii: 29. 4), with no similar mention of Arthur, it becomes difficult to allay doubts about the Prince, even without direct evidence of "lawlesse lust" or "bestiall delight" (IV. viii: 32. 3, 4).

Consequently, Arthur's absence during Britomart's adventure supports the suggestion that chastity is, as it is often considered, primarily a female virtue. The Red Crosse Knight's ability to recover from sexual lapses and the resilience of Arthur's reputation are apparently not available to Britomart, whose chastity needs to remain unscathed and unquestioned, since it is irredeemable if lost.

Although Arthur and other titular knights display moments of sexual weakness, Britomart never wavers from her quest for Artegall—except, significantly, when she suspects him of misdealings with another woman. The men, however, weaken regularly, and as we have seen, the Prince is no exception. Although Artegall is able to steel Arthur against Duessa when she threatens to soften his princely "tender hart" (V. ix: 46. 1)—"All which when as the Prince had heard and seene, / His former fancies ruth he gan repent" (V. ix: 49. 1–2)—Guyon fails to perform a similar restraining function when he and the Prince take off in "envy and gealousy" after the hapless Florimell. The duo's participation in the endless pursuit of the "chased, yet chaste" woman quickly leads them into the hidden folds of the text, while it emphasizes the contradictions which allow women to be held up as icons needing protection, even though they are endangered by the same knights.

Women are rarely portrayed as truly "present" in the epic. Perpetually iconic, demonic, in disguise, or in flight, most women remain at the distance which Derrida claims is essential, securing their identification as the *pharmakon*, that is, something simultaneously beneficial and poisonous:

> Distance is the very element of [a woman's] power. Yet one must beware to keep one's distance from her beguiling song of enchantment. A distance from distance must be maintained. Not only for protection (the most obvious advantage) against the spell of her fascination, but also as a way of succumbing to it, that distance (which is lacking) *is necessary* . . . Perhaps woman—a non-identity, a non-figure, a simulacrum—is distance's very chasm. (1978: 49)

The continual deferral of women in *The Faerie Queene* replicates this warning. Normally, the knights only have extended close contact with women when in the dangerous company of an illusory beauty such as Duessa or the False Florimell or when they visit a woman like Mercilla, whose pronounced psychological distancing and iconic status shift the threat emanating from ordinary persons of her gender. Chaste, virtuous women who are worthy and capable of the knights' affections are normally either fleeing or fleeting, with Britomart as a notable exception, whose disguise, however, reduces her erotic danger for the knights.

Women often confuse the knights in *The Faerie Queene* because they elicit such conflicting responses. Arthur, for instance, is represented in the precarious position of being strongly tempted by the crimes of concupiscence he is bound by his knighthood to prevent; in his own iconic position, he cannot openly succumb to his lust. At the same time, however, there is little effort to provide an appropriate model for "lawful lust." Thus, the many virtuous ladies who arouse erotic interest become subsumed into the same sexual category dominated by wanton women, while worthy consummations are endlessly postponed. Selected virtuous women become substitute objects of desire because others, including Gloriana, must be separated from the anxieties associated with physical sexuality.

As Derrida notes, the sexual act involved in ending a woman's virginity can engender a contradictory and complex set of emotions which a Spenserian knight might have trouble reconciling with the tenets of his quest:

> It is the hymen that desire dreams of piercing, of bursting, in an act of violence that is (at the same time or somewhere between) love and murder . . . with all the undecidability of its meaning, the hymen only takes place when it doesn't take place, when nothing *really* happens, when there is an all-consuming consummation without violence. (1981: 213)

> There is only the memory of a crime that has never been committed. (1981: 214)

Arthur's pursuits and possibly his consummations remain in the margins, therefore, in order to shield him, though not excuse him, from accusations of untoward concupiscence in his struggle with erotic responses. Women's perpetual undecidability undermines knightly attempts to differentiate between good and evil women and the proper way to deal with both groups. Hence, all women fall within the definition Catherine Clément offers for a sorceress: "She is innocent, mad, full of badly remembered memories, guilty of unknown wrongs; she is the seductress, the heiress of all generic Eves" (6). The narrative suggests that women who refuse to remain clearly demonic or iconic introduce such a jumble of emotions that they cannot be contended with openly. On such occasions, they often glide into the irretrievable folds of the text, where their fates and Arthur's activities with them hover just outside the sight of the reader.

Arthur's problems with women in the epic are far from unique, however. Countless representations of female characters reinforce perceptions of women as unreliable, indiscernible, and dangerous. The poem often suggests that women's external presentation hides internal reality, which male characters continually attempt to uncover, albeit with marginal success. In the Legend of Holiness, for example, Duessa successfully deludes the Red Crosse Knight into believing in her virtue,[20] until she is stripped of her finery:

> So as she bad, that witch they disaraid . . .
>   Ne spared they to strip her naked all.
>   Then when they had despoild her tire and call,
>   Such as she was, their eyes might her behold,
>   That her misshaped parts did them appall,
>   A loathly, wrinckled hag, ill fauored, old . . .
> Her craftie head was altogether bald,
>   And as in hate of honorable eld,
>   Was ouergrowne with scurfe and filthy scald;
>   Her teeth out of her rotten gummes were feld,
>   And her sowre breath abhominably smeld;
>   Her dried dugs, like bladders lacking wind,
>   Hong downe, and filthy matter from them weld;
>   Her wrizled skin as rough, as maple rind,
> So scabby was, that would haue loathd all womankind.
> Her neather parts, the shame of all her kind,
>   My chaster Muse for shame doth blush to write;
>   But at her rompe she growing had behind
>   A foxes taile, with dong all fowly dight;
>   And eke her feete most monstrous were in sight;
>   For one of them was like an Eagles claw,
>   With griping talaunts armd to greedy fight,
>   The other like a Beares vneuen paw:
> More vgly shape yet neuer liuing creature saw.
>
>   (I. viii: 46–48)[21]

Once Duessa's body, so "fowle deformed" is revealed,[22] the assembled company feels confident that her power is terminated and they set her loose: "Thus when they had the witch disrobed quight, / And all her filthy feature open showne, / They let her goe at will, and wander wayes vnknowne" (I. viii: 49. 7–9).[23] Subsequent events indicate that Duessa's evil has not been as fully neutralized as this decision implies, but the incident reflects a common assumption that female danger can be mitigated if the layers of clothing or deception which protect women can be stripped away. Although Duessa is portrayed as a figure exuding vice and treachery, this attitude toward women evinces itself also in situations involving virtuous female figures. Only "fully" exposed women of any moral persuasion seem to be trustworthy, and even with these, their "neather parts" generally remain loci of extreme anxiety.

Countless images of women throughout *The Faerie Queene* reflect a nervousness about potential female dissembling; an apparent belief in the difficulty of distinguishing between "good" and "evil" women; and a perpetual fear of female genitalia. Portrayals of heavily iconographic, emblematic women represent one of Spenser's most common methods of dealing with this pervasive dilemma. Such women briefly become speaking tableaux when passing knights require the information they can offer, but they always retain their emblematic qualities.[24] These emblematized women provide fundamental information regarding the presumptions and fears associated with most female figures in the epic.

Spenser's emblematized women reflect borrowings from only part of the emblem tradition, but their stasis within the clearly delineated borders of their houses and the manner of their availability to the gaze of knights and readers mark them as literary representatives of that genre. Just as Spenser relies heavily upon allegory in these instances, it is not uncommon in emblem books for women to depict mythological figures. Those chosen, such as Fortuna, Minerva, and Cassandra, are frequently those with considerable power over *man*-kind, but the details of their portrayal often demonstrate an attempt to undermine that authority and introduce numerous ambiguities regarding female sexuality. The emblems as a whole provide useful information for Spenserians, but emblematic picturae offer particularly interesting insights into Spenser's periodic appropriation of the emblematic format and its significance for women in his epic.

Goddesses and some other female figures are presented naked in many emblems from this period. Objectified as bodies, such figures draw the viewer's eye to highly marked sexual characteristics, rather than confronting the audience with images evoking these goddesses' authority.[25] While breasts receive considerable attention, especially with allusions to nurturing functions, the pubic area is also often dominantly displayed. In contrast to the adult voluptuousness of the breasts, however, genital depictions, by their lack of appropriate adult hair, frequently resemble the anatomy of young girls more closely than that of mature, sexual women. This stripping away of pubic hair further distances the threat implied by female sexuality. Instead of the treachery associated with female genitalia, maternity and vulnerability take center stage. Feminine deception can be warded off, such portraits imply, if women are given nothing to hide behind. Such complete female nudity diverts the viewer's attention from reminders of the power wielded by these women. Freud once suggested that "Nature" created female pubic hair in order to mask, with shame, the inferiority of women's sexual organs (1965a: 132). Anticipating this conclusion, many drawings of mythologized women in emblem books remove this veil, leaving the figures openly vulnerable and available for detailed male study.[26]

Virtuous women in *The Faerie Queene*, who are generally either fleeing or static, often exhibit a corollary vulnerability, though only a few of them are literally stripped in this fashion. Apart from Britomart, whose masculine garb enables her to take advantage of numerous male prerogatives, the majority of women either continually run from potential assailants in order to protect their chastity or they must remain ensconced in houses or temples to serve as iconic representations of the virtues visiting knights need to learn and assimilate. And, as Amoret learns in the Temple of Womanhood, even these enclaves may not provide safe haven. Unimpeded movement is generally reserved for men, women disguised as men, or women who eagerly seek the lawless sexual involvements which other females try to avoid.

The walls which surround these women parallel the borders encircling the emblematic picturae. Within the confines of the emblem, there is obviously no movement. The figures bound within them, replete with iconography, exist only for the gaze of the viewer and the commentary of the emblem. The numerous iconic women in Faeryland, both good and evil, are similarly impeded by such stasis. Knights who enter their environs and the readers who accompany them are drawn into deeply iconographic terrain, where the women portrayed have no existence other than as objects for male edification. Although most of these women remain clothed and appear to exercise considerable power, a closer look at their presentation demonstrates how the male visitors act to defuse apparent female strength. These emblematic woman keep their clothes on, but they offer their minds and bodies to the titular knights and others for intimate investigation. The metaphoric disrobings they endure—and often assist with—undercut their position as fully as the more conventional strippings often undergone by their counterparts in the emblem books.[27]

The women in Spenser's emblematic houses are frequently overwhelmed with allegory. In the episodes I will focus on—the House of Holiness, Alma's House of Temperance, and Mercilla's Palace—the female figures insistently declare their iconographical affiliations and generally display few distinguishing characteristics apart from those connected with their allegorical "meanings." Rarely in the epic does the allegory remain as flat and obvious as it does in association with women such as Fidelia, Speranza, and Charissa, for instance, who primarily serve to reinforce the picture of holiness being presented to Red Crosse when Una brings him to the House of Holiness.[28]

Carrying the symbols of their "trade," these women act as speaking emblems, who give succor to "wretched soules" (I. x: 3.7) via biblical representation. Their sharply limited characterizations illustrate the process through which iconic women become desexed and disempowered. Although both Fidelia and Speranza are described as betrothed, for example, they remain perpetual virgins, with the allegory suggesting that their marriages may not be solemnized on earth: "Though spousd, yet wanting wedlocks solemnize" (I. x: 4. 7).[29] Instead, they are caught between desire and fulfillment, in a state of deferred sexuality. Within this sexual no-man and no-woman's land, they are removed from the sexual realm, since they are chastely promised, though not wed. Hence, their presence is less likely to represent a sexual threat to the knights who visit them seeking enlightenment.

Likewise, poor Charissa, who drags herself from childbed in order to greet the visitors, embodies a fertility oddly distanced from sexuality. Although "Her necke and breasts were euer open bare" (I. x. 30: 7), this exposure merely facilitates her nurturing: "That ay thereof her babes might sucke their fill" (I. x. 30. 8), thereby deflecting improper responses to her "wondrous beauty."[30] Charissa's babies are presumably the result of active sexuality, yet her maternal aspect overwhelms the scene. Such desexualized representations further distance sexuality in this epic which delays wedlock whenever possible. At the same time, however, apart from physical union, the women share themselves completely with the knights. Unlike male seers, such as Merlin, who pointedly provide only limited information, these women with special knowledge offer all they possess, as Fidelia's lessons to Red Crosse indicate: "She vnto him disclosed *euery* wit" (I. x: 19. 3, emphasis added).[31]

It is interesting to note, moreover, these emblematic houses also resemble nineteenth-century French houses of ill-repute such as those recently discussed by Emily Apter. In her analysis of "cabinets" and peepshows, Apter includes a description by French historian Alain Corbin which shares salient features with Mercilla's and other emblematic houses:[32]

> Witty confections of odors, sumptuous sets, multiple mirrors, a profusion of carpets and an orgy of electricity renewed the technical arsenal of pleasure. Inside the grottos of Calypso, or the Sadean convents, nymphs and expert "nuns" refined their caresses. Tableaux vivants were the joy of the voyeur. (42)[33]

It is, of course, highly improbable that nineteenth-century French bordellos were patterned after *The Faerie Queene* and even less likely that Spenser had a prophetic vision of these arenas which he reproduced within his poem. Nevertheless, the interstices between the features of these disparate, yet similar venues help underscore the vexing aspects of the emblematic houses in Spenser's epic. As I will discuss in greater detail below, the tableaux vivants offered by Mercilla and Alma contain elements of striptease, in addition to the moral lessons provided. Furthermore, Mercilla's palace in particular emphasizes ornate display, while Guyon, Arthur, and Artegall all closely resemble the "customers" targeted by a bordello's management. The knights are invited to fill their eyes with the images of these women as they explore and learn about female mysteries. Essentially, they are being taught and encouraged in the art of voyeurism. As part of her discussion of voyeurism in *The Faerie Queene*, Theresa M. Krier notes that "Spenser's imitative depictions assume that there is no such thing as an innocent eye, pure vision and affect prior to interpretation" (8).[34] Indeed, in these acts of sponsored voyeurism, there seem to be no "innocent" parties. The male characters appear eager to look, while the female characters freely reveal.

Guyon's sojourn at Alma's Castle in the Legend of Temperance graphically illustrates this function of the virtuous, emblematic female within the epic's examination of male-centered virtues.[35] Alma not only emulates Fidelia in offering her visitor access to all that she knows, she also guides him on an extensive tour of her castle-cum-body (II. ix), encouraging intimate perusal—with the notable exception of any genital region.[36] Alma allows Guyon absolute freedom to explore her body, again reinforcing the demonstrated emblematic premise that these women's bodies exist predominantly for the education of male knights.

Alma's brand of hospitality not only highlights the voyeuristic elements of such tours, it also emphasizes the consistency with which potential female power is undermined. Privileged knowledge stands as one of the few ways for women to maintain authority over the men who entreat them for shared wisdom, but in most cases, these women generously share all they are and all they know. The only type of withholding generally perceived—represented here by the significant lack of a genital depiction in Alma's castle—raises numerous interpretive possibilities. Alma, for instance, may be providing a further denial or repudiation of adult female sexuality. As I have suggested, Arthur and the titular knights in *The Faerie Queene* encounter serious problems with achieving and maintaining their respective virtues when they come into contact with women exhibiting an unavoidable sexual presence, regardless of whether the women are primarily good or evil. Hence, although others have interpreted Alma's unacknowledged genital lack as representative of hermaphroditism,[37] it also seems likely that the omission protects Guyon from the site of potential female treachery and from a dangerous threat to his temperance. As his meeting with the bouncing naked damsels and his implied erotic interest in Florimell indicate, the epic does not offer a knight of Temperance who is insensible to female attractions. Instead of taking the opportunity to teach him and his readers about virtuous sexuality, however, the narrative begs the question by deleting an appropriate occasion for its metaphoric consideration.

The pattern of female unveiling is repeated when Arthur and Artegall visit Mercilla. Like Alma's castle, Mercilla's palace is also offered for open exploration, even though her body remains submerged beneath elaborate ceremonial trappings, not unlike the "cabinets" described above: "[Her] porch, that most magnificke did appeare, Stood open wyde to all men day and night" (V. ix: 22. 3–4). In her description of the scene, Jane Aptekar calls it "carefully orthodox":[38]

> It is a set scene, like something out of a pageant, as Mercilla sits motionless and (from a realistic point of view) absurd with jewels, scepter, sword and panoply, and with angels fluttering about her head and a bad-tempered lion beneath her. But realism is of course irrelevant. (13)

Since women remain so heavily encumbered with allegory and iconography throughout *The Faerie Queene*, Aptekar's contention that the absurdity and non-realism of the scene are "irrelevant" glosses over the gender-based centrality of these characteristics. Although the epic, like the emblems, does not attempt mimesis, the women portrayed manifest a consistent state of iconic paralysis rarely duplicated in the images of men. With infrequent exceptions, men tend to retain much more freedom of movement and receive less stylized descriptions of their appearance and purpose in the poem. Women, on the other hand, are often encrusted with myth and symbolism, restrained within close quarters, and made continually available for (k)nightly edification.

Accordingly, Mercilla acknowledges a duty to disclose herself fully to the visiting male knights when she invites them to join her at the seat of her power:

Which that those knights likewise mote vnderstand,
And witnesse forth aright in forrain land,
Taking them vp vnto her stately throne,
Where they mote heare the matter throughly scand.

(V. ix: 37. 4–7)

Elevating them to her level "and neare them none" (V. ix: 37. 9), Mercilla indicates that she is teaching equals. Reminiscent of the women discussed earlier, she intends to provide them with a clear view of all she represents. In addition, the remnants left of her status as authoritative woman are further diminished when Artegall steps in to correct her dangerous weakening toward Duessa. Her acquiescence with his implied reprimand suggests that even the most exalted female figure can require male intervention to prevent harm to the state. Mercilla remains clothed, but she strips herself of the power of her knowledge by sharing it with her visitors and by bowing to their counsel.

The prevalence of emblematic women in *The Faerie Queene* and Arthur's recurrent difficulties with virtuous sexual conduct demonstrate an intense need to keep female figures restrained and solidly fictive. Figures in emblem books are bound within elaborate borders and defined by the mottos and commentary that accompany them and by the response of the viewers encountering them. Similarly, in Spenser's epic, women are repeatedly presented for extensive literal and figurative disrobing by both knights and readers. Only male garb or exceedingly swift feet exempt female characters from such voluntary or forced revelations. While Duessa's ritual undressing appeals for readerly approbation since the witch presumably figures unrepentant evil, the numerous metaphoric disrobings of unquestionably virtuous female characters, the confinement of women within iconic houses, and the repeated excision of the locus of potential *female* pleasure as well as of male anxiety suggest that in many instances the narrative is gliding over the serious ideological implications of such scenes.

In his brief, yet insightful essay "Striptease," Roland Barthes examines that Parisian art-form in terms consistent with this process of female undressing in *The Faerie Queene*:

> Striptease—at least Parisian striptease—is based on a contradiction: Woman is desexualized at the very moment when she is stripped naked. We may therefore say that we are dealing in a sense with a spectacle based on fear, or rather on the pretence of fear, as if eroticism here went no further than a sort of delicious terror, whose ritual signs have only to be announced to evoke at once the idea of sex and its conjuration. (180)

A similar mode of detoxification imbues sites of dishabillement in Spenser's epic. Duessa, for example, illustrates Barthes's contention that in striptease "evil is *advertised* the better to impede and exorcize it" (180). As the lengthy passage detailing her unveiled loathsomeness indicates, the uncovered dissembler is no longer tempting.[39] Her allure depends upon the mystery and counterfeit provided by external garments and accessories. Once these are removed, her appearance announces her evil. Consequently, her captors set her free, mistakenly believing that her power has been neutralized.

Such stratagems are not restricted to women perceived as evil, however, since female characters often appear to exude danger, no matter how virtuous they seem or act. The ease with which knights are duped by the False Florimell and by Una's lascivious simulacrum suggests an underlying belief in the poem that all women live on the brink of dishonesty. In fact, many characters in *The Faerie Queene* seem to act from the presumption Hercule Tasso notes in his misogynistic *Of Mariage and Wiuing* (1599), "if there be any such that live thus chastely, shee is to be held as a wonder" (sig. E2v). Consequently, it is not surprising that female exemplars of righteousness such as Alma and Mercilla demonstrate their virtue by "revealing all"; if women are believed always to be hiding something wicked, allaying such fears becomes paramount before credibility can truly be established.

Curiously, the absence or displacement of the highly significant site consistently "held back" in Spenser's poem generates no spoken anxiety.[40] As noted above, women's bodies in the epic, whether presented directly or metaphorically to the knights, repeatedly appear to lack genitalia.[41] When Duessa is stripped, her genitalia are pronounced "the shame of all her kind," which the "chaster Muse [who] for shame doth blush to write" (I. viii: 48. 2). The narrator's similar elision of other women's sexual organs suggests that "her kind" refers to women of many kinds, not merely to Duessa's equals in evil. Accordingly, not only does Alma's exhaustive tour of her castle/body not include a genital region, but in Book Six, Calidore is also not sure what he saw while he was surrounded by the naked dancing damsels since "his eyes mote haue deluded beene" (VI. x: 17. 7).[42] Similarly, Fraudubio can only offer speculation about Duessa's genitals since his view of her bath was blocked by the water: "Her neather partes misshapen, monstruous, / Were hidd in water, that I could not see, / But they did *seeme* more foule and hideous" (I. ii: 41, 1–3; emphasis added). It is equally unclear how much the wanton bouncing damsels in the Legend of Temperance reveal to Guyon. Although the text states that they "ne car'd to hyde, / Their dainty parts from vew of any" (II. xii: 63. 8–9), it also suggests that the maidens eagerly showed their breasts, but "the rest hid vnderneath" (II. xii: 66. 9). Similarly, Diana's outraged response to Faunus in *The Mutabilitie Cantos* might imply that he received an unobstructed view of her body, but identifying the "some-what he did spy" (VII. vi: 46. 3) relies heavily upon readerly speculation. This recurring ambiguity accords with the uncertainty and deferral of female sexuality and sexual parts which resonate through the epic. Just as coitus seems endlessly postponed or fleeting in *The Faerie Queene*, so sightings of female genitalia generally remain absent or unverifiable. As noted, while the Garden of Adonis contains metaphoric genitalia, this locale is not available for knightly perusal.[43]

The regularity with which female sexual parts are literarily excised raises an abundance of rich interpretive possibilities and puzzles. One might wonder, for example, whether Alma's display of her metaphoric body can be termed exhibitionism if there is apparently "nothing" there to exhibit. What do the knightly voyeurs need to see in order for the show to be worthwhile or satisfying? Does her revelation constitute a virtuous or sanitized genre of exhibitionism? If so, how much castration anxiety might her censored body still generate? Is the poet perhaps responding to his contemporaries' beliefs in "the euill quality of the womb" (Sadler, sig. B1ov) by performing literary hysterectomies on some of his female characters?[44] Even more definitively than the stripper's G-string which Barthes claims "bars the way to the sexual parts like a sword of purity" (181), the absent genitalia of *The Faerie Queene* seem to keep female sexuality at a safe distance.[45] Nevertheless, although the sanctioned voyeurism encouraged here may help the poet keep his fictive knights' lustful urges at bay, it simultaneously introduces interpretive knots for his readers and reinforces common uneasiness about female genitalia and sexuality.

For example, this communal lack—and display—shared among "good," "evil," and "marginal" women once again gathers them all together, this time into a characterization which resembles Mary Ann Doane's definition of a femme fatale:

> The femme fatale is the figure of a certain discursive unease, a potential epistemological trauma. For her most striking characteristic, perhaps, is the fact that she never really is what she seems to be. She harbors a threat which is not entirely legible, predictable, or manageable. In thus transforming the threat of the woman into a secret, something which must be aggressively revealed, unmasked, discovered, the figure is fully compatible with the epistemological drive of the narrative, the hermeneutic structuration of the classical text. Sexuality becomes the site of questions about what can and cannot be known. This imbrication of knowledge and sexuality, of epistemophilia and scopophilia, has crucial implications for the representation of sexual difference. (1)

The seemingly "open" women in *The Faerie Queene* create a similar threat even as they appear to defuse it. Alma, Mercilla, and other women of their stature are not actually dubious figures of female manipulation and deceit, of course, but the absences within their ostensible "full disclosure" still reinforce the poem's ideological view of female danger and sexual confusion. Accordingly, what appears initially to be a de-eroticized striptease simultaneously emphasizes the aspect of female sexuality which psychoanalytic writings often maintain most terrifies male viewers,

as Doane describes: "For the head-on look is simultaneously pleasurable and threatening, the threat emanating from the construction which forces a reading of the female body as the site of
negativity, of lack and hence, of the possibility of castration"
(106). Consequently, the physical or metaphoric unveilings of
Duessa, Mercilla, Alma, and the other women noted re-mystify
female bodies even as they seem to de-mystify them. Hence, what
Derrida refers to as woman's "veiling dissimulation" (1978: 57) appears again: despite what seems to be a complete disrobing, somehow a veil remains. As Barthes observes, in striptease, a woman's
body actually relies on "a series of coverings" as "she pretends to
strip it bare" (180). The Faerie Queene's disrobing women exhibit
the same sleight of hand and the viewing knights are thus confronted with troubling options. Either the women do not possess
sexual organs or else the kind of absolute disclosure which might
defuse the sexual anxieties associated with females is not attainable—even metaphorically. One other possibility is offered, but
strikingly, verification is denied. Both Venus in the Temple of
Womanhood and Dame Nature in The Mutabilitie Cantos are presented as "women" who may bear male members—suggesting
perhaps that powerful women require male genitalia. Venus is described as "Both male and female, both vnder one name" (IV. x:
41. 7), while Dame Nature's sex is indeterminate: "Whether she
man or woman inly were, / That could not any creature well descry" (VII. vii: 5. 6–7). In both instances, the indecipherability of
the question is highlighted.[46] Doane notes a related phenomenon
in cinema, observing that "There is a hole in the visible" (45).

The impact of these glaring absences on the knights' imagined
psyches clearly remains fictive; nevertheless, the ideological implications for the representation of sexual difference and gender relations in the poem are considerable. Particularly within a work
whose announced foundation is behavioral education and guidance,
the continual reinscription of woman as mysteriously sexual entity
and unfathomable being deflects potential efforts to transcend gender myths and stereotypes. By freeze-framing iconic women such
as Mercilla and Alma within emblematic borders, then offering the
delusion of guided, complete perusals of their bodies and stores of

knowledge, the narrative guarantees a confused conceptualization of adult female sexuality. In Barthes's formulation, woman is "established *right from the start* as an object in disguise" (180).

This image of the disguised woman reinforces such contemporary beliefs in female duplicity as expressed through William Whateley's contention that "a thousand faults, doe lie hid in the painted box of the bosome of euerie of *Euah's* daughters" (1624: sig. D6v) and by Alexander Niccholes's advice to beware even virtuous women since "the diuell can transforme himselfe into an Angell of Light" (sig. B4v). These views are certainly supported by characters such as the False Florimell and Duessa, whose beautiful facades hide significant imperfections. Significantly, the missing pudenda of the iconic, virtuous women also support the belief that all women are hiding something and are therefore untrustworthy.

Consequently, the models of adult females remain fraught with complicated contradictions throughout *The Faerie Queene*. By ignoring even metaphoric sexuality when they reveal themselves and their secrets to the titular knights, the pedagogical emblematic women leave intact the fears, misgivings, and prurient interests about females displayed by knights of all moral calibres. Since these knights gain access to such a range of female knowledge in these scenes, the continued omission of sexual topics and anatomical representations furthers the conceptualization of woman as treacherous and unknowable. It also reinforces both the nervousness and the excitement associated with female sexuality. Although procreative sex is glorified at various moments in the epic, sexuality more commonly stays situated in the realm of the forbidden, as Guyon's vehement destruction of the Bower of Bliss exemplifies. Since these iconic women distance themselves from sexuality, their lessons do nothing to alleviate the curiosity of their visitors or to desensitize the charged atmosphere which keeps the epic's virgins in continual sexual peril. Women remain both dangerous and endangered.

Concurrently, acts of voyeurism, whether "sanctioned," "illicit," or thwarted, shape male responses to women throughout the epic. The fleeting females remain just out of sight, ever whetting the sexual and visual appetites of their pursuers, while the iconic women display themselves and less virtuous women struggle to keep male viewers from looking too closely. At the same time, women continually exhibit themselves, whether willingly or not. From Amoret as captive in Busyrane's chambers to the False Florimell at Satyrane's tournament and Alma at home, women are exposed to fascinated male eyes. Of course, the attempt to "see" women completely and thereby "know" them is doomed to failure. Hence, both voyeur and exhibitionist fall short of full disclosure or comprehension, leaving misapprehensions and skewed representations firmly in place. Ultimately, curiosity and desire remain thwarted; female characters remain elusive, and male characters continue to fill their greedy eyes with mysterious female visions.

2

Nightmares of Desire[1]

In a dream, silently, she had come to him, her wasted body
within its loose graveclothes giving off an odour of wax and
rosewood, her breath bent over him with mute secret words, a
faint odour of wetted ashes.

(*Ulysses* 12)

THE PASSAGE ABOVE from James Joyce reminds us that the
erotic, often pleasurable dreams described in the previous chapter do not exhaust the possibilities present within the world of
dreaming. In Spenser's work, as in *Ulysses*, the conjunction of
women and dreams can initiate feelings of dread and danger as well
as enticing, however frustrating, desire. Women predominate in the
dream visions featured throughout *The Faerie Queene*, and knights
and readers often share an inability to decode the elusive meanings
provided through this medium. Although men are not the only
figures in the poem who dream, their imaginings carry unique
resonances and distinctive implications for their virtue and for the
conceptualizations of women within the epic.[2]

The Red Crosse Knight's critical dream about Una in Book
One exemplifies the deception often contained within dreams visited upon male characters. Here, Archimago sends a messenger to
the underworld to obtain "a fit false dreame" (I. i: 43. 9) which
would allow the magician to plague the titular knight with "false
shewes [to] abuse his fantasy" (I. i: 46. 4). The dream, which "his
manly hart did melt away" (I. i: 47. 5), left Red Crosse "bathed in
wanton blis and wicked ioy" (I. i: 47. 6), then prompted him to
fly into a rage against the innocent Una. Though he restrains his
fury momentarily, he soon abandons the distraught virgin after
Archimago once again sends "that feigning dreame, and that faire-
forged Spright" (I. ii: 2. 2) to greet Red Crosse with a vision of

Una engaging in unlawful copulation. This image seems more real than dream and stirs his "furious ire" (I. ii: 5. 8), causing Red Crosse to leave the scene in anger.

The Red Crosse Knight's susceptibility to Archimago's magic accords with Aristotle's contention that "During sleep judgment is disabled from exercising its function. Thus, a perceptual remnant bearing some resemblance to a sense-perception is mistaken for the real one" (97).[3] Despite this possible justification for his gullibility, however, when the legend's titular knight succumbs to this "ydle dreame" (I. i: 46. 1), he begins a detour from the path of virtue which will significantly detain him from his quest. As "that troublous dreame gan freshly tosse his braine" (I. i: 55. 6), the reader realizes that Archimago's ploy has been successful—the dream vision has significantly shaken the faith of this generally virtuous knight. The repercussions for this saint-elect could be considerable, since dreams during this period often carried suggestions of infernal involvement, with many people believing, as William Perkins writes in 1610, that "Satan can frame dreames" (sig. G1).[4]

Although this illusory scene was fashioned by a male enchanter with the aid of a spright, its female subject and the threatened invocation of "the dreaded name of *Hecate*" (I. i: 43. 2–3) alert us to an important connection between such dreams and the female realm. Notably, much of the unique significance attached to male dreams arises from a powerful metaphoric code which encompasses many of the malevolent female characters in the epic. While this interrelationship is never noted explicitly, it nevertheless provides us with important further insights into the workings of sexuality, vice, and virtue. Dream visions of females in *The Faerie Queene* offer an unparalleled means for mapping the roles reserved for women within the text.

The types of dreams which seem most relevant here are those we categorize as nightmares. In contrast with familiar expectations, however, in *The Faerie Queene*, these troubling dreams are most commonly manifest materially through female personifications, rather than as mental imaginings.[5] I will discuss each of the pertinent categories in more detail below, but I begin by suggesting that, based upon etymology, most of the epic's malevolent female characters represent nightmares and that this linguistic connection alerts us to salient characteristics of their evil as well as to specific female qualities deemed most threatening.[6] Unlike virtuous women, who are often absent or in flight, evil females in the poem emerge tangibly from the spirit/dream-world, using their physical presence to cloud the judgment and the virtue of the knights they encounter.

Whether witches, hags, or succubi[7]—the three main groupings presented—these characters exhibit qualities associated with nightmares in the Renaissance.[8] In *Praxis Medicinae, or The Physicians Practice* (1639), Walter Bruel offers a standard description of the "incubvs or nightmare":

> *Incubus* is a passion wherin a man doth thinke himselfe stifled with a great weight lying on him in his sleep; likewise difficulty of speech and breathing doe accompany it, his senses are amazed, not taken away. It doth differ from the falling sicknesse herin, the matter causing the falling sicknes, is venomous, so is it not in the Hag or Mare, here is no convulsion, as is in the falling sicknesse. (sig. H_{IV})[9]

The nightmares Bruel discusses are most commonly presented as female in Elizabethan and subsequent treatises. Similarly, Faeryland is populated with nightmares personified as female, though these nightmarish figures do not restrict their activities to nighttime and do not rely upon suffocation for their treachery. Females associated with nightmares pose some of the greatest threats to virtue.[10] In contrast with the fleeting dream associated with Gloriana, the nightmares of malevolent women present apparent substance and durability. Shaped from the projections of male fears and fantasies, these embodied dreams offer numerous knights the opportunities they most desire, as well as the threats which seem most terrifying. Not surprisingly, therefore, these nightmares fit the conceptualization offered by psychoanalyst Ernest Jones: "The malady known as Nightmare is always an expression of intense mental conflict centering about some form of 'repressed' sexual desire" (44).[11] These nightmarish figures confirm both the ecstasy available through illicit lust and the danger inherent within adult female sexuality, thereby substantiating Sandra Shulman's observation that succubi arouse "feelings of voluptuousness mingled with dread" (41).

Nightmarish women largely attempt to seduce men away from the field and from virtue, using sex as their primary weapon. Their actions thus merge the early meaning of "seduce"—persuading a soldier to desert his allegiance or battle—with its subsequent sexual connotation (OED). Phaedria, for example, "with one sweet drop of sensuall delight" (II. vi: 8. 7) prompts Cymochles to "yeeld his martiall might" (II. vi: 8. 5). By flooding his senses with "false delights" and "pleasures vaine" (II. vi: 14. 2), she ensures that "of no worldly thing he care did take" (II. vi: 18. 2). This quick-thinking wanton woman even argues that Mars, the god of war, encourages knights "in Amours the passing houres to spend" (II. vi: 35. 4). As Cymochles' fury at Guyon's interruption indicates, Phaedria has convinced the knight of the joys incumbent upon "laying his head disarm'd, / In her loose lap" (II. vi: 14. 6–7). Phaedria thus provides a powerful obstacle to virtue and valor. Her argument that knightly pursuits lead Cymochles to "wast thy ioyous houres in needlesse paine" (II. vi: 17. 4) substantiates a common fear that women will divert men away from their proper tasks.

Given the frequent transience or unobtainability of sexual relations with "good" women, knights in the epic make particularly susceptible targets for such sexually voracious tempters. Jones argues that nightmares result when the object of a dreamer's wish is someone "whom the inhibiting forces of morality exclude from the erotic sphere" (76). In Faeryland, morality excludes both ladies and witches from virtuous knights' erotic sphere; hence, nightmarish females regularly appear as enactments of all such repressed sexual fantasies.[12]

These malevolent females draw their strength from this realm of male imaginings and anxieties. Similar to the femme fatales discussed by Mary Ann Doane, the power these female figures receive "is a function of the fears linked to the notions of uncontrollable drives, the fading of subjectivity, and the loss of conscious agency" (2). As the knights under the witch Acrasia's spell exemplify, those who succumb to these compelling sexual enticements fall victim to their enchanter's and their own uncontrollable drives, with the result that they do, in fact, lose subjectivity and agency—

and, for some at the Bower of Bliss, humanity. For these unfortunate knights, therefore, the cost of such allurements is very high. As Gabriele Schwab has noted in another context, the category of witches has the ability to represent both "the male fear of seductive women on the one hand, and of strong, independent women on the other" (172). In *The Faerie Queene*, these fears are often both operative. Fear of the sexual seems paramount, despite its simultaneous powerful allure. To borrow Laura Mulvey's terms, these nightmarish women, with their indeterminate appearance, perform "an amazing masquerade, which expresses a strange male underworld of fear and desire" (8).

At the same time, fashioning dangerous females into nightmares limits the scope of their power. The insubstantiability of nightmares implies that these female enemies ultimately can be melted like the Snowy Florimell, be vanquished by chivalric means, or be overcome by the return of virtuous thoughts and desires. This lack of substance also brings nightmarish women into line with misogynistic assertions such as that expressed by Hercule Tasso, who claimed in 1599 that "Woman hath no being . . . being Nothing, or a thing without substance" (sig. C3v). If human women have "no being" and demonic females emanate from psychological projections, then members of both categories can be subdued. Tellingly, these "nightmares" generally respect male hierarchical priorities and frequently subordinate themselves to a "greater" male power.[13] Since they rarely turn homicidal, their danger remains psychic and transient.[14] Knights may weaken, but their male virtue and physical prowess ultimately prevail.

Even these demonic females' lack of humanity helps limit their threatening qualities. In *The Faerie Queene*, neither witches, hags, nor succubi claim human affiliations. Instead, they emanate from the demonic/monster realm and merely adopt female human beauty as a means of seduction. Notably, these demonic origins contradict contemporary understandings of similar beings. The witchcraft treatises, for example, regularly describe witches as human women who have been lured away by the devil.[15] Consequently, the epic's insistence that witches and hags are not human alerts us to the containment which helps shape Spenserian witches.[16] Overwhelming as they often appear, they remain subject to the forces of virtue.

In most cases, when knights remember or remain true to their quests, these enemies lose most of their power, even though vicious tongues may not be silenced. While this non-human provenance may not affect the influence such figures initially exert over the knights they encounter, it does distance human women from the power and danger these demonic females represent. If human women do not have access to sorcery, except in unusual cases such as Britomart with her magic spear, knights need only learn how to pierce demonic disguises; they need not worry that any "real woman" could dominate them. They are also spared the shame accompanying defeat by a female opponent if women can triumph only with supernatural assistance. Concurrently, witches' and others' reliance upon external—male—catalysts for their treachery separates their "femaleness" from the source of their threat. As Perkins notes: "the worke is done by the help of another, namely, the Deuill, who is confederate with the Witch" (sig. A6v).[17] Hence, witches' power largely remains "male," despite their own female forms. This need for infernal cooperation places further limitations upon their malevolence because they do not act independently. While evil spirits generally appear eager to help, this lack of autonomy keeps treacherous females more vulnerable to the virtuous wrath of characters such as Arthur and Guyon. Duessa and Acrasia, for instance, both seem significantly more defenseless once their intentions are uncovered and they face their foes directly. Since their skills at deception provide most of their individual power, their authority rarely withstands the disclosure of their forgeries.

The emphasis upon nightmares which encompasses these malevolent females parallels a fascination with female spirits of the night, which was widely documented during this era. Centering upon witches and succubi, this long-standing debate and interest in demonic females regularly informs the portrayals of evil females found in *The Faerie Queene*. Initially, treatises on succubi presented these females as physical realities. Various tracts provide lengthy, detailed accounts of succubitic seduction, using ostensible case histories as evidence that such spirits operate widely within the human realm.[18] As knowledge progressed, such literal stories began to lose their credibility, but interest in succubi refused to fade. Though the tales generally did not change substantially, they were eventually accompanied either by physiological explanations or they were labeled as dreams. Hence, succubi remained "real," but their legends transformed them into less material forms, such as disease or nocturnal fantasies.[19] Philip Barrough, for example, in *The Method of Physick* (1590), describes the "Mare" or "Incubus" as "a disease, whereas one thinketh himself in the night to be oppressed with a great weight" (sig. D6)[20] and Johannes Weir (or Weyer), whose writings were contemporaneous with Spenser's, writes that "some think it [the mare or incubus] to be a mild form of epilepsy which occurs during dreams" (232).

Just as nightmares expand and amplify waking fears and anxieties, depictions of the nightmarish females in the epic often recall concerns about women discussed in contemporary documents. Succubi offer the most dramatic threat because they are closely associated with one of the predominant male fears represented; namely, actual or imagined depletions of male life forces or fluids. When Duessa convinces Orgoglio to throw the Red Crosse Knight's sexually drained and supine body into a womb-like "Dongeon deepe" (I. vii: 15. 9), for example, she focuses attention upon the enervated state of his "slombred, senceless corse" (I. vii: 15. 6).[21] Britomart's attempts to keep Artegall in conversation rather than releasing him back to the field illustrate the fairly benign version practiced by "good" women (though the length of time that men abandon such virtuous women implies that they fear the practice in any form), while Acrasia demonstrates the more terrifying extreme with Verdant, a knight she has lured into her Bower:[22]

> There she had him now layd a slombering,
>   In secret shade, after long wanton ioyes:
>   Whilst round about them pleasauntly did sing
>   Many faire Ladies, and lasciuious boyes,
> That euer mixt their song with light licentious toyes.
> And all that while, right ouer him she hong,
>   With her false eyes fast fixed in his sight,
>   As seeking medicine, whence she was stong,
>   Or greedily depasturing delight:
>   And oft inclining downe with kisses light,
>   For feare of waking him, his lips bedewd,

And through his humid eyes did suck his spright,
Quite molten into lust and pleasure lewd;
Wherewith she sighed soft, as if his case she rewd.

(II. xii: 72. 5–9; 73)[23]

The claim that "through his humid eyes [she] did suck his spright," highlights the central fear this episode addresses. The knight here displays an emasculated vulnerability similar to the Red Crosse Knight's unguarded post-coital lethargy. In both cases, and in similar episodes, women demonstrate that they can successfully deplete men of important life fluids.

The worry that women would drain men of vital fluids or energies coincides with early modern theories of sexual physiology. In Guillemeau's view, for example, even female anatomy voraciously seeks male seed: "In some Women the wombe is so greedy, and lickerish that it doth euen come down to meet nature, sucking and, (as it were) snatching the same, though it remaine only about the mouth and entrance of the outward orifice thereof" (sig. o2–o2v).[24] Although this description presents the positive image of a particularly fertile woman, the threatening implications of such female appetites remain. A belief that women possess naturally hungry vital organs makes it easy to surmise that a malicious woman might literally engulf her partner's manhood.

Such fears receive substantiation through traditional stories about succubi collecting semen from human sexual partners in order to transmit it again, either to women through the guise of incubi or by passing it on to the devil through subsequent sexual intercourse with him. The gathering of human semen was considered a critical function of these spirits, who were thought also to gather fluids emitted while men slept or masturbated. In addition, spirits were blamed for blocking men's generative capacities by creating impotence or causing temporary or permanent castration.[25]

Acrasia's confirmation of this very basic fear may help explain Guyon's "rigour pittilesse" (II. xii. 83. 2) during the destruction of her bower when he turns inquisitor and binds the witch tightly: "But her in chaines of adamant he tyde" (II. xii: 82. 6). Acrasia's threat of sexual or martial impotence could be interpreted as fuel for Guyon's ire, either on his own behalf or to protect future

Verdants. Given the setting, his actions might also signal the simultaneous allure of sexual bondage for this knight committed to temperance. Such a conclusion would correspond with those modern feminist theorists who posit a relationship between some institutionalized religions and pornography. Mary Jo Weaver, for example, suggests that "The explicitness of patriarchal warnings against sexual expression constituted a way for agitated celibates to discharge some of their sexual energy" (70).[26] Marina Warner argues further that the parade of tortured bodies which predominates in the history of female saints and martyrs conflates pornography with religiously motivated attacks against sexual transgressions:

> The particular focus on women's torn and broken flesh reveals the psychological obsession of the religion with sexual sin, and the tortures that pile up one upon the other with pornographic repetitiousness underline the identification of the female with the perils of sexual contact. (1976: 71)

The tension created by Guyon's demonstrated outrage at Acrasia's activities and the possibility of his concurrent sexual arousal could also contribute to critics' conflicted responses to this episode.[27] Like so many of the women under discussion here, Acrasia offers an enticing sexuality which is not constrained by ethics.[28] The Bower's lure of the forbidden has attracted those men who are later ensnared by dissipation, and Guyon's faint in Mammon's dwelling and his curiosity at the infamous Cissie and Flossie[29] suggest his own potential susceptibility to similar sensual temptations.[30] This element of voyeurism suggests the "desire to see" which Catherine Clément posits as essential for sorcery to succeed: "an audience, ready to satisfy its fantastic desire, is necessary for the spectacular side of sorcery" (10). Since Guyon's ocular complicity is often shared by readers, it is difficult to deny the voyeuristic delight and danger available in the Bower.

In many respects, such episodes also conform with Mulvey's contention that "Women are simply the scenery onto which men project their narcissistic fantasies" (13). The seemingly endless indeterminacy which characterizes these nightmarish females reinforces the suggestion that Acrasia and others possess no fixed image and that male fantasies determine the contours these females present. Thus, Guyon's display of anger at the Bower signifies shame at the contribution of his own weakness as well as from the licentious activities he encounters.

Guyon's rage could also be in reaction against Acrasia's facility with replicating the natural realm.[31] Clément's comment upon this brand of sorcery seems particularly relevant for this witch and for the Legend of Temperance: "The sorceress, who in the end is able to dream Nature and therefore conceive it, incarnates the reinscription of the traces of paganism that triumphant Christianity repressed" (5). Acrasia's recreation in her Bower of the best that "natures worke by art can imitate" (II. xii: 42. 4) demonstrates her dual ability to delude the senses with forged nature and to disrupt the transition from the pagan/classical world to the Christian world which this legend frequently models.[32] Thus, like Duessa, Acrasia seems to offer heresy along with her sensual temptations.

She also introduces the possibility of particularly heinous sins, since the witch's rapacious sexuality changes men into animals:

These seeming beasts are men indeed,
Whom this Enchauntresse hath transformed thus,
Whylome her louers, which her lusts did feed,
Now turned into figures hideous.

(II. xii: 85. 1–4)

Like many witchcraft treatises, *Malleus Maleficarum* devotes several pages to the vexing Homeric question of "whether witches can by some Glamour Change Men into Beasts" (61). More recently, Clément traces a connection between scenes of seductive sorcery and "animality, men changing into beasts . . . the supreme transgression—bestiality" (13). Clearly, the Bower's linking of sexuality with animality marks it as a site of unmanageable lusts. Grill's decision to remain with delight "in filth and foule incontinence" (II. xii: 87. 7), moreover, highlights the attractions accompanying this decadent existence. Challenging Acrasia's allure, it seems, requires strong measures.

Acrasia's life-sucking predilections also foreground the danger associated with other succubitic females, including Duessa's confederate "*Ate*, mother of debate" (IV. i: 19: 1), who craves "liuing food" (IV. i: 26. 2): "For life it is to her, when others sterue /

Through mischieuous debate, and deadly feood, / That she may sucke their life and drinke their blood" (IV. i: 26. 3–5). There are no English references to vampires until the eighteenth century, but succubi are mentioned as far back as the fourteenth century and witches and hags were often said to suck blood, as John Webster relates during an anecdote from *The Displaying of Supposed Witchcraft* (1677): "I met an old Witch, one of those that are said to enter houses in the night time, and there to suck the blood of little children lying in their Cradles" (sig. K3). According to early modern understandings of physiology, blood and semen were considered to be interrelated life-force entities. Thomas Vicary, for example, writes in 1577 that "[sparme] is made and gathered of the most best and purest drops of blood in all the body" (sig. M3v). Consequently, the succubi/witches' focus upon draining either of these fluids triggers primal terrors of death or castration/impotence.

"Female" powers of seduction and deception join forces here in order to draw men into these vulnerable positions. Since the giving of semen can be pleasurable, the women attract men with open promises of sexual encounters, while concealing their intention to deplete their victims' life fluids or to sap male energy through sexual satiation. In either case, the women ensure that the knights withdraw from the chivalric realm, sometimes permanently. Anticipating modern psychoanalytical writings which discuss male fears about the enervating possibilities of sexuality, *The Faerie Queene* offers literal confirmation for the threat Lacan describes as "the castrating and devouring, dislocating and astounding effects of feminine activity" (92).

This threat is so powerful in Spenser's formulation that it even outlasts its female sources, as the Red Crosse Knight learns when he unwittingly rests by the Nymph's perilous fountain:

> Hereof this gentle knight vnweeting was,
>   And lying downe vpon the sandie graile,
>   Drunke of the streame, as cleare as cristall glas;
>   Eftsoones his manly forces gan to faile,
>   And mightie strong was turnd to feeble fraile.
>   His chaunged powres at first them selues not felt,
>   Till crudled cold his corage gan assaile,

And chearefull bloud in faintnesse chill did melt,
Which like a feuer fit through all his body swelt.

(I. vii: 6)

His own circumstances make Red Crosse susceptible to this danger, but Diana's wrath with the Nymph who "therein wont to
dwell" (I. vii: 4. 8) triggers his lethargy. By the time he "vp-
started lightly from his looser make" (I. vii: 7. 8), he has already
been "pourd out in loosnesse on the grassy grownd" (I. vii: 7. 2)
and his dissipated state retards his reaction time: "But ere he could
his armour on him dight, / Or get his shield, his monstrous enimy
/ With sturdie steps came stalking in his sight" (I. vii: 8. 1–3).
The narrative suggests that neither Diana nor the Nymph need
be present or even aware of the Red Crosse Knight in order for
the water to take effect.

Succubitic females in *The Faerie Queene* often seem more concerned with such draining of vital fluids from their partners than
with gathering them for future diabolical uses. The focus of their
actions remains upon the immediate goal of depleting the knights,
rather than returning to the devil with human blood, breath, or
seed. With possible resonances from the biblical injunction against
the spilling of seed, Red Crosse, Arthur, and others lose energy
and the capacity for arms after these encounters, but they apparently are spared the possibility of infernal progeny.

This deviation from the folkloric norm for succubi helps ensure
that when the titular knights recover from their moral lapses, there
will be no literal residue remaining which could further compromise them. These "bitches from hell"[33] keep the knights from battle
and hope to enlist them for lascivious ends, but the implications
of an infernal sperm bank holding the semen of the central figures
of virtue in the poem could be devastating. Accordingly, gender
once again has its privileges. Females represented in the epic, such
as Chrysogone and Satyrane's mother, find it difficult to escape
progenerative consequences from their involuntary sexual intercourse with non-human figures, but the prominent men represented in the poem appear to be immune from similar results,
despite their own eager participation in the illicit activities.
This aspect of a familiar double standard never receives com-

ment, regardless of its repetition. According to Geoffrey of Monmouth, for instance, Merlin's mother was a nun who became pregnant after being raped by an incubus.[34] Spenser's narrative does not comment on the famous seer's parental ties to the underworld, however, despite the impact this relationship might have upon the important advice Merlin offers central characters. Offspring produced after such rapes by gods or spirits generally do not inspire much discussion.[35] Equally unnoted is the discrepancy between the fertility rates after male-infernal voluntary copulations and female-infernal/deific rape. Since mutual pleasure was commonly considered physiologically necessary for conception to occur (Eccles 33), this outcome defies contemporary gynecological theories. Nevertheless, protection of the men against productive use of their bodily fluids apparently carries more importance than physiological accuracy or statistical probability.

As has often been noted, the narrative in *The Faerie Queene* keeps knights and ladies separate as much as possible, even when the pairings promote virtue, as Una's and the Red Crosse Knight's coupling doubtless does. The poem continually indicates that women keep men from their knightly duties; hence, conjugal time needs to be postponed. This emphasis upon women's distracting qualities helps explain why Duessa and her fellow hags and witches often seem primarily concerned with keeping the knights out of the field. Such diversions provide roadblocks for knights en route to sainthood or the completion of their quests without the permanent immoral ramifications of fruitful copulation with confederates of the devil. Neverthless, suspect women share an important goal with the evil men who prey upon women in Faeryland; that is, they attempt to lure their victims to sin. It is not always sinful to lose in battle, but succumbing to unlawful lust brings virtue into question. Obviously, within allegory, opponents often represent sins or temptations, but the loss of the *literal* fray does not inevitably constitute a moral transgression. Some challengers primarily test prowess at arms, not virtue; others turn out to be unrecognized comrades. Hence, serious moral repercussions do not always accompany defeats on the battlefield, despite the allegorical emphasis upon virtuous behavior.

The temptations offered by malevolent women, on the other

hand, typically carry immediate moral consequences. These opponents tend to offer seduction, not battle—though they may rely upon fiercesome knights to facilitate their sexual advances and they periodically encourage men to battle with each other. Generally, they form allegiances which enable their sensual manipulations, luring knights into sinful pleasures and away from their commitment to arms. The description of Arachne in the Legend of Temperance illustrates a common model favored by these deceptive temptresses: "And ouer them *Arachne* high did lift / Her cunning web, and spred her subtile net, / Enwrapped in fowle smoke and clouds more blacke then let" (II. vii: 28. 7–9). Though male opponents, including Guyon, also rely upon nets occasionally, they tend to be more straightforwardly recognizable than the women. A knight approaching rapidly on horseback with weapons drawn provides an evident target, whereas physically attractive women give little hint of their true intentions. Consequently, the webs of deceit spun by the disguised enemies often prove much stronger and more enduring than feats of arms. Lacking the narrator as a guide, the knights frequently demonstrate little understanding of the dangers they face in these situations until they have already committed an unvirtuous sexual act. Libidinal temptations remain the most difficult to resist.

According to the familiar double standard, however, men can easily recoup their reputations and their places as virtuous knights —even saints—despite sexual indiscretions. Thus, female tempters such as Duessa who represent true dedication to the downfall of these men, not simply to the satisfaction of their own sexual desires, use their seductive powers primarily to entice their victims into extended or permanent dissipation, with occasional further spiritual consequences as well. Coupling with Duessa, for instance, introduces threats of apostasy and treason along with its illicit sexuality through her association with the evils of Catholicism[36] and with Mary, Queen of Scots.[37] As the villain with a thousand faces, Duessa magnifies the dangers perceived as inherent within the female sex. She also combines the treacheries associated with the witches, hags, and succubi triad. In common Elizabethan or Spenserian usage, witches may also be termed hags or act as succubi, though hags are only rarely perceived in succubitic roles. Duessa is one of the few characters who straddles each of these categories, once again demonstrating her finesse in adapting to contingencies, although in the text, she is most commonly called a witch.

In its definition for "witch," the OED includes a typical reference from 1585 which refers to an incubus as "a kind of disease called the nightmare or witch." Once again, this association with nightmares suggests a close connection between such figures and their victims' imaginings.[38] Like the witches described elsewhere, witches in the epic devote themselves to wreaking havoc on others, but this link with their targets' psyches makes them particularly virulent.

Surprisingly few of the numerous concerns about witches found in *The Discoverie of Witches, Malleus Maleficarum,* and similar contemporary treatises on witchcraft, however, emerge as significant topics of interest in *The Faerie Queene.* Although witches' marks, sabbats, and familiars prompt extended debates and discussions in these other writings and in the witchcraft trials, they do not figure prominently in Spenser's poem. Instead, the witches' involvement in sexual issues receives the most attention. Spenserian witches work to seduce knights away from righteousness, using their powers of sexual forgery and their affiliation with darker forces to draw knights away from virtuous and chivalric pursuits. They exhibit protean qualities, alternately presenting alluring beauty, then metamorphosing into the harshness of hags.

Duessa's portrayal, for example, illustrates familiar cautionary statements about the dangers related to female beauty. As the anonymous *Discourse of the Married and Single Life* (1621) demonstrates, many treatises urge guarded responses to female appearance, attacking its effect upon men whether beauty is present or not:

> If she be faire, all thy businesse abroad is sure to go to wracke: for her bewitching and attracting beauty will inforce thee to stay within dores. If she be foule, thy business at home will go worse: for that by reason of her noysomnesse, thou wilt haue but little list to bee at home. (sig. B8^v)

Knights in the poem give no indication of having read such tracts, however. Instead, their behavior is apparently based upon very literal interpretations of Neoplatonic doctrine, readily and simplistically equating physical with spiritual beauty. In Neoplatonic thought, as Pico della Mirandola observes, "the desire for beauty is the one which by us is called love" (45). Unfortunately, these knights often interpret any beautiful woman as an appropriate object of love. This mistake guarantees their entrancement by what Pico terms "vulgar love," or "the desire to possess such beauty" (63), which "can occur only in those souls which are immersed in matter and in some fashion dominated by the body" (65). In order to reach beyond this attachment to physical beauty toward "angelic" love, the knights need to learn how simultaneously to "see the intelligible things and see to the sensible" (65–66). As Pico notes, however, few men reach such an "image of heavenly love" (64). While the titular knights are presumably striving toward this "perfect" love (64), their portrayals often show them driven by desires for the physical.[39]

Baldasar Castiglione's Pietro Bembo discusses this lure of physical beauty specifically as it plagues such aspiring young courtiers: "The mind is seized with a desire for the beauty which it recognizes as something good, and, if it allows itself to be guided by what its senses tell it, it falls into very grave errors, and judges that the body is the chief cause of the beauty which it enshrines" (326). Although Bembo claims that "true love of beauty is good and holy" (327), he also maintains that young men's "vigour . . . easily persuade[s] the soul to yield to desire" (327).

In recognition of this tendency, Elizabethan writers regularly caution that beauty cannot be trusted. *A Discourse of the Married and Single Life*, for example, argues that "beauty and chastitie seldome dwell vnder one and the same roofe" (sig. Cı), while Alexander Niccoles reports that "An honest woman dwels at the signe of an honest countenance, and wilde lookes (for the most part) accompany wilde conditions" (sig. Cı). Given such conflicting responses to female beauty, it is not surprising that lauded women in the poem, such as Una and Britomart, are often presented covering their hair and faces, as Thomas Buoni, among others, recommends: "Hauing receaued so great a blessing, shee should learne of her mother nature, to hide it, which couereth euery faire, and pretious thing, vnder a thousand shells, and barks: yea in hard rocks and bottomles depthes, and not to lay it open as a thing common" (sig. C3). Still, despite these warnings and the example set by virtuous women, the knights in *The Faerie Queene* rarely display any distrust of physical appearances, and the unchaste demonstrate that seductive beauty can overcome the strongest male resistance.

Duessa, of course, justifies all the caution displayed above. This chameleon-like tempter has mastered the art of beautifying disguise so well that even her confederates can be fooled, as her need to identify herself to Night indicates:

> I that do seeme not I, *Duessa* am,
> (Quoth she) how euer now in garments gilt,
> And gorgeous gold arayd I to thee came;
> *Duessa* I, the daughter of Deceipt and Shame.
> Then bowing down her aged backe, she kist
> The wicked witch, saying; In that faire face
> The false resemblance of Deceipt, I wist
> Did closely lurke; yet so true-seeming grace
> It carried, that I scarse in darkesome place
> Could it discerne, though I the mother bee
> Of falshood, and root of *Duessaes* race.
> O welcome child, whom I haue longd to see,
> And now haue seen vnwares. Lo now I go with thee.
>
>   (I. v: 26. 6–9; 27)

The mildly comic tone overlaying this scene where Night fails at first to recognize the daughter of her old friend and relative Deceipt only briefly deflects its implications. As the two evil women kiss and join forces, the reader realizes that Duessa's consummate skill in camouflage amplifies her danger for the knights and ladies she encounters. If "that dreaded *Night*" (I. v: 24. 4) cannot pierce Duessa's disguise unaided, the regularly duped knights gain some justification for their seemingly endless susceptibility to Duessa's "faire face." The literal-minded reader may wonder why no one ever catches on to the repeated deception, but Night's puzzled reaction suggests that Duessa's costuming defies betrayal. Since the bad guys cannot discern one of their own company, there seems to be little hope for the virtuous, although these difficulties do not spare them the moral consequences of succumbing.

Such "forged beauty" (I. ii. 36. 1) constitutes one of the most common and treacherous perils encountered by the knights portrayed in *The Faerie Queene*. By the time Duessa is finally judged and sentenced to death in The Legend of Justice, she and her confederates have shaken the faith and virtue of countless knights. A master of dissimulation, Duessa is always ready and able to key into her victims' weakest points. By fashioning the images they most desire, she consistently offers the temptation most likely to insinuate itself into the knights' imaginations.

Duessa displays the seminal aspects of her sorcery during her interactions with Fraudubio and Fraelissa (I. ii). Here, the witch draws upon her abilities to refashion her own appearance as well as to camouflage the beauty of another. Noting that Fraelissa's lovely appearance blocks the witch's access to Fraudubio, Duessa creates a fog, which casts a shadow of deception over the scene and mars Fraelissa's features:

> And by her hellish science raisd streight way
> A foggy mist, that ouercast the day,
> And a dull blast, that breathing on her face,
> Dimmed her former beauties shining ray,
> And with foule vgly forme did her disgrace:
> Then was she faire alone, when none was faire in place.
>
> (I. ii: 38. 4–9)

Convinced by Duessa that Fraelissa was indeed a "deformed wight, / Whose borrowed beautie now appeareth plaine" (I. ii: 39. 1–2), Fraudubio recreates the Red Crosse Knight's mistake, leaving his own lady behind in order to follow "euer false Duessa" (I. ii: 37. 9). The parallels between the duping of Fraudubio and the Red Crosse Knight's belief in Archimago's dream demonstrate how readily beautiful simulacra can deceive knights' senses. Much of the time, even the most virtuous knights react to female beauty as though it provides incontrovertible evidence of value.

The most dramatic demonstration of witches' ability to manufacture or destroy female beauty may be when the son of the unnamed witch in Book Three falls in love with Florimell. In order to appease her son's murderous rage when Florimell flees, the "accursed Hag" (III. viii: 2. 1) calls upon her sprights and with their help "deuiz'd a wondrous worke to frame" (III. viii: 5. 2). After the spright chosen to inhabit that "carkasse dead" (III. viii: 7. 9) takes up residence, the simulacrum becomes so believable that "who so then her saw, would surely say, / It was her selfe, whom it did imitate, / Or fairer then her selfe" (III. viii: 9. 3–5). As we later learn, the Snowy Florimell becomes a smashing success despite its maleness, demonstrating that witches' skillful shaping of reality to accommodate male desire makes them formidable opponents.[40]

Ate figures less prominently in the epic than Duessa,[41] but her characterization also highlights the ills associated with witches and with women, as the description of her approach with Duessa indicates:

> But Ladies none they were, albee in face
> And outward shew faire semblance they did beare;
> For vnder maske of beautie and good grace,
> Vile treason and fowle falshood hidden were,
> That mote to none but to the warie wise appeare.
>
> (IV. i: 17. 5–9)

Ate's "face most fowle and filthy" (IV. i: 27. 1) initially seems to offer knights a clue to her loathsome ways, but her appearance shifts, keeping pace with her intentions and successes:

> To hurt good knights, was as it were her baude,
> To sell her borrowed beautie to abuse.
> For though like withered tree, that wanted iuyce,
> She old and crooked were, yet now of late,
> As fresh and fragrant as the floure deluce
> She was become, by chaunge of her estate.
>
> (IV. i: 31. 3–8)

Duessa and Ate together present a formidable impediment to knightly virtue.[42]

Naturally repulsive, malevolent females consistently transform themselves in order to exploit this knightly weakness. Ate, for example, possesses "squinted eyes" (IV. i: 27. 2) and a "loathly mouth" (IV. i: 27. 3), which would reveal her venom, if kept visible:

. . . vnmeete a mouth to bee,
That nought but gall and venim comprehended,
And wicked wordes that God and man offended:
Her lying tongue was in two parts diuided,
And both the parts did speake, and both contended;
And as her tongue, so was her hart discided,
That neuer thoght one thing, but doubly stil was guided.

(IV. i: 27. 3–9)

Recognizing that her true appearance reveals her intentions, she also resorts to disguises as needed. Ate and Duessa thus represent many of the qualities characterizing the continuum of witches, hags, and succubi. Duessa spends most of the poem in disguise, presenting herself behind a show of beauty. Ate, on the other hand, only rarely chooses such dissemblance, preferring instead to vent her spleen openly.

Beautiful females lacking in virtue nearly always turn out to be such "forged beauties." With few exceptions, their physical charms are illusory, hiding deformities which virtuous knights eventually uncover. This division between "truly" beautiful women and fraudulent beauties thus concurrently supports those writers who equate beauty with virtue and those who warn against deception. Since the dishonestly beautiful females in the poem tend not to be human, the Neoplatonic ideal is not disturbed. Knights need to learn to distinguish between human and demonic beauties, but they can generally keep their belief in the inner beauty of attractive human women.

The poem upholds this correlation by insisting that human females who become bad lose their beauty—especially those turned haughty, such as Mirabella. The mermaids in Book Two exemplify this pattern:

They were faire Ladies, till they fondly striu'd
    With th'*Heliconian* maides for maistery;
Of whom they ouer-comen, were depriu'd
Of their proud beautie, and th'one moyity
Transform'd to fish, for their bold surquedry.

(II. xii: 31. 1–5)

The fate of these prideful women also parallels Munera's destiny,[43] whose golden hands and silver feet were "chopt off" (V. ii: 26. 9) by Talus in Book Five "withouten pitty of her goodly hew" (V. ii: 25. 8).[44] The violence Talus displays here indicates the severity of this type of "crime." The common impulse to deprive beautiful women of their looks when they transgress against knightly values implies a belief that women who stray do not deserve to be attractive. Vindication against the women's audacity seems as important as safeguarding future knights from similar deceptions.

Unlike Munera, whom Talus "drowned in the durty mud" (V. ii: 27. 4), the mermaids retain their power to lure unwary travelers:

> But th'vpper halfe their hew retained still,
> And their sweet skill in wonted melody;
> Which euer after they abusd to ill,
> T'allure weake trauellers, whom gotten they did kill.
>
> (II. xii: 31. 6–9)

Their propensity toward murder distinguishes the mermaids from most of the other treacherous females; nonetheless, they figure as a brief reminder of the potential perils accompanying uncontrolled women.

Fortunately for Guyon's virtue, however, the Palmer is able to dissuade the tempted knight from answering their call: "But him the Palmer from that vanity, / With temperate aduice discounselled" (II. xii: 34. 1–2). Guyon typifies knights in the poem by his continued susceptibility to temptation. Even this close to the end of the book devoted to his own virtue, Guyon needs the Palmer to lead him away from the mermaids. Guyon's response signals the recalcitrance of this problem, which partially accounts for the many violent responses to women in the epic.

While the knights only have intercourse or flirtations with the array of beautiful women who hide their physical deformities, their encounters with other demonic women are significant even without sexual involvement. Most often described as "hags," these women openly project the images hidden beneath the succubi's forged beauty.[45] As Bruel indicates, nightmares were often attributed to "an old Hagge riding us" (H2).[46] The OED defines "hag" as an "infernal being, in female form"; "applied to manes . . . and other terrors of the night"; and "A woman supposed to have dealings with Satan and the infernal world; a witch." Only after these citations does it list the definition most familiar to modern audiences, namely, "an ugly, repulsive old woman: often with implications of viciousness or maliciousness." In Faeryland, according to Fraudubio's tale, witches must periodically reveal their own hag-like features: "that day is euery Prime, / When Witches wont do penance for their crime" (I. ii: 40. 4–5). On one such occasion, he sees Duessa become "the diuelish hag" (I. ii: 42. 1) he had mistaken for a beauty. His revelation comes too late, however, and Duessa transforms him into the "wretched man, wretched tree" (I. ii: 33. 4) who later reveals the witch/hag's true intent. As Artegall also learns, exposure to hags often signals a dramatic shift in a knight's status.

In general, hags in the epic serve as markers pointing to knights who have already fallen into dishonor or disrepute. At this stage, the seductive allure of a beautiful woman is no longer needed. Hags act with a forthrightness rarely ascribed to succubi. They channel their energies into open venom against their targets and allow their appearance to reflect their nature with loathsome accuracy, as Envy and Detraction demonstrate when they pursue Artegall:

> The one of them, that elder did appeare,
>> With her dull eyes did seeme to looke askew,
>> That her mis-shape much helpt; and her foule heare
>> Hung loose and loathsomely: Thereto her hew
>> Was wan and leane, that all her teeth arew,
>> And all her bones might through her cheekes be red;
>> Her lips were like raw lether, pale and blew,
>> And as she spake, therewith she slauered;
> Yet spake she seldom, but thought more, the lesse she sed.
> Her hands were fould and durtie, neuer washt,
>> In all her life, with long nayles ouer raught,
>> Like puttocks clawes: with th'one of which she scracht
>> Her cursed head, although it itched naught;
>> The other held a snake with venime fraught,

On which she fed, and gnawed hungrily,
As if that long she had not eaten ought;
That round about her iawes one might descry
The bloudie gore and poyson dropping lothsomely.

(V. xii: 29–30)

The disgusting description of "these Hags," "so vnhandsome drest" (V. xii: 38. 1) notes the severity of Artegall's decline by the time he is recalled to Court at the end of Book Five. His harassment by "two griesly creatures" (V. xii: 28. 6) who make no move to cover their "faces most foule and filthie" (V. xii: 28. 6–7), may suggest that Artegall is no longer vulnerable to female charms, but it also exemplifies his great distance from glory here. The insult for Artegall of being accompanied by such foul figures is compounded by their decision not to bother with disguise.[47]

The hags portrayed in the epic still retain recognizably human-like forms, though misshapen and unattractive. Denied female beauty, however, they are also largely removed from any non-allegorical existence. Hags in the poem usually provide vivid personifications of emotions, attitudes, and situations which plague the inhabitants of Faeryland, as Maleger's companions exemplify:

Maleger was his name, and after him,
   There follow'd fast at hand two wicked Hags,
   With hoarie lockes all loose, and visage grim;
   Their feet vnshod, their bodies wrapt in rags,
   And both as swift on foot, as chased Stags;
   And yet the one her other legge had lame,
   Which with a staffe, all full of litle snags
   She did support, and *Impotence* her name:[48]
But th'other was *Impatience*, arm'd with raging flame.

(II. xi: 23)

Others, including Occasion and Slander serve as hags with predominantly allegorical functions, although femaleness is emphasized even in these cases.[49] Occasion, for example, is not only an allegorical hag, she is a mother,[50] while Slander is said to bring shame upon her sex:

. . . that same Hag, his aged mother, hight
Occasion, the root of all wrath and despight.

(II. iv: 10. 8–9)

That shamefull Hag, the slaunder of her sexe.

(IV. viii: 35. 2)

A foule and loathly creature sure in sight,
And in conditions to be loath'd no lesse:
For she was stuft with rancour and despight
Vp to the throat, that oft with bitternesse
It forth would breake, and gush in great excesse,
Pouring out streames of poyson and of gall
Gainst all, that truth or vertue doe professe,
Whom she with leasings lewdly did miscall,
And wickedly backbite: Her name men *Sclaunder* call.

(IV. viii: 24)

The poem's insistence upon marking the sex and gender of these
creatures allows a thread of misogyny to weave through denunci-
ations of their behavior. In fact, it is often difficult to distinguish
slurs against individual hags or witches from those against women
in general.

Hags assault their victims with lies and vituperation. Revealing
their nightmarish roots, they often operate relentlessly and without
warning, though in the poem they do not suck blood from infants
as their folkloric counterparts do.[51] Hags epitomize the worst characteristics attributed to aging, quarrelsome women, with none of
the feigned charms writers warn against.

Predictably, the most prevalent feature which hags share with
contemporary negative depictions of women is a hyperactive
tongue. Women in the period are often advised to be "true tonged
and of fewe wordes,"[52] probably to discourage the type of speech
reported by Joseph Swetnam, among others. Swetnam, for example,
warns against marrying a widow because "with her cruel tongue
she will ring thee such a peal that one would think the devil were
come from Hell."[53] Such cautionary tales receive physical confirmation through the verbal outpouring of hags such as Occasion: "And
euer as she went, her tongue did walke / In foule reproch, and
termes of vile despight" (II. iv: 5. 1–2). The standard iconographical

representation of Occasion, which is replicated in the poem, portrays her as a partially bald woman.[54] This diminishment of conventional female beauty clearly reveals her allegorical character, but
once again, situates her as a "female" danger.

Many of these hags seek similar "occasions" for harm through
energetic use of their poisoned tongues, as the description of Ate
and then of Enuy make evident:

> Ate: Her lying tongue was in two parts diuided,
>   And both the parts did speake, and both contended;
>   And as her tongue, so was her hart discided,
>   That neuer thoght one thing, but doubly stil was guided.
>
> (IV. i: 27. 6–9)

> Enuy: Her face was vgly, and her mouth distort,
>   Foming with poyson about her gils,
>   In which her cursed tongue full sharpe and short
>   Appear'd like Aspis sting, that closely kils,
>   Or cruelly does wound, whom so she wills.
>
> (V. xii: 36. 1–5)

Enuy also wields a very literal representation of a stinging tongue:

> so false sclaunders at him threw.
> And more to make them pierce and wound more deepe,
> She with the sting, which in her vile tongue grew,
> Did sharpen them, and in fresh poyson steepe.
>
> (V. xii: 42. 5–8)

Similarly, Guyon finds that in order to stop Occasion's vilification
he must physically impede her voice: "And catching hold of her
vngratious tong, / Thereon an yron lock did fasten firme and
strong" (II. iv: 12. 8–9). Resorting to a lock to stop her speech,
Guyon literalizes a familiar strategy offered for the containment
of female speech.

Such maneuvers draw attention to the sex of these particularly
virulent attackers. Unlike most male opponents, who rely upon
physical feats in their battles against the virtuous, hags generally
respect the physical limits and stereotypes prescribed for members
of the female gender, exercising their verbal rather than their phys-

ical prowess. However injured the knights' pride may be after such encounters, the culturally assigned privileges and distinctions for the two genders are normally not disturbed or are restored expeditiously. Furthermore, as Duessa's bargaining and pleas to Orgoglio demonstrate, even the most treacherous female figures tend to respect traditional gender roles:

> *Duessa* loud to him gan crye;
> O great *Orgoglio*, greatest vnder skye;
> O hold thy mortall hand for Ladies sake,
> Hold for my sake, and do him not to dye,
> But vanquisht thine eternall bondslaue make,
> And me thy worthy meed vnto thy Leman take.

> (I. vii: 14. 4–9)

Notably, despite her status as irredeemable reprobate, Duessa remains ensconced here in a traditional gendered hierarchy, serving as Orgoglio's "deare" (I. vii: 16. 1). Though "dreaded more of men" (I. vii: 16. 6) she is still placed in a subsidiary role to the "hideous Geant horrible and hye" (I. vii: 8. 4). Regardless of Duessa's status as female arch-villain in the poem, she generally demurs from upsetting male-female hierarchies. Instead, she works her evil from within a conventional gender role, regularly changing or betraying the man she "serves," but stopping short of gender anarchy.

Radigund could be argued as an exception to this surprisingly common pattern, but even she fits into the familiar, containable category of "Amazon" and she resorts to "feminine wiles" when she tries to seduce Artegall. Although she supports gender inversion by cross-dressing her captive, she also displays stereotypical female behavior during her interactions with him. For the most part, no matter what other codes of appropriate behavior are violated, female detractors do not upset the firmly established hierarchies of gender. Instead, they magnify the flaws associated with women during this period and consistently emphasize their roles as *female* enemies.

In contrast, the male equivalent of the hag in the epic, the Blatant Beast whose "hundred tongues did bray" "so dreadfully"

(V. xii: 41. 7) is depicted as non-human, not specifically as a man, except through the use of male pronouns.[55] His maleness receives no particular mention, unlike the women whose sex is often noted in detailed physical terms. Physical strength is the primary recurring "masculine" attribute associated with male foes. Genital maleness usually only becomes relevant during sexual assaults against females, as the anatomically-based portrait (IV. vii: 5–9) of the "wilde and saluage man" (IV. vii: 5. 1) attacking Amoret exemplifies. Most of the time, male genitals receive little notice.[56] In addition, figures described as half human male/half non-human do not appear with the frequency of half female characters. This disparity suggests that "femaleness" is always a charged category, while "maleness" may not be relevant in every instance.

Among the female characters presented in the epic, it often appears that those portrayed as half humanly beautiful/half foul are considered the most evil, as though this additional indetermination heightens female treachery. Although allegorical representations could presumably be asexual, hermaphroditic or some non-specific gender, the importance of femaleness remains evident in these cases. In Book One, for example, the allegorical figure Error is presented in female guise:

> . . . the vgly monster plaine,
> Halfe like a serpent horrible displaide,
> But th'other halfe did womans shape retaine,
> Most lothsome, filthie, foule and full of vile disdaine.
>
> (I. i: 14. 6–9)

Hamilton glosses this passage as portraying Error "iconographically as a serpent with a woman's face" (1977: 34), but this depiction actually gives Error *half* a woman's body, not simply female facial features. In addition, it is not easy to discern whether this particular female form is being called "Most lothsome, filthie, foule and full of vile disdaine" or whether these terms refer to a more generic understanding of female figures. A similar description presents the monster Echidna in Book Six:

> *Echidna* is a Monster direfull dred,
> Whom Gods doe hate, and heauens abhor to see;

So hideous is her shape, so huge her hed,
That euen the hellish fiends affrighted bee
At sight therof, and from her presence flee:
Yet did her face and former parts professe
A faire young Mayden, full of comely glee;
But all her hinder parts did plaine expresse
A monstrous Dragon, full of fearefull vglinesse.

(VI. vi: 10)

Echidna, mother of the Blatant Beast (VI. vi: 12. 1–2), exemplifies the recurrent conflation of the female and maternal with the monstrous. So horrible is Echidna that "euen the hellish fiends affrighted bee (VI. vi: 10. 4). Her power partially resides in her ability to mask her strength and her viciousness behind a convincing show of young, female beauty, though her monstrosity is so evident that she predominantly relies upon power rather than duplicity.

One of her other offspring, however, once again demonstrates that female beauty normally carries adequate allure to hide the most ghastly evils:

An huge great Beast it was, when it in length
Was stretched forth, that nigh fild all the place,
And seem'd to be of infinite great strength;
Horrible, hideous, and of hellish race,
Borne of the brooding of *Echidna* base,
Or other like infernall furies kinde:
For of a Mayd she had the outward face,
To hide the horrour, which did lurke behinde,
The better to beguile, whom she so fond did finde.

(V. xi: 23)

In practice, Echidna's daughter makes no effort to hide her wickedness and when Arthur encounters her in Book Five, she figures prominently as a monstrous female threat, but she also possesses the power to forge beauty.

The blow which finally kills her once again signals the centrality of sex even during battles with non-human creatures. Arthur initially hacks off her lion's claws, but his fatal maneuver combines coital imagery with generative symbolism: "Vnder her wombe his fatall sword he thrust" (V. xi: 31. 2). By attacking her womb in combative perversion of a sexual act, Arthur highlights his opponent's sex. Numerous other blows could have ended the fray, but his choice (which is not paralleled by the castration of male enemies) suggests that her female aspect warrants a particularly forceful attack. Given the frequent absence of female generative parts discussed in the previous chapter, it seems significant that the womb of this evil creature should be identified as the point of its destruction. Subsequently, the lines detailing this monster's death further the reader's awareness of her anatomical sex: "out of her infernall sinke, / Most vgly filth, and poyson therewith rusht" (V. xi: 31. 6–7). This image of her poisoned womb recalls contemporary tracts warning about the ills accompanying female reproductive anatomy, such as John Sadler's pronouncement in 1636 that "Amongst all diseases incident to the body, I found none more frequent, none more perilous then those which arise from the ill affected wombe . . . there is no disease so ill but may procede from the evill quality of it" (sig. A4ᵛ-A5). Such easy correspondences between descriptions of ordinary women's anatomy and that of monstrous females shows us how readily these figures can be conflated—especially in the psychic domain of dreams and nightmares, where normal divisions quickly fall away.

Similarly, although she is not physically monstrous, Excesse is also presented as distinctly female in *The Faerie Queene*: "a comely dame did rest, / Clad in fair weedes, but fowle disordered, / And garments loose, that seemd vnmeet for womanhed" (II. xii: 55. 7–9). Standing guard at the entrance to the Bower of Bliss, Excesse unsuccessfully attempts to entice Guyon into the enjoyment of her "sappy liquor" (II. xii: 56. 3). When she fails in her efforts, Guyon goes forth to destroy the Bower, leaving little trace of its signature superfluity. In allegorical terms, a figure such as Excesse can represent overabundance of all kinds; nevertheless, its manifestation as female links it explicitly within a tradition connecting femaleness with excess—in speech, in sexuality, and elsewhere.[57] As Doane remarks in another context, "the feminine body is insistently allegorized and mythified as excess" (2). Indeed, Spenser is joining a host of contemporary and modern writers when he presents a female image of excess. John Sadler, for instance, pointedly advises prospective Jacobean mothers that "Excesse in all things is to be avoyded" (sig. Gl); Thomas Becon announces in 1577 that "excesses bee called vices" (sig. D6); and an edition of *Malleus Malleficarum* announces in 1608 that "There are three things in nature, the Tongue, an Ecclesiastic, and a Woman, which know no moderation in goodness or vice" (42).

Spenser's presentation of Excesse as female also affiliates her with Derridean and other postmodern explorations of woman as "the dangerous supplement" (1976: 141–64), including Irigaray's conceptualization of woman's "plural" sexuality (1985b: 28), which marks her as *"never being simply one,"* appearing instead as "a sort of expanding universe to which no limits could be fixed" (1985b: 31).[58] Although the "excess" of Spenser's character is represented specifically by drink, her placement at the entrance to Acrasia's Bower also attaches her to the sexual indulgences represented therein. Camille Paglia, in fact, reads Excesse in distinctly sexual terms: "Excess, a 'comely dame' in disordered clothes, crushes scrotal grape clusters (a Dionysiac symbol) into a vaginal cup of gold, the male squeezed dry for female pleasure" (187). Not surprisingly, characters thus portrayed as luring others into libidinal or other excesses are often female.

This assortment of nightmarish females in *The Faerie Queene* helps illuminate the epic's version of "the myriad ways in which the female form has been used as a mould into which meanings have been poured by a male-dominated culture" (Mulvey 11). Just as succubi, witches, and hags in early modern Europe remained poised between the material world, the spiritual or physiological realm, and the domain of the imaginary, their nightmarish counterparts in Spenser's poem hover in a state of endless malleability, ready to change function or appearance in response to individual male fears or desires. As nightmares, these spirits have ready access both to personal and to communal psychic anxieties or desires. It is easy to imagine them transferred to the modern medium of animation, where their features could remain in continual transformation.

One factor, however, remains constant through each of these transmutations; namely, the "femaleness" of the specter. No matter how monstrous and disfigured these characters become, they do not lose their gender specificity. The emphasis upon the maternity of the hags Occasion and Slander, for example, implicitly heightens their already overwhelming ferocity.[59] Similarly, the simulacra designed to lure knights from righteousness are always presented in female form and the range of nightmares presented manifest stereotypical "female" characteristics, such as excessive speech or lust. In nearly every case, these figures magnify recognizably "female" attributes and use them to tempt or terrify male characters.

Given the correlation between these nightmarish females and fundamental male terrors, it is not suprising that the punishment of that ultimate female "lumpe of sin" (VI. i: 23. 7) Duessa differs dramatically from the fates of her male equivalents. Despite Arthur's brief weakening at her trial (V. ix: 46. 1–6), Duessa is sentenced to death and then killed in the Legend of Justice (V. ix: 49. 6; V. x: 4). In contrast, Busyrane, Scorne, and Disdaine all remain alive—thanks to the pleading of their female captives (III. xii: 34; VI. viii: 30)—and even the Blatant Beast eventually "got into the world at liberty againe" (VI. xii: 38. 9).

These variations are not incidental; they testify to the perceived enormity of "female crimes" against men and the lesser importance granted to crimes against female bodies. Since the Duessa in Book Five bears a closer resemblance to Mary Stuart than to the witch of previous episodes it can become difficult as a reader to correlate the testimony against her with her activities in prior books. Although she is convicted on charges against the state, the predominant "crime" we witness before the trial remains her pattern of successful seduction through masquerade. She has offered sex and the men who accepted have paid the price of dissipation. For the most part, however, although she has relied upon the false pretenses of forged beauty, Duessa has allowed her victims freedom to choose or decline her temptations. Nevertheless, her tenacity apparently mandates her execution.

In contrast to Duessa's victims, Amoret and Mirabella are tortured brutally by their male captors.[60] Mirabella's tormenters laugh as they beat her (VI. vii: 44–45), while Amoret is "bounden fast" with "yron bands" (III. xii: 30. 7; 30. 8) and her heart is "entrenched deepe with knife accursed keene" (III. xii: 20. 6). None of these acts of pornographic sadism result in the death penalty, however. Amoret interferes when Britomart moves to kill Busyrane, and Mirabella is presented as too afraid of the unknown to allow Arthur to intervene in her abuse. Consequently, those responsible for these beaten and butchered female bodies pass unpunished, while the nightmarish Duessa is killed—largely for successfully enticing knights into consensual sex and for retaining her power both through beauty and after unmasking.[61]

The accumulated configurations discussed in this chapter accord with Mulvey's Freudian contention that women only *seem* to be "the subjects of an endless parade of pornographic fantasies, jokes, day-dreams and so on" (11), when in fact, "most male fantasy is a closed-loop dialogue with itself" (11). Representations of females in *The Faerie Queene* confirm this hypothesis. Just as the epic's "good" women seem most important as the basis for homosocial narrative, the "bad" women enable the perpetuation of male sexual myths. Duessa and Acrasia, for instance, offer the heights of sexual ecstasy, but concurrently figure as what modern parlance might term "ball-busting, castrating bitches." Numerous women provide evidence to support warnings about deceptive beauty, and the parade of deformed female bodies justifies fears of female genitalia. In addition, the various hags spewing forth vitriolic speech offer amplified personifications of imagined quarrelsome old women.

Since none of these females are human, however, they enable male characters to retain their Neoplatonic ideals about the coincidence of inner and outer beauty. Nightmarish women emanate from interior demons and terrors, but the virtuous women in the epic confirm other expectations. Hence, once these challenged knights arise from their lethargy and vanquish their nightmares, they can rejoin the realm where beauty does signify virtue. Even Artegall, who departs the epic in the company of hags, can look forward to his prophesied marriage with Britomart.

This company of nightmares gives rein to the most terrifying and desirable male fantasies, while keeping the female figures who fulfill them ultimately manageable. To borrow Mulvey's terms again, "women are no more than puppets" (11) in this scenario.

Recalling the good women who vanish into the margins, these nightmarish women generally either evaporate like the Snowy Florimell or fall back under male domination. After playing their part in the testing of male resolve, they are no longer needed. Hence, they recede into the background of the male psychic pageant.

3

The Importance of Being Fairest
Kidnapping and Courtship in Faeryland

THE CONFLICTING ATTITUDES toward women in *The Faerie Queene* discussed in the previous chapters become particularly evident when designations of virtue are assigned by the narrator or by other characters in the poem. In the Proem to Book Three, chastity is called "that fairest vertue." By choosing the term "fairest" to describe the virtue most often associated with women, the narrator foregrounds the unacknowledged symbiosis linking female "virtue" with attractiveness, subtly alluding to the tendency for chastity and other ostensibly honored female traits to depend upon beauty for recognition. The poem frequently displays an emphasis upon physical beauty disconnected from demonstrated virtue. This disjuncture often seems to undermine Neoplatonism's standard formulation of earthly beauty as reflective of heavenly beauty.[1] Nevertheless, it exemplifies the gendered foundation of such conventions which Ann Rosalind Jones notes: "Neoplatonism and Petrarchism were systems of metaphor and rhetoric organized around a male gaze, constituting and affirming male erotic fantasy as the governing frame of reference" (4). The inextricability of such male erotic fantasies from the poetic conventions contributing to *The Faerie Queene* guarantees that physical attractions will commonly overshadow actions and demeanor when female value is calculated.[2] Other qualities may be praised, but beauty usually reigns supreme. What Claudine Herrmann terms "the virile system" (41) dominates the landscape, ensuring that male prerogatives receive top billing and consideration. Female characters, in contrast, tend to display an empty or malleable signification.[3] Their largely conventional aspects adapt to accommodate wide-ranging male projections and desires.[4] Hence, the interpretations of female behavior offered by narrator and characters most often reflect the needs of this "virile system" rather than female intentions or actions.[5]

Beauty, in fact, performs a major function in the allocation of the labels "good" and "bad" to women.[6] Despite the common assertion that "chastity" has readily identifiable attributes and enemies, it usually proves impossible to fix definitive boundaries between female characters who adhere to the ruling precepts and those who break them. Maidenheads can sometimes be "repaired" for women who have acted unchastely, while undeniably chaste women remain prey to perilous rumors against their virtue. Often, the physical attributes and matrimonial accessibility of these characters outweigh their virtuous or reprehensible activities.

These tendencies are particularly apparent in the patterns and practices affiliated with kinship and courtship. What Gayle Rubin notably described as "the traffic in women" organizes and shapes female destinies. Sexual and marital decisions are made for female characters based on criteria which are predominantly outside their own experiences. It often matters more which interpretation best suits the needs of male individuals or structures rather than whether presumed transgressions or virtues are real or fictive. The presence or absence of male familial ties, for example, regularly determines whether females are considered virtuous, while the most blatant female indiscretions can be overlooked when there are pressing male reasons for doing so. Female characters are rarely shown fashioning their own destinies and the concept of female agency remains as transitory and illusory as the virtue of the Snowy Florimell.

These prominent patriarchal needs include the homosocial bonding which helps govern female circulation in Faeryland's marital economy.[7] This formulation is exemplified vividly in the Chaucerian tale of Cambell and Canacee in Book Four.[8] Here, with recurrent, though unacknowledged incestuous implications, a brother battles over possession of his sister,[9] while her own considerations—including her longstanding refusal to accept a marriage partner—largely evaporate from view. Cambell maintains that his participation in her marital negotiations results from her failure to choose a spouse, but it is clear that his own sexual and homosocial concerns contribute significantly to his involvement:[10]

Yet she to none of them her liking lent,
Ne euer was with fond affection moued.

(IV. ii: 36. 2–3)

Which, whenas *Cambell*, that was stout and wise,
Perceiu'd would breede great mischiefe, he bethought
How to preuent the perill that mote rise,
And turne both him and her to honour in this wise.

(IV. ii: 37. 6–9)

Cambell's largely unspoken personal stake in the outcome overshadows the irony of instituting a ferocious tournament in order
to "preuent the perill."[11] He also never acknowledges the deeply
sexual nature of the battle, which is represented in part by the
symbolic talisman Canacee sends her "dearest frend" (IV. iii: 35.
5) for protection in combat: "Conceiued by a ring, which she him
sent, / That mongst the manie vertues, which we reed, / Had
power to staunch al wounds, that mortally did bleed" (IV. ii: 39.
7–9).[12] The ring's reputation and sexual connotations terrify most
of Canacee's suitors, who decide that her beauty does not justify
the danger: "That dread thereof, and his redoubted might / Did
all that youthly rout so much appall, / That none of them durst
vndertake the fight" (IV. ii: 40. 2–4). So long as the "ring" representing Canacee's virginity keeps her suitors at bay, Cambell is
protected from giving her up—an exchange he resists however
much he needs it.[13]

When "three brethren bold" (IV. ii: 41. 1)[14] accept the
challenge, they further signal the tourney's complex signification
as a scene of female exchange with homosocial implications.[15] Cambell's resistance to their status as suitors highlights his own sexual
ties to Canacee while magnifying the fraught nature of the exchange system. Tournaments in the poem purport to identify and
connect the most beautiful woman with the most valiant knight
and "For to lose a Lady, were great shame" (IV. iv: 9. 3). Accordingly, in this battle for a woman's possession, both individual and
familial egos are at stake:

It hath bene through all ages euer seene,
That with the praise of armes and cheualrie,

> The prize of beautie still hath ioyned beene;
> And that for reasons speciall priuitie:
> For either doth on other much relie.
> For he me seemes most fit the faire to serue,
> That can her best defend from villenie;
> And she most fit his seruice doth deserue,
> That fairest is. . . .
>
> (IV. v: 1)

No matter how important it may be to marry off Canacee, Cambell's knightly pride resists relinquishing his claim to one of the "fairest" ladies. Consequently, Cambell fights for his sister's celibate chastity against the determined brothers who attack it as part of the sanctioned courtship ritual: "chalenging the Virgin as [their] dew" (IV. iii: 14. 8).[16] These jumbled motivations result in a monumental conflict, which seems more likely to lead toward massacre than filial bonding (especially since the brothers eventually merge):

> With that they both together fiercely met,
> As if that each ment other to deuore;
> And with their axes both so sorely bet,
> That neither plate nor mayle, whereas their powre
> They felt, could once sustaine the hideous stowre,
> But riued wer like rotten wood a sunder,
> Whilest through their rifts the ruddie bloud did showre
> And fire did flash, like lightning after thunder,
> That fild the lookers on attonce with ruth and wonder.
>
> (IV. iii: 15)

When the battle begins, its ferocity and the early likelihood that no one will survive exemplify the need for society's incest taboo. Cambell's intensive battle against Canacee's suitors implies that he would keep her for himself if that were allowed. The tournament's peaceful end, on the other hand, demonstrates the increased profit men receive when they intermarry rather than form unions within their sibling group—a desirable outcome stressed by Lévi-Strauss's informant in *Elementary Structures of Kinship*: "Don't you realize that if you marry another man's sister and another man marries your sister, you will have at least two brothers-in-law, while if you marry your own sister you will have none? With whom will you hunt, with whom will you garden, whom will you go visit?" (485). Cambell's and Canacee's devotion for each other also explains the particularly strong filial tie to Triamond which results from Cambell's sacrifice of his sister. Once Cambell has transferred his most precious "possession," he gains a powerful homosocial bond with the victor.[17]

Though tournaments to determine the ownership of women abound in Faeryland, this tourney most openly portrays the role these competitions play within the epic's kinship structures, in part because it illustrates the importance of Lévi-Strauss's dictum that "The prohibition [of incest] is not merely a prohibition . . . because in prohibiting it also orders. Like exogamy, which is its widened social application, the prohibition of incest is a rule of reciprocity" (51). Faeryland is a society like those Lévi-Strauss discusses, wherein "rank and fortune are rated highly" (47); furthermore, the matrimonial exchange depicted portrays "a particular case of those forms of multiple exchange embracing material goods, rights, and persons" (113). At the outset of the battle, Cambell presents Canacee to the assembled knights "to be seene, as his most worthie wage, / That could her purchase with his liues aduentur'd gage" (IV. iii: 4. 8–9), in correspondence with Lévi-Strauss's assertion that "purchase must be seen as a form of exchange" (138) and in accordance with Faeryland's equation between women and property. In addition, at the conclusion of the fray, we recognize what Lévi-Strauss posits as the primary impetus for marriage alliances:

> Exchange—and consequently the rule of exogamy which expresses it—has in itself a social value. It provides the means of binding men together, and of superimposing upon the natural links of kinship the artificial links—artificial in the sense that they are removed from chance encounters or the promiscuity of family life—of alliance governed by rule. (480)

When the virulent enemies "plighted hands for euer friends to be" (IV. iii: 49. 5), they cement their kinship ties and cancel their earlier enmity. Canacee's gains or losses do not warrant much consideration. Though a chief element of the system involved, Canacee functions only as objectified "woman" without an active voice in the determination of her future. Thus, her role accords with Gayle Rubin's description of this system: "the woman [is] a conduit of a relationship rather than a partner to it . . . women are in no position to realize the benefits of their own circulation" (174).

Despite this marginalization of the female, however, the happy conclusion would not be possible if another woman, Cambina, had not provided the trust and symmetry which Lévi-Strauss also finds crucial for successful female exchanges: "Generalized exchange always contains an element of trust . . . There must be the confidence that the cycle will close again, and that after a period of time a woman will eventually be received in compensation for the woman initially surrendered" (265).[18] Since the ferocity of warfare is generally not conducive to the growth of such trust and mutual exchange, outside help is needed, here provided by the figure Lévi-Strauss posits as the most appropriate person to facilitate this kind of exchange: "The prohibition on the sexual use of a daughter or a sister compels them to be given in marriage to another man, and at the same time it establishes a right to the daughter or sister of this other man" (51). When Triamond's sister Cambina arrives to complete this equation,[19] she enables the harmony and feasting which traditionally accompany such couplings:

> Where making ioyous feast theire daies they spent
> In perfect loue, deuoide of hatefull strife,
> Allide with bands of mutuall couplement;
> For *Triamond* had *Canacee* to wife,
> With whom he ledd a long and happie life;
> And *Cambel* tooke *Cambina* to his fere,
> The which as life were each to other liefe.
> So all alike did loue, and loued were,
> That since their days such louers were not found elsewhere.

(IV. iii: 52)

After the battle is resolved, Cambina quickly becomes a static figure. Like the narrator, she offers no protest against Canacee's "purchase" as Triamond's "worthie wage" (IV. iii: 4. 8–9). When Cambell established the tourney, he validated the premise that "the victour should his sister take" (IV. ii: 38. 9). The homosocial foundation of this structure precludes female vocalization, even as it enables "friendship."

Despite the harmonious ending, however, the less felicitous elements of this and other combats revolving around women remind us of the contentious aspects of tournament etiquette and of the structures of marital exchange. As an abundance of bloody encounters in the epic indicates, the stealing of another man's woman cannot be countenanced, even though she may be won—with or without her concurrence. Female characters typically only figure as booty in these tournaments. Accordingly, while men may challenge each other in combat, women have recourse to punitive action against a man only when he breaks the rules, as Calidore illustrates when he sympathizes with a jilted woman after she narrates the story of her rejection:

> Whom when my knight did see so louely faire,
>   He inly gan her louer to enuy,
>   And wish, that he part of his spoyle might share . . .
> He with strong hand down from his steed me throw'th
> And with presumpteous powre against that knight streight go'th.
>
> (VI. ii: 17. 1–3; 8–9)

By disrespecting the accepted regulations of female exchange, this fickle beloved provokes the wrath of those who have vowed to maintain order. Nevertheless, women's typical lack of choice in such matters illuminates the system's grounding in male concerns.[20]

This preeminence of patriarchal needs comes into the limelight also during episodes where knights ignore physical reality in order to preserve the illusion of female integrity. Despite the supposed importance of female virginity, Arthur and others demonstrate the ability to "undo" female sexual transgressions, with the stories of Pœana and Priscilla providing the most striking examples of such discretionary absolution.[21] Here, Arthur and Calidore each choose to preserve specific female reputations rather than hold the women responsible for illicit sensual encounters. In each instance, the women's sexual indulgences are "erased," thereby avoiding unwanted social repercussions which could seriously damage the men involved in their lives.[22]

Pœana, for instance, clearly her father Corflambo's daughter, receives this consideration despite her evil ways. Though "giuen is to vaine delight, / and eke too loose of life, and eke of loue too light" (IV. viii: 49. 8–9), Pœana exudes beauty: "So faire, as euer yet saw liuing eie" (IV. viii: 49. 5). Regardless of the subsequent proviso limiting her appeal: "And were her vertue like her beautie bright, / She were as faire as any vnder skie" (IV. viii: 49. 6–7), she benefits from the familiar knightly tendency to disregard the difference between true and feigned beauty.

Placidas, in fact, revels in Pœana's embraces even though her dubious character is well known to him: "There with great ioyance and with gladsome glee, / Of faire *Pæana* I receiued was, / And oft imbrast, as if that I were hee [Amyas]" (IV. viii: 59. 6–8). This loyal friend stresses the unimportance of Pœana's wanton nature when he announces that nothing bars him from her love since he is not already pledged to another woman:

> Which I, that was not bent to former loue,
>   As was my friend, that had her long refusd,
> Did well accept, as well it did behoue,
>   And to the present neede it wisely vsd.
>
> (IV. viii: 60. 1–4)

Since female characters remain most notable for their interchangeability, the ease with which Placidas decides to ally himself with this beautiful, but hazardous woman suits the tenets governing sexual affiliations. For Placidas, encouraging Pœana's affections offers welcome sensual delights; saves his best friend from infidelity; and provides him with the lovely woman every knight requires. Corflambo's daughter is clearly dangerous, but "the sweetnesse of her rare delight" (IV. ix: 6. 6), which also nearly incites Arthur into untoward lust (IV. ix: 6. 7), proves sufficiently alluring that concern about her treacherous nature vanishes.

The power of patriarchal structures to determine "virtue" regardless of the facts comes into play when Arthur decides to forgive Pœana's despicable activities, so long as she accepts his censure— and, significantly, his allocation of her lands and person:

He with good thewes and speaches well applyde,
Did mollifie, and calme her raging heat.

(IV. ix: 14. 6–7)

That trusty Squire he wisely well did moue
Not to despise that dame, which lou'd him liefe,
Till he had made of her some better priefe,
But to accept her to his wedded wife.
Thereto he offred for to make him chiefe
Of all her land and lordship during life.

(IV. ix: 15. 3–8)

Though the idea of female reform only rarely surfaces in contemporaneous writings, Arthur plants the concept in the couple's minds, then actively encourages its realization. This maneuver accords with other societal expectations, however. In whatever context women are considered in the epic—and in the period—the most important attribute remains male affiliation. Since a woman *must* be married, betrothed, overseen by a parent or male sibling, or enclosed within the Church, a successful marriage can override other considerations.

Not surprisingly, therefore, Pœana's scourge upon the countryside is conveniently interpreted as resulting from the absence of a suitable male to keep her in line, not from an innately evil nature. The narrative suggests that her history of hard living results primarily from sexual frustration: "Sith loue was first the ground of all her griefe" (IV. ix: 15. 2). Consequently, by urging the marriage between Placidas and Pœana, Arthur neutralizes her venom, while simultaneously removing her from the inherently dangerous realm constituted by unattached women. Since there is a man available and willing to wed her, all recollection of Pœana's "lewd loues and lust intemperate" (IV. ix: 16. 7) can be suppressed beneath renewed appreciation for "she whom Nature did so faire create, / That she mote match the fairest of her daies" (IV. ix: 16. 5–6).

The salient role of such alliances in female reputations should not be underestimated. If Mirabella, for instance, had a father, brother, or other affiliated male, she might have avoided perpetual torment. Here, as elsewhere, ostensibly rigid guidelines for virtue prove surprisingly malleable. Women generally only benefit from this flexibility, however, when their absolution concurrently grants a male ally relief or reprieve.

Such shifts to accommodate women with men ready to marry them help explain Calidore's willingness to lie on behalf of Priscilla.[23] Although our sympathies may be engaged here in favor of the thwarted young lovers, it is still difficult to justify the disregard for truth modeled by one of the epic's titular knights,[24] however lacking in our respect he might already be (acting the buffoon as he normally does is not inherently immoral, however regrettable).[25]

Calidore deliberately represses knowledge of Priscilla's actions when he reports to her father:

> There he arriuing boldly, did present
> The fearefull Lady to her father deare,
> Most perfect pure, and guiltelesse innocent
> Of blame, as he did on his Knighthood sweare,
> Since first he saw her.
>
> (VI. iii: 18. 1–5)

Regardless of his supposed knightly commitment to the truth, this blatant lie is not shown to concern the courteous, but imperturbable knight, who has already demonstrated that he can "sleepe all night through weary trauell of his quest" (VI. iii: 9. 9) despite the restless despair of those around him, who "all the night for bitter anguish weepe" (VI. iii: 10. 4). Since Priscilla would not be the only one to suffer, Calidore can overlook her indiscretions.

Calidore "mends" Priscilla's lost virginity when he "her restored trustily" (VI. iii: 19. 6) to her father's protection, suggesting that chastity results from societal affirmation, not from physical integrity. Furthermore, the feckless knight appears quite pleased with his ability to concoct a plausible story, which cannot be doubted without bringing his supposedly unassailable knightly honor into question:

> He passed forth with her in faire array,
> Fearelesse, who ought did thinke, or ought did say,
> Sith his own thought he knew most cleare from wite.
> So as they past together on their way,

He can deuize this counter-cast of slight,
To giue faire colour to that Ladies cause in sight.

(VI. iii: 16. 4–9)

Unlike Calidore's other questionable activities—such as his repeated blundering upon couples happily involved in amorous trysts—his cloaking of Priscilla's adventures on the road does not result from cheery ineptitude. He is presented as understanding fully what he is doing, choosing to sidestep truth in order to smooth things over for Priscilla at home.

In addition, the narrative suggests that Calidore is quite content with his decision. Though he is not portrayed as being particularly blessed with insight, he presumes that he can decide people's futures however he pleases. Accordingly, he frequently ignores facts in order to produce desirable conclusions. Surprisingly, moreover, basic goodness is not a prerequisite for receiving Calidore's help.

Among those allowed to live peaceably despite a history of promoting rack and ruin, Briana stands out as one of the most virulent prior to her neutralization by Calidore. At her behest, the evil Maleffort, "a man of mickle might, / Who executes her wicked will, with worse despight" (VI. i: 15. 8–9), pursues a "faire Damzell" (VI. i: 16. 2):

They saw the Carle from farre, with hand vnblest
Hayling that mayden by the yellow heare,
That all her garments from her snowy brest,
And from her head her lockes he nigh did teare,
Ne would he spare for pitty, nor refraine for feare.

(VI. i: 17. 5–9)

Calidore, of course, immediately sets out "for to pursue that villaine, which had reft / That piteous spoile by so iniurious theft" (VI. i: 18. 4–5), eventually easily overcoming the entire rout of wicked folk operating under Briana's auspices: "As doth a Steare, in heat of sommers day, / With his long taile the bryzes brush away" (VI. i: 24. 4–5).

When Briana angrily objects that Calidore has unjustly "Murdred my men, and slaine my Seneshcall" (VI. i: 25. 3), he answers

with a tirade against evil which leaves little apparent space available
for reform:

> Bloud is no blemish; for it is no blame
> To punish those, that doe deserue the same;
> But they that break bands of ciuilitie,
> And wicked customes make, those doe defame
> Both noble armes and gentle curtesie.
> No greater shame to man then inhumanitie.
>
> (VI. i: 26. 4–9)

His attitude hardly seems conducive to a truce with the woman
responsible; nonetheless, he immediately follows his call for blood
with an appeal for "that discourteous Dame" (VI. i: 30. 4) to
reform:[26]

> Then doe your selfe, for dread of shame, forgoe
> This euill manner, which ye here maintaine,
> And doe in stead thereof mild curt'sie showe
> To all, that passe.
>
> (VI. i: 27. 1–4)

Calidore's offer fails to move the haughty woman, however.[27] Still,
the courteous knight decides to settle the dispute with Crudor,
rather than demanding immediate recompense from Briana.[28] His
rationale is not stated explicitly, but it seems likely that a possible
coupling provides sufficient reason to pursue reform rather than
punishment. The benefits possible for society outweigh the pair's
crimes so long as they settle down together.

Eventually, both Crudor and Briana agree to revise their conduct, the former clearly out of gratitude for Calidore's decision not
to murder him:

> The wretched man, that all this while did dwell
> In dread of death, his heasts did gladly heare,
> And promist to performe his precept well,
> And whatsoeuer else he would requere.
>
> (VI. i: 43. 1–4)

Crudor is allowed to attone by taking "*Briana* for his louing fere,
/ Withouten dowre or composition" (VI. i: 43. 7–8), with the pre-

sumption that this action will "release his former foule condition"
(VI. i: 43. 9). In accordance with common practice in Faeryland,
Briana is not consulted, but since her reprehensible acts are attrib-
uted to a passion for Crudor, it seems likely that she will happily
accept being given to the forcibly chastened knight. Her reaction,
"Whereof she now more glad, then sory earst" (VI. i: 45.

1–2),
however, might still catch the reader off guard because Briana
quickly transforms Calidore into a deific figure to whom she offers abundant obeisance (as well as her Castle):

> Before his feet her selfe did proiect,
> And him adoring as her liues deare Lord,
> With all due thankes, and dutifull respect,
> Her selfe acknowledg'd bound for that accord.

(VI. i: 45. 5–8)

Presumably, Briana here acknowledges the wisdom of Calidore's
decision, even though he leaves her no voice in her future. Typically, readers are deprived of any insight into her reasoning. Since
she is choosing the sanctioned solution, all is considered well with
no need for explanation.

Amidst the subsequent frenzy of feasting and gratitude, when
"most ioyfuly she them did entertain" (VI. i: 46. 2), one critical
aspect of her transformation easily becomes lost, however; namely,
Calidore's subtle use of a torment which is often used to gain
female cooperation: "For his exceeding courtesie, that pearst / Her
stubborne hart with inward deepe effect" (VI. i: 45. 3–4). Even
when they are largely metaphorical, such piercings of female hearts
signal moments of substantial distress, though they may initiate
virtuous and necessary conjunctions. Britomart experiences significant pain, for example, after swallowing "vnawares the hidden
hooke with baite" (III. ii: 38. 9) which will make her love Artegall.[29] In extreme cases, including Busyrane's torture of Amoret,
when her "dying hart / [was] seeming transfixed with a cruell dart"
(III. xii: 31. 4–5), such female agony is admitted, but the frequency
of this approach remains unacknowledged.[30] Both good and evil
men rely upon such pain in order to "encourage" women to concur
with male desires. Since Briana does not garner much sympathy
from readers, her pain receives little notice. The prevalence of such

sadistic practices, however, once one notices them lurking in previously overlooked figurative language as well as in "minor" episodes, is deeply problematic.[31] In such instances, the literalness of the object conjoins with its metaphoric resonances, highlighting the simultaneous prominence of "piercing" in both literal and literary realms in the epic.

Calidore's decisions concerning Priscilla and Briana reflect another surprisingly common practice within this epic which claims to promulgate virtuous behavior. Similar emphases upon contingency over moral standards unite numerous disparate incidents concerned with women, their beauty, their virtue, and their paramours or spouses. Male characters occasionally suffer from their self-interest in this regard, but the negative consequences for them remain minimal. Women, on the other hand, fall victim to the vagaries of male opinion with sufficient regularity to keep many of them in continual flight. Despite the benefits of discretionary absolution, for instance, no history of chastity seems strong enough to guard against the lies of those who target an Una, an Amoret, or a Florimell for misrepresentation. Furthermore, the results deemed "everything turning out for the best," ignore the lack of female control over the lives others choose for them.

The problematic consequences women face as a result of such privileging of male prerogatives and desires are nowhere more evident than at Satyrane's tournament.[32] Here, the knights abandon any pretense of honoring chastity in order to promote libidinous delight in female beauty. From the beginning, this inversion of stated values is evident through the male characters' behavior and responses:[33]

> Then first of all forth came Sir *Satyrane*,
>   Bearing that precious relicke in an arke
>   Of gold, that bad eyes might it not prophane.
> (IV. iv: 15. 1–3)

> That same aloft he hong in open vew,
>   To be the prize of beautie and of might;
>   The which eftsoones discouered, to it drew
>   The eyes of all, allur'd with close delight,
> (IV. iv: 16. 1–4)

The startling shift in perspective here regarding Florimell's gir-dle[34] replicates a similar conflict permeating attitudes toward fe-male chastity. When Satyrane first appears for the tournament, he guards the girdle from potentially harmful glances, but as soon as he enters the arena, he not only sheds the protective covering, he also displays the "gorgeous girdle, curiously embost" (IV. iv: 15. 6) to the assembled company, with predictable results: "hearts [were] quite robbed with so glorious sight, / That all men threw out vowes and wishes vaine" (IV. iv: 16. 5–6). The great care for the item initially suggested is thus undermined with a vengeance only a stanza later.[35]

When the motley composition of the gathering is revealed, it appears unlikely that anyone would assume an absence of "bad eyes" among those at the tournament; nonetheless, no other excuse for violating the girdle's sanctity presents itself. Consequently, the "precious relicke" becomes the source and object of the lustful urges it technically resists as emblem of true chastity. By classifying the object as a "relique," moreover, the narrator signals a com-memorative function, suggesting that it memorializes a lost sexual state. "Relic" and "relique" normally connote remembrances of things past, including "that which remains or is left behind—es-pecially after destruction or wasting away" (OED). Here, there is a dual implication that both chastity and any regard for the "virtue" have dissipated.

The girdle's symbolic power is further subverted at the close of the tournament. Ever since Venus, the original owner, ironically and cunningly undid the girdle "when so she vsd her looser sport" (IV. v: 3. 9), the "goodly belt" (IV. v: 5. 9) has ostensibly separated chaste women from their less scrupulous counterparts:

> That girdle gaue the vertue of chast loue,
>   And wiuehood true, to all that did it beare;
> But whosoeuer contrarie doth proue,
>   Might not the same about her middle weare.
>
> (IV. v: 3. 1–4)

This miraculous garment attracts many contenders: "For peare-lesse she was thought, that did it beare" (IV. v: 6. 5). Despite such appeal, none of the women present except Amoret can "find it fit,

withouten breach or let" (IV. v: 19. 5). Upon discovering this inability of "chaste" women to wear the girdle, the judges decide
to give it to the False Florimell despite her unworthiness: "Yet
nathemore would it her bodie fit; / Yet nathelesse to her, as her
dew right, / It yeelded was by them, that iudged it" (IV. v: 20.
1–3).[36] The judges here determine that beauty, not virtue, deserves
commendation: "that golden belt by doome of all / Graunted to
her [False Florimell], as to the fayrest Dame" (IV. v: 16. 1–2).[37]
This separation of truth from beauty was foreshadowed by the
universal acclaim and wonder greeting the snowy Florimell when
she entered as Blandamour's escort: "For all afore that seemed fayre
and bright, / Now base and contemptible did appeare, / Compar'd
to her, that shone as Phebes light" (IV. v: 14. 1–3). Not until the
true Florimell reappears and dissolves her fraudulent double in
Book Five do most of the knights even question the disturbing
disparity between the False Florimell's perceived matchless beauty
and her inability to prove her virtue. From her choice of companions to her angry demeanor at the tournament (IV. v: 19. 7–9), the
illusory beauty gives no indication that she deserves the praise
lavished upon her. On the contrary, she offers ample cause for
suspicion—particularly to the poem's readers, who know "she" is
male.[38] Still, none of the dazzled knights are worried, except fleetingly when the girdle refuses to stay fastened, and "all the men
wondred at the vncouth sight" (IV. v: 17. 1).[39]

Since female beauty constitutes a woman's most salient characteristic, knights rarely pause to consider that beautiful women
can be lethal. Hence, despite endless fights over women who often
turn fraudulent, these battles never lose their value for proving the
dominance of particular men over other knights desiring the same
beauty. This desire is often non-specific, however, and the fairest
beauties tend to merge into each other, as the procession at the
Snowy Florimell's tourney suggests: "so many faire did see" (IV.
v: 12. 9). Nevertheless, "since the day that they created beene, / So
many heauenly faces were not seene / Assembled in one place" (IV.
v: 12. 4–6), and the need to ascertain the absolute fairest consumes
each of the gathered knights. This designation depends entirely
upon the agreement of those involved, however, not on an immutable measure. Thus, the False Florimell wins by "doome of all"

(IV. v: 16. 1), regardless of her evident unworthiness and in spite of the suspect nature characterizing many of those involved in the decree. Although several of the men represented, such as Braggadocchio, hardly qualify as judges of virtue, their voices count equally with those belonging to men of more indisputable stature. At Satyrane's tournament, readers not only realize that female virtue is less esteemed than pulchritude, they also note that knights never hesitate to offer women as "prizes."[40] No one questions the organization of a competition to match the greatest beauty with the most renowned knight, even though the "honored" woman is only consulted during an extreme crisis, notably when all the apparent male victors leave in dejection or dismay without anyone claiming the reward:

> Which troublous stirre when *Satyrane* auiz'd,
>> He gan to cast how to appease the same,
>> And to accord them all, this meanes deuiz'd:
>> First in the midst to set that fayrest Dame,
>> To whom each one his chalenge should disclame,
>> And he himselfe, his right would eke releasse:
>> Then looke to whom she voluntarie came,
>> He should without disturbance her possesse:
> Sweete is the loue that comes alone with willingnesse.

(IV. v: 25)

The irony of the sentiment expressed in the stanza's last line eludes everyone at the tournament, possibly since the deceptive maid chooses Braggadocchio, a man well suited for consorting with a fraudulent partner. Since the allocation of women proposed here corresponds with other courtship customs in Faeryland, no one is troubled.

Still, suspect characters such as Braggadocchio are not the only men drawn by the False Florimell's charms: "All that her saw with wonder rauisht weare" (IV. v: 14. 5). The substitute beauty is, in addition, so incomparably lovely that the only question raised ponders whether she is *too* perfect to be Florimell: "*Florimell* her selfe in all mens vew / She seem'd to passe: so forged things do fairest shew" (IV. v: 15. 8–9).[41] Only Britomart, the sole woman in a position to cast judgment upon the occasion, refuses to succumb to the snowy maiden's charms: "For that strange Dame, whose beauties wonderment / She lesse esteem'd, then th'others vertuous gouernment" (IV. v: 20. 8–9).[42] This emphasis upon the overwhelming importance of female beauty—"that daz'd the eyes of all, as with exceeding light" (IV. v: 10. 9)—remains common. Beauty draws knights to prospective brides (even marriages determined by fate, such as Britomart's with Artegall, depend upon beauty to encourage compliance) and provides evidence of virtue—the massive weight of contrary examples notwithstanding. Beauty constitutes both the lure and the reward of female companionship—while concurrently prompting male responses which endanger chastity.[43]

For example, in addition to the pervasive current of amusement which surrounds clearly wanton women, such as Hellenore and the women encountered by the Squire of Dames, open laughter at real or perceived female sexual indiscretions also occurs at several critical moments in the epic.[44] Although those initiating the frivolous reactions are often men of ambiguous distinction, such as Sir Satyrane,[45] these jovial interchanges point toward women's tenuous positions in Faeryland, irrespective of individual female claims to "crowne[s] of heauenly praise with Saints aboue" (III. viii: 42. 7).

The infamous Sir Satyrane and the Squire of Dames instigate two of these episodes.[46] The pair shake with laughter through the Squire's account of his quest to find chaste women, then initiate a wave of male amusement at the tournament when only a single demonstrably chaste woman can be found: "Which when that scornefull *Squire of Dames* did vew, / He lowdly gan to laugh, and thus to iest" (IV. v: 18. 1–2); and, "Therat all Knights gan laugh" (IV. v: 19. 1). The laughter permeating this scene,[47] which causes the "Ladies [to] lowre" (a deprecating description which increases their debasement in the episode) resonates with an atmosphere similar to that described by Freud when he discusses the implications of smutty jokes in *Jokes and Their Relationship to the Unconscious*:[48]

> Smut is thus originally directed towards women and may be equated with attempts at seduction. If a man in a company of men enjoys telling or listening to smut, the original situation,

which owing to social inhibitions cannot be realized, is at the same time imagined. A person who laughs at smut that he hears is laughing as though he were the spectator of an act of sexual aggression. (97)

Recollections of sexual situations such as Freud describes figure most prominently in the first encounter between the two men, when Satyrane "full hartely laughed" (III. vii: 58. 5) at the Squire's account of his failure to find more than one chaste woman:

> Perdy, (said *Satyrane*) thou *Squire of Dames*,
> Great labour fondly hast thou hent in hand,
> To get small thankes, and therewith many blames,
> That may emongst *Alcides* labours stand.
>
> (III. vii: 61. 1–4)

The Squire's story prompts amusement because it alludes directly to his many sexual successes: " . . . ere the yeare his course had compassid, / Three hundred pledges for my good desartes, / And thrise three hundred thanks for my good partes" (III. vii: 55. 3–5). It also lightheartedly deflates any pretensions to virtue for two of the three women who denied him their bodies:

> The first which then refused me (said hee)
> Certes was but a common Courtisane,
> Yet flat refused to haue a do with mee,
> Because I could not giue her many a Iane . . .
> The second was an holy Nunne to chose,
> Which would not let me be her Chappellane,
> Because she knew, she said, I would disclose
> Her counsell, if she should her trust in me repose.
>
> (III. vii: 58. 1–4; 6–9)

The laughter shared by this duo clearly emanates from salacious imaginings about the women who provided sexual favors. Even the two women who refuse conjure venerous thoughts since they operate freely within the sexual marketplace, despite the Squire's failure to gain access to them. As Freud points out, this brand of entertainment originates from sexual aggression; accordingly, these men dismiss the possibility that women ever exhibit sexual restraint. The Squire's amazement that the lowly, but beautiful

chaste woman could refuse him further emphasizes the widespread belief that female chastity exists only among unappealing
women.

Consequently, the Squire loudly scoffs when the tournament
produces only one woman pure enough to wear the girdle of chastity. In mocking derision, he attacks the manufacturer of the garment, sarcastically implying that the standard, not the competing
women, is at fault for the failure of the test:

> Alas for pittie that so faire a crew,
> As like can not be seene from East to West,
> Cannot find one this girdle to inuest.
> Fie on the man, that did it first inuent,
> To shame vs all with this, *Vngirt vnblest.*
> Let neuer Ladie to his loue assent,
> That hath this day so many vnmanly shent.
>
> (IV. v: 18. 3–9)

As the narrator indicates, many join in the lecherous amusement
prompted by the Squire's disdain for the concept of chastity:
"each one thought, as to their fancies came" (IV. v: 17. 2).

This deflation of the virtue's esteem continues through the
comic description of the women's disgruntlement at being openly
revealed as sexually incontinent. As they "lowre" (IV. v: 19. 1), they
locate the source of their distress in unrighteous indignation, not
in outrage at wrongful accusations. Furthermore, the Snowy Florimell—here only designated by the name she has purloined—responds with parodic fury when Amoret is revealed as the only
woman able to fasten the belt successfully around her waist: "But
Florimell exceedingly did fret, / And snatching from her hand halfe
angrily / The belt againe, about her bodie gan it tie" (IV. v: 19.
7–9). When the fraudulent woman receives the girdle, despite her
evident inability to claim it rightfully, this amusement at the dearth
of chaste women receives legitimation. There is no congruent recognition of the consequences facing women who fail to live virtu-
ously, however. Nor does the narrator comment on the problem
of using beauty as the primary means of determining virtue:

All which who so dare for to enchace,
　Him needeth sure a golden pen I weene,
　To tell the feature of each goodly face.
For since the day that they created beene,
　So many heauenly faces were not seene
Assembled in one place: ne he that thought
　For *Chian* folke to pourtraict beauties Queene,
　By view of all the fairest to him brought,
So many faire did see, as here he might haue sought.

　　　　　　　　　　　　　　　　　(IV. v: 12)

The humor accompanying this complete dismissal of chastity
draws attention to a pervasive devaluation of women.[49] Since chastity often receives little respect outside rhetoric, it is not surprising that the personification of womanhood is recognizable by "her
sad semblant" (IV. x: 49. 6). Male characters regularly do more
to undermine female reputations and safety than to protect them;
therefore, men in the epic are not generally trustworthy sources
of information or succor for women.

Florimell's story often illustrates this pattern. Shortly after the
narrator abandons Florimell in Book Three (III. viii: 43), for instance, Satyrane intrudes upon Paridell's efforts to save her by announcing that she has died:

Ah gentle knight (said then Sir *Satyrane*)
　Thy labour all is lost, I greatly dread,
　That hast a thanklesse seruice on thee ta'ne,
And offrest sacrifice vnto the dead:
　For dead, I surely doubt, thou maist aread
Henceforth for euer *Florimell* to be,
　That all the noble knights of *Maydenhead*,
　Which her ador'd, may sore repent with me,
And all faire Ladies may for euer sory be.

　　　　　　　　　　　　　　　　　(III. viii: 47)

He further intimates that her virtue has been irretrievably dam-
aged, offering as evidence the mangled, *bloody* remains of the famous girdle of virginity: "I found her golden girdle cast astray,
/ Distaynd with durt and bloud, as relique of the pray" (III. ix:

49. 8–9). Far removed from the "precious relicke" displayed at the tournament in Book Four, this "relique of the pray" suggests that Florimell has "died" sexually and mortally. The confusion of subjects and verbs within the stanza further implies that the wronged woman can be held responsible for her defilement. The girdle has been "cast astray" by an unnamed person; hence, the shadow of suspicion encompasses everyone there, including Florimell. Paridell (an unlikely champion!) refuses to accept the tale "Till triall doe more certain truth bewray" (III. viii: 50. 5), but since the knights later accept her duplicitous substitute without demur, even failing to register surprise when the false maiden allies herself with the clearly unworthy Braggadocchio, Florimell cannot expect her "goodly chastitee" (III. viii: 43. 3) to protect her from false report. The narrator may claim that "white seemes fairer, macht with blacke attone" (III. ix: 2. 4), but besieged virgin women commonly suffer intensely from comparison with their blacker counterparts.[50]

This recurrent subversion of female chastity takes on a particularly disturbing cast when Scudamour is finally reunited with Amoret. Male domination imbues this scene, completely denying female autonomy or self-determination, while emphasizing that even "virtuous" men may have an investment in publicly undermining female chastity.[51] The violation which causes some modern readers to recoil at this scene fails to horrify anyone within the epic, however, and Scudamour escapes with the reluctant Amoret, while eluding significant rebuke.[52]

Scudamour's abduction of Amoret closely matches Busyrane's abuse of the defenseless maiden, but it rarely provokes as outraged a response.[53] Nevertheless, even Scudamour initially seems aware of this parallel: "my hart gan throb, / And wade in doubt, what best were to be donne: / For sacrilege me seem'd the Church to rob" (IV. x: 53. 1–3). Amoret's feelings do not figure here.[54] Scudamour's combined lust and sense of manly honor urge him not to leave without accomplishing his task: "folly seem'd to leaue the thing vndonne, / Which with so strong attempt I had begonne" (IV. x: 53. 4–5).

Having overcome his awe at the sanctity of the Temple, Scudamour presses onward without hesitation, ignoring objections to his intrusion and to his plans for kidnapping the woman seeking sanctuary there:

> . . . that formost matrone me did blame,
> And sharpe rebuke, for being ouer bold;
> Saying it was to Knight vnseemely shame,
> Vpon a recluse Virgin to lay hold,
> That vnto *Venus* seruices was sold.
>
> (IV. ix: 54. 1–5)

The reckless Scudamour cannot be stopped at this point, however, and not only carries on with his mission, but denies the validity of the Temple:

> Nay, but it fitteth best,
> For *Cupids* man with *Venus* mayd to hold,
> For ill your goddesse seruices are drest
> By virgins, and her sacrifices let to rest.
>
> (IV. ix: 54. 6–9)

When Scudamour denounces the Temple, he justifies whatever actions he deems necessary, even if that means threatening the women guarding Amoret:

> With that my shield I forth to her did show,
> Which all that while I closely had conceld;
> On which when *Cupid* with his killing bow
> And cruell shafts emblazond she beheld,
> At sight thereof she was with terror queld,
> And said no more.
>
> (IV. x: 55. 1–6)

Scudamour's pride at successfully terrifying the guardians of female virginity correlates with the aggressive laughter discussed above. He is jubilant at his ability to frighten Venus's female priests. Personifying a machismo ideal, Scudamour triumphantly proves that might and perseverence easily triumph over mere "recluse virgin[s]."[55]

Scudamour's initial trangression becomes even more distressing when the Goddess urges him on:

> And euermore vpon the Goddesse face
>   Mine eye was fixt, for feare of her offence,
>   Whom when I saw with amiable grace
>   To laugh at me, and fauour my pretence,
>   I was emboldned with more confidence,
>   And nought for nicenesse nor for enuy sparing,
>   In presence of them all forth led her thence,
>   All looking on, and like astonisht staring,
> Yet to lay hand on her, not one of all them daring.
>
> (IV. x: 56)

Even Scudamour's audacious revelry in his own effrontery pales next to Venus's laughing complicity in the kidnapping of her adopted daughter and faithful virgin follower.[56] Venus here ensures that Amoret will become Scudamour's wife and destroys any hope for unthreatened female sexual integrity. Since Amoret was "sold" (IV. x: 54. 5) to her, she confirms the maiden's designation as property with no voice in her own future. Scudamour hesitates at the prospect of Venus's intervention: "[his] eye was fixt, for feare of her offence" (IV. x: 56. 2), but her convivial acquiescence with his violation of the hallowed space provides him with permission for his enterprise. Venus's laughter models the female complicity often found in the poem.[57] Her amused approval of Scudamour's brutality and his use of her son Cupid on his shield combine to produce the image of a powerful woman aiding in her gender's own belittlement by a man.

The goddess' apparent pleasure at the episode's conclusion cannot be shared by readers sensitive to Amoret's plight, however.[58] Critics often suggest that Amoret's troubles result either from her fear of sex or from her incomplete sexual maturation, but her anguished pleas belie such readings. It is unsettling for readers to dismiss her abductions and torture as part of the process of growing up, even in this fictive world. Scudamour is no more compassionate than Amoret's critics, moreover, and he ignores her pleadings:

> She often prayd, and often me besought,
>   Sometimes with tender teares to let her goe,
>   Sometimes with witching smyles: but yet for nought,

That euer she to me could say or doe,
Could she her wished freedome fro me wooe;
But forth I led her through the Temple gate,

(IV. x: 57. 1–6)

Amoret's empassioned resistance holds no weight against Scudamour's insistence, especially since he meets no forceful opposition:

No lesse did *Daunger* threaten me with dread,
When as he saw me, maugre all his powre,
That glorious spoyle of beautie with me lead,
Then *Cerberus*, when *Orpheus* did recoure,
His Leman from the Stygian Princes boure.
But euermore my shield did me defend,
Against the storme of euery dreadfull stoure:
Thus safely with my loue I thence did wend.

(IV. x: 58. 1–8)

Once Amoret is completely subsumed into her physical attributes,
becoming "that glorious spoyle of beautie," she retains no hope,
leaving the reader to note the painful irony of the knight's assur-
ance that the pair's exit was accomplished "safely." Only from
Scudamour's violently-based perception of love does "*Cupid* with
his killing bow / and cruell shafts emblazond" (IV. x: 55. 3–4), in
conjunction with the manifest reluctance of the bride, constitute
a commendable retreat into an admirable marriage.[59] Amoret's
version of the story would undoubtedly sound very different.[60]

The context within which the reader learns of this episode once
again foregrounds the familiar centrality of narrative sex within
this epic of postponed consummations. For the knights involved,
there are repeated indications that the intense pleasure of telling
their tales of conquest far exceeds their desire for specific women,
whether for sexual or dynastic purposes. As Arthur's rendition of
his erotic dream exemplifies, the dominant locus of sensuality resides within the story rather than with the actual physical encounter, even when the woman involved is the Queen of Faeryland.

Appropriately, therefore, Arthur himself introduces Scudamour's tale of the battle for Amoret by asserting that everyone
should be able to exercise self-determination while contracting am-

orous affiliations: "That of their loues choise they might freedom
clame" (IV. ix: 37. 8). This pronouncement, though contrasting
significantly with Amoret's experience, prompts Sir Claribell to
request an accounting of the events at the Temple of Venus:

> Mote we entreat you, sith this gentle crew
> Is now so well accorded all anew;
> That as we ride together on our way,
> Ye will recount to vs in order dew
> All that aduenture, which you did assay
> For that faire Ladies loue: past perils well apay.
>
> (IV. ix: 40. 4–9)
>
> So gan the rest him likewise to require.
>
> (IV. x: 41. 1)

Claribell's entreaty, which is supported by the entire company,
brings the focus of Scudamour's quest where they feel it belongs;
namely, on Amoret's beauty and upon the knight's spectacular
escapades. Amoret's considerable pain and hardship receive no
mention; instead, she is represented as "the spoils" claimed by the
knight who has survived considerable peril: "this shield of loue I
late haue wonne, / And purchased this peerelesse beauties spoile"
(IV. x: 3. 2–3). Since, as Scudamour remarks, his goal was never
to find a particular woman, but rather "To winne me honour by
some noble gest, / And purchase me some place amongst the best"
(IV. x: 4. 4–5), the emphasis of the story remains with the vigor
of Scudamour's pursuit and the enviable physical charms of his
target, not with Amoret's feelings or trials, except those demonstrating that Scudamour has obtained a woman of unsullied virtue:
"Since of my loue at length I rest assured, / That to disloyalty she
will not be allured" (IV. x: 2. 8–9). Once again, this elision of the
woman's perspective receives female approval, this time through
Britomart's eager insistence that Scudamour comply with the company's requests for his story: "*Britomart* did him importune hard,
/ To take on him that paine" (IV. ix: 41. 2–3). Her language reinforces the erotic nature of the narrative enterprise through the
sexual connotations of "that paine," as well as by the implication

that Scudamour will prove capable of assuaging Britomart's sensual longings with his words: "[Britomart] whose great desire / He glad to satisfie, him selfe prepar'd / To tell what misfortune he had far'd" (IV. ix: 41. 3–5).

This emphasis upon narrative rather than physical sex suggests again that male characters are most interested in sexual alliances because of the stories they create. Scudamour's obvious delight in the telling of his tale of conquest not only underscores the important function such narratives perform in securing homosocial bonds between virtuous men, it also highlights the narrator's dominant role in manipulating the reader's response into similar configurations. Without regular, pointed narratorial intervention, a reader could easily fail to discern the purportedly substantial variations between Scudamour's condoned behavior and the maligned activities of other men in the epic, such as Busyrane. From Amoret's viewpoint, there may not be a significant difference between her treatment by the two men, but the narrator works to elicit the audience's sympathy for Scudamour, while vigorously denouncing the magician's abduction of the virgin from the scene of her nuptials.[61] Such distinctions would not always be apparent to an unadvised reading audience, who might well concur with Scudamour's earlier self-denunciation—"thou vile man, vile *Scudamore*" (III. xi: 11. 6)—when they witness his disregard for his chosen lover's desire to continue as a virgin within the Temple of Venus.

The boundaries supposedly separating the two categories of men blur repeatedly. The argument opening the episode at Busyrane's Castle, for example—"the house of Busyrane, where *Loues spoyles* are exprest" (III. xi; emphasis added)—echoes through Scudamour's account of his adventures. While caught under Busyrane's control, Amoret suffers the effects of a sadistic torturer, but even here, there are striking parallels between Scudamour's tactics and the magician's strategy of "strong enchauntments and blacke Magicke leare" (III. xi: 16. 7). As the sanctioned lover relates, Busyrane "with wicked hand" (III. xi: 10. 7) relentlessly subjects "My Lady and my loue so cruelly to pen . . . and the sharpe steele doth riue her hart in tway" (III. xi: 10. 9; 11. 4). Until Britomart boldly intervenes, Busyrane's scriptorial sex constrains Scudamour's

powers of sexual narrative, highlighting the correlation between
the two rhetorical modes of sexual expression. Busyrane's method,
moreover, is able to silence Scudamour:

> There an huge heape of singultes did oppresse
> His [Scudamour's] strugling soule, and swelling throbs em-
> > peach
> His foltring toung with pangs of drerinesse,
> Choking the remnant of his plaintife speach.
>
> > (III. xi: 12. 1-4)

In further ironic contrast, Busyrane's cruelty, unlike Scudamour's,
aligns itself with that of several other despised male characters,
whose desires curiously focus upon capturing the love of various
abducted maids, rather than their physical ravishment.[62] Although
Busyrane's procedures cannot be countenanced, he still exhibits a
startling interest in Amoret's response and his writing is designed
"all perforce to make her him to loue" (III. xii: 31. 6). Scudamour's rhetoric, on the other hand, presents Amoret as a trophy
rather than an object of love. Nevertheless, Britomart chastises
Busyrane's despicable nature rather than Scudamour's: " . . . Thou
wicke man, whose meed / For so huge mischiefe, and vile villany
/ Is death . . . " (III. xii: 35. 1-3). Still, as Hamilton notes, "The
worker of her [Amoret] smart is as much Scudamour as Busirane"
(1977: 418). Though Scudamour may function as Amoret's fated
mate, he remains culpable for transgressions which seem congruent with the enchanter's crimes. Neither male character deserves
praise or emulation, but only one receives significant criticism in
the narrative.

Similar abductions often help organize Faeryland's "kinship
structure" and support the homosocial exchange economy upon
which Faeryland depends for stability. Since order within the realm
is ensured through the mechanics of the "traffic in women," readers
are calmed by purported differences between kidnappings motivated by "love" or "lust." It is unclear, however, whether the stolen
women could appreciate such subtle distinctions.

The importance of beauty remains the one constant as male
characters maneuver to assert authority by claiming one of the
numerous "fairest" maids alive. In Irigaray's formulation, "The use

made of women is thus of less value than their appropriation one by one" (1985b: 174). The ease with which snowy maidens, dream women, and disguised hags fool knights, as well as Calepine's apparent inability at night to recognize Serena, the ostensible object of his quest (VI. viii: 48–51), suggest that despite the multifold sighs devoted to various—absent—individual ladies, women are eminently interchangeable. This plethora of undifferentiated women counters the notion that Faeryland is structured around feats to honor specific women; instead, the endless transference of female bodies allows male figures to exert masculine supremacy and to display generalized desire.

The circulation of women through the poem often becomes literal as characters such as Florimell traverse Faeryland in perpetual flight. Since even officially approved tournaments can offer Florimell as the "prize" and since "good" knights, including Arthur and Guyon, join in the frenzy pursuing the frightened maid, wary women never stop. The chases only end when the narrative changes its focus.

Amoret and Florimell, of course, serve as the most prominent examples of women passing from man to man through Faeryland. Each woman's normal routine includes abduction and lengthy captivity. Linked further by their virtually unique ability to wear the sacred girdle, the lives of these two fair maidens exemplify the patterns of kinship and homosocial behavior which support male society in the epic. As Florimell and Amoret travel through the text, the reader perceives the importance of female exchange within the marital and chivalric economy depicted. Florimell, of course, never stops her literal circulation except when she is being held captive.[63] Even then, her vaporous double begins a less frenzied circulation while the worthy woman languishes under involuntary subjugation.

In addition, Florimell's adventures highlight the evident interchangeability not only between female characters, but also with the symbols representing them. In a perplexing, yet interpretively rich episode, Florimell is chased by a hyena-monster, who has been commissioned by the witch/hag of III. vii to destroy the maiden who has recently fled from the witch and her son. When the sexually symbolic hyena (Hamilton 1977: 369; 71) is unable to catch

Florimell, he diverts his rage to "her Palfrey tired lame, and slew him cruelly" (III. vii: 28. 8–9). By the time Sir Satyrane arrives on the scene, he is too late to rescue the palfrey or to assist Florimell, but he ties the beast up with the departed maiden's "golden ribband" of chastity (III. vii: 36. 1),[64] further emphasizing the sexual foundations of the transaction. Here, Florimell's person and virginity metonymically transfer to the "milke-white" palfrey (III. vii: 30. 8), which the hyena disembowels (III. vii: 29. 1). This conflation of Florimell's body and chastity with the devoured corpse of her abandoned mount makes it clear that the importance of her function within the exchange system transcends the significance of her physical reality in the poem. Not surprisingly, therefore, when the hyena returns with the girdle, the witch can successfully craft another substitute—the Snowy Florimell—to appease her son's outrage at his loss of the virgin (III. viii: 4–9). The true Florimell is not needed, so long as her place in the system is maintained.

Amoret also embodies many of the central characteristics of this exchange economy. Her strikingly abnormal conception and immediate abduction after her unusual birth underscore a seminal feature of this structure. The women who are consistently stolen tend to have obscure or absent families, making it unclear from whom or what they are stolen. Unlike attached women who have familial protection, these interchangeable women function predominantly as property. They possess few rights over themselves, leaving the crucial question of their ownership up for grabs. In this respect, these women invoke the Derridean "trace,"[65] representing an origin which can never be located, just as they often resist identification or even physical substantiation.

The narrator draws attention to these pervasive thefts at key moments, including the middle of Book Four, where he queries Cupid about these common, painful events:

> Great God of loue, that with thy cruell dart
>   Doest conquer greatest conquerors on ground,
>   And setst thy kingdome in the captiue harts
>   Of Kings and Keasars, to thy seruice bound,
>   What glorie, or what guerdon hast thou found
>   In feeble Ladies tyranning so sore;

And adding anguish to the bitter wound,
With which their liues thou lanchedst long afore,
By heaping stormes of trouble on them daily more?

(IV. vii: 1)

In saluage forrests, and in deserts wide,
With Beares and Tygers taking heauie part,
Withouten comfort, and withouten guide,
That pittie is to heare the perils.

(IV. vii: 2. 6–9)

By diverting responsibility to Cupid for these abductions, the narrator hints that love is their impetus, but the strategies demonstrated, as well as the consequences for knights, miscreants, and women, propel the reader to a substantially different conclusion. Love of beauty rather than love of women prompts most of these kidnappings, just as the strengthening of homosocial bonds or potential social ascension generally determines the configuration of the exchanges.

The role of homosocial bonding in the exchange of women re-emerges subtly through the familial ties of female victims, as well as through the divergent fates of the women discussed above. Since affiliation with a male figure supersedes other concerns, it should come as no surprise that fatherless women suffer more intensely from unwanted attentions than women with fathers, even absent fathers. The unusual amnesty from sexual consequences proffered to Priscilla and Pœana accords with their situation as women of identified paternity—even Corflambo's suspect nature does not eliminate his daughter from the special privileges granted to females with known fathers. Although the connection between their fates and their parentage is never noted explicitly, their amnesty from penance is consonant with the fates of other women within this category. This immunity makes sense within the environment portrayed, since attacking or chasing a woman with a father or brother correspondingly includes that male in the fray. Women who have men to protect them are not free; therefore, there is less immediate benefit to be gained by targeting them through unlawful means. Unaffiliated women, on the other hand, appear to be fair game.[66]

Britomart seems impervious to many of these dangers, as befits a king's daughter with an important generative service to perform. Though Glauce does not inspire much confidence as a protective force, Britomart's male guise, as well as the company of her nurse, helps distance her from the traumatic chases endured by the other women. Britomart's function within the marital economy is too important for her to become mixed up in the troubles facing other virtuous women—even Una, for instance, suffers temporary disrepute.

Una's history, however, highlights her privileged, though threatened position. Her beauty and hence her identity and reputation can be stolen, but she remains relatively protected against the sexual attack by Sansloy, who foregoes raping her in order "her to perswade, that stubborne fort to yilde" (I. vi: 3. 7):[67]

> With fawning wordes he courted her a while,
>   And looking louely, and oft sighing sore,
>   Her constant hart did tempt with diuerse guile:
>   But wordes, and lookes, and sighes she did abhore,
>   As rocke of Diamond stedfast euermore.
>   Yet for to feed his fyrie lustfull eye,
>   He snatcht the vele, that hong her face before;
>   Then gan her beautie shine, as brightest skye,
>   And burnt his beastly hart t'efforce her chastitye.
>
> (I. vi: 4)

Although Una's remarkable beauty further incites Sansloy's lust and urges him to battle for the "rich spoile of [her] ransackt chastetee" (I. vi: 5. 5), it also prompts the narrator to call forth divine intervention "Ah heauens . . . How can ye vengeance iust so long withold" (I. vi: 5. 6, 8) which arrives precipitously in the unlikely guise of an unusually gallant group of satyrs:

> Who when they hear that pitteous strained voice,
>   In hast forsooke their rurall meriment,
>   And ran towards the far rebownded noyce,
>   To weet, what wight so loudly did lament.
>   Vnto the place they come incontinent:
>   Whom when the raging Sarazin espide,
>   A rude, misshapen, monstrous rablement,

Whose like he neuer saw, he durst not bide,
But got his ready steed, and fast away gan ride.

(I. vi: 8)

Unlike Florimell—or most women in Faeryland—Una does not come under renewed attack from this unseemly rabble. Instead, they are overcome by her beauty and her plight and choose immediately to offer succour, "gently grenning," rather than laughing with lust or derision: "And gently grenning, shew a semblance glad / To comfort her, and feare to put away, / Their backward bent knees teach her humbly to obay" (I. vi: 11. 7–9).

There is never any overt connection drawn between Una's treatment and her parentage, but it correlates with a common pattern in the epic. Florimell, Amoret, and Serena seem no more worthy of continual abuse than Una does, yet their potential rescuers regularly prove to be as treacherous as any other foes. The connection between fate and family is emphasized directly, moreover, when Duessa attempts for one final time to undermine the match between Una and her beloved. When the paragon of evil confronts the court with accusations designed to stop the betrothal, Una's dynastic role overwhelms the scene, as the King introduces his daughter: "Then forth he called that his daughter faire, / The fairest *Vn'* his onely daughter deare, / His onely daughter, and his onely heyre" (I. xii: 21. 1–3). This emphasis upon her role as sole heir and "goodly royall Mayd" (I. xii: 33. 1) further enhances her beauty, underscoring the relationship between these two attributes, as the Red Crosse Knight notes: "Oft had he seene her faire, but neuer so faire dight" (I. xii: 23. 9). Duessa proves no match for Una in her familial surrounding and the holes in her story are readily exposed. There is nothing to be gained by accepting the claims of Duessa's prior entanglement with the Red Crosse Knight, since believing her could bring disaster to the realm. The bestowal of an only heir to a worthy mate takes precedence; therefore, Duessa's manufactured charges cannot be believed, even though less credible accusations are often accepted elsewhere. Since male accord determines most of the serious decisions in the environment portrayed, patrilineal considerations can be difficult to subvert.

Male acclamation continually plays dramatic roles in the structure of this society. Families rely upon societal cooperation in order to confirm the worthiness of their marriageable daughters. Similarly, for knights, snaring one of the "fairest dames alive" requires common agreement that the prized woman belongs in this category. When the women are absent, knights need strong narrative skills in order to convince their comrades that their beloveds qualify. Such ties between women and words are critical aspects of the entire system, as Lévi-Strauss comments: "Passing from speech to alliance, i.e., to the other field of communication, the situation is reversed. The emergence of symbolic thought must have required that women, like words, should be things that were exchanged" (496).

Given the prominent role of narrative sex and homosocial affiliations within the marital economy and kinship structure illustrated, it is singularly appropriate that the stealing of text and the stealing of women are linguistically connected. To "plagiarize," a term which came into usage at the turn of the sixteenth century, not only means to steal another's words, it also draws from the Latin "kidnapping" and "seduction" (OED).[68] In Spenser's epic, the theft or capture of a knight's words and of his lady are congruent activities, since the lady's primary worth resides in her ability to supply anecdotal material for her knight.[69] Knights accumulate value not from the physical aspects of their couplings, but from their use of language in the homosocial and sexual realms. In contrast, women merely circulate through the text, serving as receptacles for male fantasies and tender for the kinship market. Despite the narrative's insistence upon the value of female virtue, the fates of female characters in the epic make it evident that their most significant responsibilities revolve around the importance of being "fairest."

4

'Fayre of face . . . though meane her lot'

The Worth of Virtue

THE INTERCONNECTIONS BETWEEN beauty and the judgments
of female virtue discussed in the previous chapter reflect only
part of the criteria used to determine women's virtue. Just as
knights in *The Faerie Queene* are often measured by their "valor,"
female characters are also judged by theirs, although that term is
not used specifically when women fall under scrutiny.[1] Nevertheless, assessments of female behavior and virtue generally demonstrate an affinity for the qualities associated with valor, with the
concept of "worth" figuring most prominently. Male figures, however, are most often evaluated in accord with definitions emphasizing "courage and bravery" (OED). Status and proven feats of
courage thus determine the esteem granted by the narrator or the
characters to men in the epic. Female "valor," on the other hand,
more closely reflects those definitions which stress "intrinsic worth
or merit"; it also invokes the related term "valoir" and its associations of "value, worth, [and] price" (OED). In a female exchange
economy such as that represented in *The Faerie Queene*, the many
facets of "worth" carry more significance for women than courage
or the other elements associated with valiant men. Birth often joins
beauty, for instance, to help decide how female characters are
treated and classified, as permutations of "worth" insinuate themselves throughout determinations of female "virtue."[2] Although
female characters may be praised or derided according to ostensible
perceptions of their "virtue," their station in life joins their physical
appearance in contributing most forcefully to these judgments.[3]

Linguistically, "worth" can denote material value or value to
a person, in either material or less tangible respects. It also indicates

whether something is important; whether someone is entitled to respect; or whether an individual deserves punishment. In addition, when considering the connections between worth and sexual relations in Spenser's epic, it becomes significant that "worth" can also mean paying honor to a person or deity (OED). Throughout the epic, it is difficult to differentiate between references to material worth and the concept of worth associated with virtue. When a knight or lady is deemed "worthy" or "unworthy" of another's affections, both connotations surface concurrently. Such evaluations, moreover, shift repeatedly since they are linked to the relative standing between two particular people, rather than to unchanging states or circumstances. When "worth" enters the picture, "virtue" once again adapts to accommodate priorities which often owe much to gender.

The prevalence of this pattern appears in part through countless references to female individuals' "degree" or "estate," which help mark connections between genealogy and moral evaluations. The categories particularly important here divide persons of "meane" circumstances; those of higher or nobler status; "metahuman" figures;[4] and deific characters. Though explicitly signifying standing in the political, social, or heavenly world, these designations also determine expectations and evaluations of individual virtue. The workings of this system and the mutability of virtue in conjunction with female "worth" particularly come to the forefront when we consider the varying fates and responses to three female figures; namely, Mirabella, Pastorella, and Belphoebe. References to "worth" circulate throughout the descriptions of these three disparate, yet related characters. Concurrently, each benefits or suffers in direct response to her combined birth and beauty, while the variations between their stories suggest that the importance of behavior fades in comparison with these more vaunted attributes. The epic provides ample justification for Irigaray's contention that *"woman has value on the market by virtue of one single quality: that of being a product of man's 'labor'"* (1985b: 175); in these stories, "man's labor" refers to a range of activities, including his wooing or his gazing. Hence, by looking closely at equations between beauty, birth, and designations of "worth," we can bring into focus one of the dominant patterns impeding female characters in the epic from achieving the mode of "virtue" available to their male counterparts. Mirabella illustrates this process most dramatically. Her change in status clearly was designed to accommodate the men drawn to her beauty. Subsequently, assessments of her virtue become based upon her acceptance of or resistance to the accompanying behavioral prescriptions. Her story exposes not only the gender bias we might expect to find beneath its Petrarchan and Neoplatonic conventions, it also underscores the epic's common promotion of similar tenets.[5] The importance of social and political rank in early modern England is replicated in the poetry especially forcefully where the prerogatives and responsibilities of female characters are concerned.[6]

Consequently, despite her inflated standing, Mirabella's tale soon loses its early optimistic flavor:

> She was a Ladie of great dignitie,
>   And lifted vp to honorable place,
>   Famous through all the land of Faerie,
>   Though of meane parentage and kindred base,
>   Yet deckt with wondrous giftes of natures grace,
>   That all men did her person much admire,
>   And praise the feature of her goodly face,
>   The beames whereof did kindle louely fire
> In th'harts of many a knight, and many a gentle squire.
> But she thereof grew proud and insolent,
>   That none she worthie thought to be her fere,
>   But scornd them all, that loue vnto her ment,
>   Yet was she lou'd of many a worthy pere,
>   Vnworthy she to be belou'd so dere,
>   That could not weigh of worthinesse aright.
>   For beautie is more glorious bright and clere,
>   The more it is admir'd of many a wight,
> And noblest she, that serued is of noblest knight.
>   (VI. vii. 28–29)

When the narrator chastizes Mirabella for refusing her suitors, he grants male characters authority to designate her position and treatment since "noblest she, that serued is of noblest knight."

According to this proposition, male adulation determines female nobility. As we have already seen with the Snowy Florimell, this construction often leaves virtue by the wayside; nevertheless, it still operates centrally. In Mirabella's case, it saddles her with an obligation to choose male companionship in gratitude for her elevated status. At least where lowly born women are concerned, her story illustrates Irigaray's assertion that "the circulation of women among men is what establishes the operations of society, at least of patriarchal society" (1985b: 184). When Mirabella decides to remain autonomous, her virtue is impugned, even though there is no suggestion that her chastity or honesty have been tainted. Her accusers, however, quickly label her rejection of male values as a heinous crime, deserving of severe punishment.[7]

This insistence in the narrative that Mirabella ally herself with one of these countless suitors illustrates the charged emotions linked with the idea of female autonomy. It also keeps our attention focused upon the concept of "worth." The term's repetition in the second stanza above is indicative of its prominence in this system. Mirabella is deemed incapable of judging "worthinesse" for herself because she rejects many deemed "a worthy pere" by the narrator. As a consequence, she is classed "vnworthy" and suffers accordingly.

The accusations that Mirabella has grown "proud and insolent" also highlight this structuring. In association with warriors, "proud" denotes "valiant and brave" behavior (OED). Here, however, its proximity to "insolent" unmistakably marks the rationale for its more familiar, negative application to Mirabella. In contemporary usage, "insolent" actions were those which were "contemptuous of the rights of others." As this episode indicates, access to female beauty and potential sexual favors is considered a "right" for male suitors of appropriate standing in the poem, so long as the woman is not claimed by another man. This incident also illustrates how quickly "virtue" dissolves into what might be called "vir"-tue, with women facing judgment according to their recognition and respect for ostensible male prerogatives.[8]

Mirabella is labeled "proud and insolent" only after her beauty incites sexual longings in the men around her: "The beames whereof did kindle louely fire / In th'harts of many a knight, and many a gentle squire" (VI. vii: 28. 8–9).[9] Prior to this, she was known as "a Ladie of great dignitie" whose demeanor and beauty caused her "to be lifted vp to honorable place" (VI. vii: 28. 1–2) and led numerous knights to overlook her "mean parentage and kindred base" (VI. vii: 28. 4) in deference to her "wondrous giftes of natures grace" (VI. vii: 28. 5). Henceforth, she was expected to welcome these suitors with respect and gratitude for their willingness to disregard her humble origins. When "this coy Damzell thought contrariwize" (VI. vii: 30. 1), her perceived effrontery quickly becomes intolerable.

Mirabella is faulted for not acknowledging the "worth" of her suitors whose claims to status are founded more securely than her own: "Vnworthy she to be belou'd so dere, / That could not weigh of worthiness aright" (VI. vii: 29. 5–6).[10] The damsel denies that their stature grants them special access to her person, and "none them worthie thought to be her fere" (VI. vii: 29. 2). In response, the narrator proclaims that "vnworthy she to be belou'd so dere" (Vi. vii: 29. 5), and her punishment ensues.

The danger accompanying Mirabella's mutable position is further emphasized when she is described as "coy" (VI. vii: 30. 1). "Coy" can intimate actual or feigned modest shyness, as well as a disdainful demeanor. Additionally, a "coy" woman can either be one "not responding readily to familiar advances" or one who is "not demonstrative" (OED). Thus, a "coy" woman could be appropriately modest or reprehensibly aloof. Ambiguity resonates through these definitions, each of which was current in the sixteenth century, and Mirabella's carriage and actions could be interpreted to fit any of them.

Remarkably, Mirabella's diffidence drives none of her suitors away. Instead, they "languish long in lifeconsuming smart, / And at the last through dreary dolour die" (VI. vii: 31. 3–4). This consternation, outrage, and widespread demise—"they were all betrayd, / And murdred cruelly by a *rebellious* Mayd" (VI. vii: 34. 8–9; emphasis added)—generated by Mirabella's decision to remain unattached illustrates the power concentrated within unrestrained female beauty. Were Mirabella's punishment less severe, one might read such passages as glimpses of anti-Petrarchan irony.[11] Far from representing a standard disdainful Petrarchan beauty, however, Mirabella provokes enormous anxiety. Cupid's intense "wroth," which impels him to unbandage his eyes "That he might see his men, and muster them by oth" (VI. vii: 33. 9) and his hasty gathering of a jury to inquire into the "missing of his crew" (VI. vii: 34. 1) underscore this facet of her story. When the narrator moralizes against Mirabella as "the Ladie of her libertie," he condones the general outrage. Initially, he describes her "crime" in neutral terms: "She was borne free, not bound to any wight, / And so would euer liue" (VI. vii: 30. 8–9). In later reports, however, he supports Cupid's decision: "What could the Gods doe more, but doe it more aright?" (VI. vii: 31. 9). Guarding against an audience who might sympathize with the chastised lady, the narrator helps direct the reader's response by introducing Mirabella as a figure in disgrace:

> . . . they met
> With a faire Mayden clad in mourning weed,
> Vpon a mangy iade vnmeetely set,
> And a lewd foole her leading thorough dry and wet.
>
> (VI. vi: 16. 6–9)

He then tantalizes his readers by withholding the story behind her woeful circumstances: "But by what meanes that shame to her befell, / And how thereof her selfe she did acquite, / I must a while forbeare to you to tell" (VI. vi: 17. 1–3). He also includes Mirabella's version of events only after she is punished.[12] The narrator thus prepares his audience to concur with the court's judgment against the lady, where Cupid (characterized as "myld by kynd" [VI. vii: 37. 1]) "did the rigour of his doome represse . . . [and] vnto her a penance did impose" (VI. vii: 37. 4, 6). Her "reduced" sentence and the presumed impossibility of reparation: "Aie me, how could her loue make half amends therefore?" (VI. vii: 38. 9) suggest that a death sentence was warranted. The narrator's adept swaying of the evidence helps incline the audience against Mirabella. By focusing upon the alleged wickedness compelling her disdain for those "who sighed for her sore" (VI. vii:

30. 5), and by omitting any negative reaction to Cupid's response, the narrator becomes complicit with the love god's severity. The poem solidifies the portrait of Mirabella as a woman whose suffering is just when Mirabella decides to remain in bondage and Arthur silently accepts that she "needes must by all meanes fulfill / this penaunce" (VI. viii: 30. 2–3).[13] Although Arthur offers to free the woman from the "villaines" who torment her, he does so without comment on the legitimacy or duration of the punishment. Instead, he offers the ambiguous, morally neutral observation that "sith your fortunes thus dispose . . . if ye list haue liberty, ye may" (VI. viii: 29. 6–7). While she may be offered mercy, the justice governing her situation is never questioned.[14]

Once again, the Squire of Dames' story helps illuminate the system determining Mirabella's fate.[15] Both the horrified reactions to her activities and the benign attitudes toward her penance are highlighted when her story is contrasted with the Squire's encounter with Sir Satyrane, where both knights laugh at the questing Squire's plight: "Safe [one], I neuer any woman found, / That chastity did for it selfe embrace" (III. vii: 60. 1–2). Far from expressing dismay, Satyrane is delighted—"Thereat full hartely laughed Satyrane"—and jokingly commiserates: "Great labour fondly hast though hent in hand, / To get small thankes" (III. vii: 61. 2–3).[16] The widespread sexual generosity found among Faeryland's women elicits no obvious concern, even from the narrator. And, as already noted, the squire's immoral quest receives no criticism from other characters.

This connection between status and sexuality is further underscored by the attitude expressed toward the three who refuse the squire: "ill they seemed sure auizd to bee, / Or brutishly brought vp" (III. vii: 57. 8–9). In particular, the one chaste woman's resistance surprises the erstwhile lover, who unexpectedly needs to work at seduction: "Long thus I woo'd her with dew obseruance" (III. viii: 59. 7). Eventually he concedes defeat, however, recognizing that victory "was as farre at last, as when [he] first begon" (III. vii: 59. 9).

Significantly, this "faire" woman's steadfastness catches the squire off guard because it conflicts with the expectations accompanying her social standing:

> [the] Damzell was of low degree,
> Whom I in countrey cottage found by chaunce;
> Full little weened I, that chastitee
> Had lodging in so meane a maintenaunce.
>
> (III. vii: 59. 1–4)

Since the dictum "noblest she, that serued is of noblest knight" pervades the epic, one might expect this lowly damsel to seek some elevation of her status by joining with the eager squire, yet "in her countenance / dwelt simple truth in seemely fashion" (III. vii: 59. 5–6).

The narratorial approval which this maiden's chastity attracts does not transfer to the hapless Mirabella, however. Instead, angry, disgruntled responses to the lady's physical abstinence reflect the obverse expectations tethered to her inflated status. Rather than generating approving commentary for her sexual continence, this aloof beauty is subjected to the scorn detailed above. Her consistent refusal to recognize any unusual "privilege" represented by her popularity with the men of the upper ranks remains chief among her crimes.

The insistence upon reparation also foregrounds the economic basis of the episode, which accords with Irigaray's belief that in female exchange economies "women" are not exchanged as such, but instead "women [are] reduced to some common feature—their current price in gold, or phalluses" (1985b: 175). Mirabella's autonomy not only keeps her from participation in this system, it also illuminates the potential fragility of the structure and interferes with the expected production of male esteem.[17] The interminable nature of her punishment mirrors the gravity of this offense. After her chastisement, in fact, even Mirabella insists that it would be impossible for her to display adequate grief or remorse for her actions:

> Here in this bottle (sayd the sory Mayd)
> I put the teares of my contrition,
> Till to the brim I haue it full defrayd:
> And in this bag which I behinde me don,
> I put repentaunce for things past and gon.

Yet is the bottle leake, and bag so torne,
That all which I put in, fals out anone;
And is behinde me trodden downe of *Scorne*.

(VI. viii: 24. 1–8)

This monetary rhetoric continues when Mirabella presents her penance: "all is now repayd with interest againe . . . [Cupid] Causde me be called to accompt therefore" (VI. viii: 21. 9; 22. 2). Such language makes it particularly apparent that the economics of female exchange are the central focus here.

This emphasis upon "worth" does not always transfer to the male realm. Mirabella, for instance, stops Arthur from killing Scorn even though the vile creature deserves a messy end based both upon his worth and his behavior: "Slay not that Carle, though *worthy* to be slaine" (VI. viii: 17. 7; emphasis added). The victim disregards the villain's "actual" worth, since her life has become bound up with his fate: "My life will by his death haue lamentable end" (VI. viii: 17. 9). Despite Scorn's history, her judgment is greeted without much dismay, though Arthur briefly inquires, "What meaning mote those vncouth words comprize" (VI. viii: 18. 4).

Her pleas to keep Disdain alive emanate from terror rather than mercy: "For more on him doth then him selfe depend; My life will by his death haue lamentable end" (VI. viii: 17. 8–9). She clearly fears that no matter how painful her torture might be, the alternative could be worse: "I needes must by all meanes fulfill / This penaunce, which enioyned is to me, / Least vnto me betide a greater ill" (VI. viii: 30. 2–4).

The Prince, however, echoes the narrator's contentment with Mirabella's punishment and repentance. Arthur, in fact, appears quite impressed by Cupid's handling of the situation:

The Infant hearkned wisely to her tale,
And wondred much at *Cupids* iudg'ment wise,
That could so meekly make proud hearts auale,
And wreake him selfe on them, that him despise.

(VI. viii: 25. 1–4)

Mirabella's fruitless task apparently corresponds with Arthur's sense of justice; even when he offers to free her from her wretched companions, he never suggests that Cupid has been too harsh. Instead, the reader senses that Arthur's ire results wholly from his distaste for Scorn and Disdain, not from any particular sympathy for the lady. The Prince clearly would have liked to destroy Disdain, "had not the Ladies cry / Procur'd the Prince his cruell hand to stay" (VI. viii: 29. 1–2). Though he immediately diverts his fury upon Mirabella's intervention: "But being checkt, he did abstaine streight way" (VI. viii: 29. 4), the energy of his attack upon the vile giant—"He would with whipping, him haue done to dye" (VI. viii: 29. 3)—indicates that it monopolizes his attention; the woes of the lady remain secondary.[18] When she makes her choice, he immediately accepts her decision without comment and turns back to more compelling affairs at hand: "So humbly taking leaue, she turnd aside, / But *Arthure* with the rest, went onward still / On his first quest" (VI. viii: 30. 6–8).

The commentary discussing Mirabella's choices stops once she has been chastised and punished by Cupid. Instead of the numerous narratorial interjections which accompanied the earlier tales of her disdain for men, her quiet acquiescence with her torture receives no response. In significant contrast, the story of her prior life received two tellings; hence, readers are well aquainted with the supposedly "correct" moral interpretation of her behavior. Mirabella's version of the tale, however, does not come until after she has been forced to capitulate at Cupid's court; thus, we hear her voice only after she concurs with the sanctioned version of events. By the time she enters the narrative, she has been "converted"; therefore, she never explains her choices.

In addition, neither the narrator nor the Prince offer concern that her capitulation arises from a horror of further torture, not from contrition. Since her beauty has disappeared through the process of "wasting her goodly hew in heauie teares" (VI. vii: 38. 3) and her attire has fallen into "in such misseeming foule array" (VI. vii: 39. 3), the danger she poses to future knights has diminished dramatically and her spirit is clearly broken as she spends "her good dayes in dolorous disgrace" (VI. vii: 38. 4). Mirabella is no longer a threat.

All voices agree that she must suffer the vicious fool who now
abuses her in perpetuity, however,[19] since she would not accept the
love of those who earlier pursued her: "Ne list me leaue my loued
libertie, / To pitty him that list to play the foole" (VI. viii: 21. 3–4).
Indeed, even if someone were inclined to pity the forlorn woman,
her anguished words suggest that no one could save her: "Nor
heauens, nor men can me most wretched mayd / Deliuer from the
doome of my desart, / The which the God of loue hath on me
layd" (VI. viii: 19. 5–7).

Though equally unacknowledged by the narrator or by Arthur,
this already pitiful figure becomes an unwilling participant in a
twisted form of the sexual relationships she declined.[20] In retribu-
tion for leaving her suitors suffering with thwarted sexual desire,
Mirabella now provides perpetual sadistic sexual pleasure for her
captors,[21] similar to modern depictions of "bondage and discipline"
such as those Linda Williams describes, which show "the binding
and torture of the victim" (197). In these situations, Williams notes,
"everything is focused on the highly ritualized forms of violence
and domination enacted on the body of a woman." Such sadistic
acts closely resemble the violence committed against Mirabella:

. . . that angry foole
Which follow'd her, with cursed hands vncleane
Whipping her horse, did with his smarting toole
Oft whip her dainty selfe, and much augment her doole.

(VI. vii: 39. 6–9)

Ne ought it mote auaile her to entreat
The one or th'other, better her to vse:
For both so wilfull were and obstinate,
That all her piteous plaint they did refuse,
And rather did the more her beate and bruse.
But most the former villaine, which did lead
Her tyreling iade, was bent her to abuse.

(VI. vii: 40. 1–7)

The sexual imagery here—particularly the use of the "smarting
toole" to abuse her flesh—emphasizes the prominence of rape in
Mirabella's torture. Nevertheless, this sexual violation generates no
outrage, despite the horrifying magnification of Mirabella's at-

tacker, who illustrates Williams's thesis through seeking to "aggressively master [Mirabella's] threat of difference through various forms of sadistic punishment" (204):

> For he was sterne, and terrible by nature,
> And eeke of person huge and hideous,
> Exceeding much the measure of mans stature,
> And rather like a Gyant monstrous.
>
> (VI. vii: 41. 1–4)

Amazingly, Mirabella is lauded for accepting this abuse, becoming a warning for female readers, not a rallying point against similar sexual tortures:

> Ye gentle Ladies, in whose soueraine powre
>   Loue hath the glory of his kingdome left,
>   And th'hearts of men, as your eternall dowre,
>   In yron chaines, of liberty bereft,
>   Deliuered hath into your hands by gift;
> Be well aware, how ye the same doe vse,
>   That pride does not to tyranny you lift;
>   Least if men you of cruelty accuse,
> He from you take that chiefedome, which ye doe abuse.
> And as ye soft and tender are by kynde,
>   Adornd with goodly gifts of beauties grace,
>   So be ye soft and tender eeke in mynde;
>   But cruelty and hardnesse from you chace,
>   That all your other praises will deface,
>   And from you turne the loue of men to hate.
> Ensample take of *Mirabellaes* case,
>   Who from *the high degree* of happy state,
> Fell into wretched woes, which she repented late.
>
> (VI. viii: 1–2; emphasis added)

As these stanzas suggest, sexual torture figures as a sanctioned rejoinder to perceived female insubordination.

The intense physicality of Mirabella's punishment thus confronts the reader with a glaring example of the poem's moves to suppress female agency—at considerable cost to female bodies. The brutality of the male revenge depicted underscores the seriousness of Mirabella's alleged transgression. At this point, Mirabella's tale invokes modern discussions of masochism and sadomasochism, subjects which have been explored in numerous recent feminist and psychoanalytic texts.[22] Illuminating correlations can be found, for example, between this episode in *The Faerie Queene* and Pauline Réage's *Story of O*, a novel which details a woman's willing submission to extreme forms of sexual domination. In discussions of this modern work, we can locate repeated parallels between O's subjection and Mirabella's chastened acceptance of her torture. Although the two female characters become engaged in abusive situations through different avenues, the goals of their torturers seem quite similar. Consequently, the critical commentary on *Story of O* can help us interrogate the details of Spenser's presentation of sadomasochism in *The Faerie Queene*.[23]

Although Mirabella does not initially subject herself to sadism with the same willingness O displays, the two stories show marked commonalities. Like O, Mirabella is "to be always available and open" (Benjamin 57) to the abuse offered by Scorn and Disdain. Her articulate rejoinders to Arthur's questioning suggest that she also resembles O in learning "to be deaf and dumb to the feelings and cries of her flesh" (Griffin 219). The male characters in *Story of O* maintain that their supremacy emanates from their anatomical sex; consequently, O often sees only the genitalia, not the faces of those who torment her, emphasizing her subjugation to all men. Similarly, since Mirabella's "crime" has been interpreted as an affront against all men, Scorn and Disdain serve as conduits for a generalized male fury. Mirabella has been judged and sentenced by "men"; Cupid's tribunal merely serves as a rallying ground.

Throughout Mirabella's scenes of torture, her body exemplifies a process which Kaja Silverman finds in Réage's tale. The narratives of Mirabella and O demonstrate a similar discursive construction of female bodies: "That body is charted, zoned and made to bear meaning, a meaning which proceeds entirely from external relationships, but which is always subsequently apprehended both by the female subject and her "commentators" as an internal condition or essence" (1984: 325). Just as O's capitulation with her torture signals her agreement with the meanings attached to her body by her male tormenters, Mirabella's acceptance of perpetual abuse suggests that she has abandoned her own interpretation of her body and actions in favor of the male readings placed upon them. Once branded as "proud and insolent," Mirabella internalizes these labels, and we receive no information regarding the meanings she placed upon her actions prior to her arrest.

As Mirabella's story unfolds, readers are continually confronted with a decision which also faces Réage's audience; namely, "are our sympathies with the beater or the beaten?" (Massé 52). The crafting of this episode strongly suggests that the narrator is seeking to thwart any sympathy on behalf of the victim. The variety of voices which speak against Mirabella help discourage any acknowledgment of her torment which might enlist supporters for her cause.

In fact, Mirabella's own powers of speech also serve to distance the audience further from any sympathy with her plight.[24] By fashioning Mirabella as an articulate representative of the *Mirror for Magistrates'* tradition, the poet separates readers from the immediacy of the scene. As Elaine Scarry has observed in her noteworthy study *The Body in Pain*, pain can often seem "unreal to others" no matter how "indisputably real to the sufferer" (56). Since Mirabella's torture is surrounded so completely with narrative and moralizing, it seems probable that her pain and its sadistic origins lose much of their impact, even though exhibiting what Scarry terms pain's "obscene conflation of private and public" (53), whereby Mirabella experiences: "all the self-exposure of the utterly public with none of its possibility for camaraderie or shared experience" (53). Mirabella's episode emphasizes this solitude, even when she is with the Prince. Once sentenced by Cupid, the woman is completely alone in her torment, though constantly available for public viewing. As Arthur's actions exemplify, although her punishment may initially elicit concern, her own rendition of its origins diminishes the sympathy she attracts. Once chastened, Mirabella adds her own voice to those which condemn her.

Significantly, however, Scarry argues that severe torture actually destroys speech: "Intense pain is also language-destroying: as the content of one's world disintegrates, so the content of one's language disintegrates; as the self disintegrates, so that which would express and project the self is robbed of its source and its subject" (35). This description underscores the significant gap separating the representation of Mirabella's abuse and reality. While we should never expect verisimilitude from a work of this kind, this suppression of the effects of female torture furthers the poem's complicity with the acts represented. By keeping our focus upon her purported offenses and not on the visceral impact of her penalty, the poem deflects our awareness of the implications of her story.

Thus, Mirabella's tale can be framed not only as the tale of a disdainful Petrarchan beauty or of a woman whose perceived "worth" demanded capitulation to male desires. It can also be interpreted from the perspective Silverman offers for O's story: "It is the history of the female subject—of the territorialization and inscription of a body whose involuntary internalization of a corresponding set of desires facilitates its complex exploitation" (1984: 346). Mirabella's history details a similar process; although, as we shall see below, not all female characters in *The Faerie Queene* are equally subject to the terms of this system.

As Mirabella's situation starkly demonstrates, the "gift" of status she received came heavily encumbered with rules and expectations—the predominant constituent being an inability to use it to her own advantage. This is particularly true since her position was raised in order to make her "worthy" of the men seeking her favors. The narrator tells women that men's love is theirs as a "dowre" (VI. viii: 1. 3), presumably as an aid toward matrimony.[25] Consequently, as the text indicates, rejected men can legitimately appeal to Cupid, asking that her "soueraine power" (VI. viii: 1. 1) be revoked:

> Be well aware, how ye the same doe vse,
> That pride doe not to tyranny you lift;
> Least if men you of cruelty accuse,
> He from you take that chiefedome, which ye doe abuse.
>
> (VI. viii: 1. 6–9)

In addition, any woman who trangresses against this system offers herself up to what Benjamin labels "sadomasochistic fantasy, the most common form of erotic domination" (55). Both Arthur's limited response and the apparent complicity of the narrator in Mirabella's subjugation mark her position within this realm of male fantasy.

Since women's status in the epic depends upon their reputation in the male world, the threats that "men [will] you of cruelty accuse" and that "all your other praises will deface" carry considerable persuasive weight. In this economic system, women can scarcely afford to challenge male authority. Since their beauty ultimately determines women's position, the possibility of "defacement" is particularly poignant, while the severity of Mirabella's torture imposes a substantial deterrent against similarly autonomous women. Mirabella's case makes it clear that female power will be destroyed if it is ever truly exercised.

Divergent reactions to other female characters in *The Faerie Queene*, however, further demonstrate that the virulent rancor against Mirabella results largely from her transgressions against status, not simply her rejection of the suitors. Other female characters who treat men similarly do not receive congruent punishments—provided that they outrank the men they spurn. As I discuss below, Belphoebe is a particularly prominent example of this construct, but the pattern also includes women without deific connections, such as Pastorella.[26] Similar to Mirabella, her beauty and bearing contrast markedly with the expectations accompanying her presumed social standing. At the same time, her pastoral environment and professed antipathy toward courtly affectations correspond with Belphoebe's distancing herself from court. Pastorella also evinces a Belphoebean immunity from societal and narratorial criticism, while the parallels between her situation and Mirabella's diminish as her tale progresses.

Pastorella receives substantial praise, for example, despite her initial reluctance to encourage any of the "many a one [who] burnt in her loue" (VI. ix: 10. 2–3) because she believed that none of them were *worthy* of her: "Yet neither she for him [Coridon], nor other none / Did care a whit, ne any liking lend: / Though meane her lot, yet higher did her mind ascend" (VI. ix: 10. 7–9).[27] Later commentary amends this reading by suggesting that she also shies away from Calidore's attempted gallantry because she "had euer learn'd to loue the lowly things" (VI. ix: 35. 5); nevertheless, her early disdain still seems part of a general distaste for her suitors: "His layes, his loues, his lookes she did them all despize" (VI. ix: 35. 9). Rather than creating resentment or provoking wrath, Pastorella's rejection of her ardent admirers and her claim to a higher station attracts admiration, since common consent finds her worthy, as Calidore exemplifies: "he in his mind her worthy deemed, / To be a Princes Paragone" (VI. ix: 11. 4–5) Her upward pretensions figure prominently, in fact, without negative comment, in the description of Calidore's initial viewing of his future love, where she displays both a royal—"[she] did weare a crowne" (VI. ix: 7. 7)—and a celestial aura:

> That all the rest like lesser lamps did dim:
> Who her admiring as some heauenly wight,
> Did for their soueraine goddesse her esteeme.
>
> (VI. ix: 9. 5–7)
>
> As if some miracle of heauenly hew
> Were downe to them descended in that earthly vew.
>
> (VI. ix: 8. 8–9)

Pastorella is raised both literally and figuratively above her pastoral companions: "Vpon a litle hillocke she was placed / Higher then all the rest" (VI. ix: 8. 1–2). Such separation from those sharing her reputed birth-rank reinforces the consistent linkage between appearance and innate behavior with social standing. Since Meliboe "was to weet by common voice esteemed / The father of the fayrest *Pastorell*" (VI. ix: 14. 1–2), the shepherds do not know that Pastorella's actual parentage places her outside of their realm;[28] still, their responses indicate that her exalted status is readily perceptible. Her nurse later notes that her stature is obvious, "Most certaine markes . . . do it me teach" (VI. xii: 18. 3), but even those without previous knowledge quickly recognize her standing. Hence, she becomes the object of intense, but general adoration: "Ne was there heard, ne was there shepheards swayne / But her did honour" (VI. ix: 10. 1–2); "And caroling her name both day and night, / The fayrest *Pastorella* her by name did hight" (VI. ix: 9. 8–9). Coridon, however, "For her did languish, and his deare life spend" (VI. ix: 10. 6), because he cannot accept her disdainful response to him: "Fit to keep sheepe, vnfit for loues content" (VI. x: 37. 4).

Aspersions against this forlorn suitor's integrity do not appear until well into the narrative of his competition with Calidore over Pastorella, however. Evidence of insufficient virtuous worth appears only after the suitor has been found materially unsuitable. In Canto ix, when Coridon is introduced, Pastorella's disdain for him is linked to his inferior ranking, not moral turpitude: "Though meane her lot, yet higher did her mind ascend" (VI. ix: 10. 9). The hapless shepherd then foolishly challenges Calidore to feats more fitting with a knight's training: "But *Calidore* he greatly did mistake; / For he was strong" (VI: ix. 44. 1–2). Only late in the next canto does Coridon's deficient status and prowess become equated with a dearth of virtue. Here, the charges against him ring with intimations of his lowly status in addition to his purported moral lapses: "Through *cowherd* feare he fled away as fast" (VI. x: 35. 3; emphasis added). The dual meaning implied by this spelling of the word brings ranking into consideration again, particularly since Coridon's earlier activities do not appear to be especially unseemly. Once a lowly status has been posited, however, less admirable behavior becomes expected.

Henceforth, everyone ignores Coridon's longstanding efforts to serve Pastorella honorably: "[all the shepherds] did their labours share, / To helpe faire *Pastorella*, home to driue / Her fleecie flocke; but *Coridon* most helpe did giue" (VI. ix: 15. 7–9), concentrating instead upon his failure to protect the maiden from the improbable raging tiger:

> Which *Coridon* first hearing, ran in hast
> To reskue her, but when he saw the feend,
> Through cowherd feare he fled away as fast,
> Ne durst abide the daunger of the end.
>
>   (VI. x: 35. 1–4)

Once the narrator establishes that Coridon's lowly status relieves Pastorella from any obligation to him, the text focuses on Calidore's more successful efforts at impressing her. Coridon sinks from notice except through Calidore's suspect courtesy, which offers Coridon solace, though not the girl.[29]

Calidore also demonstrates that acceptable romantic involvements result primarily from matches of compatible social stature. Calidore is "vnwares surprised in subtile bands / Of the blynd boy"

(VI. ix: 11. 6–7), not only because of Pastorella's "comely carriage" (VI. ix: 9. 4), but also because he believes that her value far exceeds that of her companions, who must therefore be displaced:

> Her whyles Sir *Calidore* there vewed well,
> And markt her rare demeanure, which him seemed
> So farre the meane of shepheards to excell,
> As he that in his mind her worthy deemed,
> To be a Princes Paragone esteemed.
>
> (VI. ix: 11. 1–5)

Thus, "although his quest were farre afore him gon" (VI. ix: 12. 3), he determines to remain near her, ironically donning the garb and manners of those shepherds he intends to supplant:

> [Calidore] thought it best
> To chaunge the manner of his loftie looke;
> And doffing his bright armes, himselfe addrest
> In shepheards weed, and in his hand he tooke,
> In stead of steelehead speare, a shepheards hooke.
>
> (VI. ix: 36. 1–5)

Since Pastorella does not invite the favors of real shepherds and balks at Calidore's courtly manners, she predictably softens toward the knight's new bearing, whereby, like herself, he presents a pastoral appearance, but carries courtly credentials.

Even though Pastorella does not yet realize her own origins, the significance of her hidden birthmark announces itself through her crafty protection of her value on the marriage market. By twice pretending to be other than she actually is—that is, interested in the Captain's attentions, "She thought it best, for shadow to pretend / Some shew of favour" (VI. xi: 6. 5–6); and then ill, "to faine a sodaine sicknesse" (VI. xi: 7. 8)—she unwittingly replicates her actual dual existence. Having lived a deceptive life, she easily fashions successful deceits. She and her pastoral companions have intuitively discovered her true "worth"; therefore, she responds as virtue and society would dictate for one of her birth.

Even when her safety is in question, moreover, the emphasis remains upon her "worth." When the merchants eye Pastorella, for instance, the brigands respond by dickering over her value: "gan her forme and feature to expresse, / The more t'augment her price, through praise of comlinesse" (VI. xi: 11. 8–9). Pastorella needs to ensure that she is properly assessed in order to attract the appropriate suitors. Otherwise, the only alternative is to join Mirabella: " . . . with foule despight / Abusde, against all reason and all law, / Without regard of pitty or of awe" (VI. viii: 6. 3–5).

Pastorella neatly escapes such a fate, however. Unlike Mirabella, Pastorella is never criticized for her choices in love, regardless of her many sorrowful suitors.[30] Neither does she incite adverse comment when she resorts to lies in order to fend off the brigand's captain, ignoring his unusual choice to woo her initially rather than rape her: "[he] sought her loue, by all the meanes he mote; / With looks, with words, with gifts he oft her wowed" (VI. xi: 4. 7–8). Pastorella's deceptions raise no questions, just as her rejection of pastoral suitors does not send her to Cupid's court. So long as Pastorella does not violate the expectations of her position, in other words, her reputation rests secure. Unlike Mirabella, Pastorella remains the focus of adulation and praise.

However striking this contrast between Mirabella and Pastorella may be, it only hints at the hierarchical distinctions separating the former from Belphoebe, whose relationship with Timias emphatically demonstrates the variation between privileges granted to women of different ranks.[31] Unlike the unlucky Mirabella, the virgin hunter leaves her smitten squire to languish under the burden of hopeless love with complete impunity.[32] Instead of heaping censure upon Belphoebe's head, most critical and narratorial commentary suggests that Timias deserves to suffer for audaciously succumbing to the high-born virgin's beauty.[33] As punishment, Timias is relegated to an unusual fate for men; namely, a life of sexual abstinence whereby he must remain faithful, though distant, to his inaccessible object of desire.[34] Although the narrative surrounding these events ignores the parallel, the argument for IV. vii suggests that Timias closely resembles Mirabella's rejected suitors: "The squire her [Belphoebe] loues, and being blam'd his days in dole doth lead."[35]

The circumstances which keep Belphoebe so privileged are signaled before her birth. In Book Six, the men who succumb to Mirabella's love appeal to Cupid, who comes to their aid. The very

nature of Belphoebe's upbringing, however, was determined by
Cupid's absence. Not surprisingly, therefore, his jurisdiction does
not readily provide protection for Timias. If Venus and Diana had
not joined forces after the disappearance of the youthful love god,
they would never have stumbled across Chrysogone's newborn
daughters nor taken them away to be raised in their own images.
Amoret most directly substitutes for Cupid, since she is adopted
by Venus, but in many respects, Belphoebe fulfills a similar function for the virgin goddess. The infant's unnatural conception and
birth make her a singularly apt child for Diana to appropriate, since
the chaste goddess exists outside the environs of standard physical
sexual relations.

The effects of Diana's fostering are clearly reflected in Belphoebe's behavior. It is ironic, therefore, that Diana's attitude toward the bereft Venus, when the latter sets out to find her errant
son, closely resembles the arrogant tone which haunts Mirabella:

> Thereat *Diana* gan to smile, in *scorne*
> Of her vaine plaint, and to her scoffing sayd;
> Great pittie sure, that ye be so forlorne
> Of your gay sonne, that giues ye so good ayd
> To your disports: ill mote ye bene apayd.
>
> (III. vi: 21. 1–5; emphasis added)

Venus, however, denounces Diana's snide dismissal of her bereave-
ment, reminding the sylvan goddess that misfortune eventually
visits everyone:

> But she [Venus] was more engrieued, and replide;
> Faire sister, ill beseemes it to vpbrayd
> A dolefull heart with so didainfull pride;
> The like that mine, may be your paine another tide.
>
> (III. vi: 21. 6–9)

Despite this timely reminder of the value of compassion, neither Venus nor Diana show any signs of worry that Chrysogone
might suffer upon discovering that her mysterious babies have disappeared. Although the stanza in which they decide "from her
louing side the tender babes to take" (III. vi: 27. 9) contains numerous allusions to remorse, including such phrases as "nigh of

sense *bereaued*" and "her seeming *grieued*" (III. vi: 27. 5, 7; emphasis added), the goddesses do not hesitate to kidnap the infants, although they do pause at the "wonder" of the scene: "And gazing each on other, nought bespake" (III. vi: 27. 6). The irony of stealing two babies to relieve the grief over losing one's own is never discussed. Instead, agreeing "Out of her [Chrysogone] heauy swowne not to awake" (III. vi: 27. 8), "Vp they them [the infants] tooke, each one a babe vptooke" (III. vi: 28. 1).

This story of her origins provides important insights into Belphoebe's traditional escape from criticism.[36] The miraculous origin of Chrysogone's impregnation, for example, establishes the faerie's twin daughters' extraordinary positions both within and outside the human realm. Although Titan is implicated in the conception, "*Titan* faire his beames did display" (III. vi: 6. 5), there is an equally strong suggestion that it was simply miraculous:

> But wondrously they were begot, and bred
> Through influence of th'heauens fruitfull ray,
>
> (III. vi: 6. 1–2)
>
> The sunne-beames bright vpon her body playd,
> Being through former bathing mollifed,
> And pierst into her wombe, where they embayd
> With so sweet sence and secret power vnspide,
> That in her pregnant flesh they shortly fructifide.
>
> (III. vi: 7. 5–9)

Venus and Diana readily assume that this spontaneous pregnancy exempts them from honoring maternal rights, and without evident qualm, they choose "from her louing side the tender babes to take" (III. vi: 27. 9). Years later, Belphoebe often similarly distances herself from common moral and behavioral codes without self-consciousness or narratorial criticism.

Since her genealogy is dramatically indeterminate, Belphoebe's social and political status defies categorization. Non-humans do not fit easily into standard hierarchies, even within *The Faerie Queene*. Her links with divinity, moreover, free her from the constraints impeding Mirabella's self-determination. In addition, Diana's early decision that she is "to be vpbrought in perfect Maydenhed" (III. vi: 28. 4) situates Belphoebe outside the rules and boundaries of ordinary sexual exchange. The hunter's affiliation with the gods grants her special license.

Unlike Belphoebe, who thus remains exempt from many behavioral codes, Timias suffers repeatedly for his adherence to chivalric codes, as exemplified by his thwarted rescue of Mirabella as well as by his doomed love for Belphoebe. He spends much of the epic being punished for "wrong" choices involving women, although his mistakes seem to result from misjudgments regarding status, rather than from moral blunders.[37] As the narrator warns, however, this type of mistake carries serious repercussions:

> Well said the wiseman, now prou'd true by this,
>   Which to this gentle Squire did happen late,
>   *That the displeasure of the mighty is*
>   Then death it selfe more dread and desperate.
>   For naught the same may calme ne mitigate,
>   Till time the tempest doe thereof delay
>   With sufferaunce soft, which rigour can abate,
>   And haue the sterne remembrance wypt away
> Of bitter thoughts, which deepe therein infixed lay.
> Like as it fell to this vnhappy boy,
>   Whose tender heart the faire *Belphebe* had
>   With one sterne looke so daunted, that no ioy
>   In all his life, which afterwards he lad,
>   He euer tasted, but with penaunce sad
>   And pensiue sorrow pind and wore away,
>   Ne euer laught, ne once shew'd countenance glad;
>   But alwaies wept and wailed night and day,
> As blasted bloosme through heat doth languish and decay.
>   (IV. viii: 1–2; emphasis added)

Timias suffers intensely from an unwanted passion, which is classed as wrong because of his "meane estate":[38]

> when her excellencies he did vew,
>   Her soueraigne bounty, and celestiall hew,
>   The same to loue he strongly was constraind:

But when his meane estate he did reuew,
He from such hardy boldenesse was restraind.

                                        (III. v: 44. 4–8)

Calling himself "foolish," Timias reinforces the already prominent
parallels between his sorry situation and the woeful position of
Mirabella's rejected lovers. His reaction varies only because he
does not hold Belphoebe responsible and because he plans to ded-
icate his impending death to her honor.[39] Unlike Mirabella's suitors, however, whose plights arouse narrative and deific sympathy,
Timias prompts relatively uninvolved narration. He is never con-
tradicted when he asserts that dishonor rightfully accompanies his
love for Belphoebe. Instead, the poem seems to favor Timias's ad-
monitions to himself: "But foolish boy, what bootes thy seruice
bace / To her, to whom the heauens do serue and sew?" (III. v:
47. 1–2).

Timias also believes without question that his status bars him
from wooing Belphoebe, accepting that her unworldly origins grant
her an unassailable, however heartless, code of conduct.[40] Concurrently, Belphoebe apparently expects immunity from unwanted so-
licitations.[41] Hence, she remains oblivious to the source for Timias's
anguish, since it defies her world-view. In an arena where female
insight draws fear rather than admiration, Belphoebe's incredible,
yet implicitly admired, blindness helps ensure her continuance as
an emblem of "dew perfection." In fact, the narrator implies that
only "enuy" could lead to criticism against Belphoebe: "Ne poysn-
ous Enuy iustly can empaire / The prayse of her fresh flowring
Maidenhead" (III. v: 54. 5–6).

Belphoebe is described as a paragon continually through the
epic.[42] She is designated, for instance, as the locus of "all the gifts
of grace and chastitee" (III. vi: 2. 5):[43]

Well may I weene, faire Ladies, all this while
    Ye wonder, how this noble Damozell
So great perfections did in her compile,
    Sith that in saluage forests she did dwell,
    So farre from court and royall Citadell,
The great schoolmistresse of all curtesy:
    Seemeth that such wild woods should far expell

All ciuill vsage and gentility,
And gentle sprite deforme with rude rusticity.
But to this faire *Belphoebe* in her berth
The heauens so fauourable were and free,
Looking with myld aspect vpon the earth,
In th'*Horosocope* of her natiuitee,
That all the gifts of grace and chastitee
On her they poured forth of plenteous horne.

(III. vi: 1; 2. 1–6)

This idealization of Belphoebe encourages the narrator and critics to blame Timias for subsequent events and to relieve Belphoebe of any responsibility, despite indications of her involvement:

She his hurt thigh to him recur'd againe,
But hurt his hart, the which before was sound,
Through an vnwary dart, which did rebound
From her faire eyes and gracious countenaunce.
What bootes it him from death to be vnbound,
To be captiued in endlesse duraunce
Of sorrow and despaire without aleggeaunce?

(III. v. 42: 3–9)

Although Belphoebe may be incompletely aware of her effect upon the squire, the choice implied when she issues a "dart" of love,[44] as well as the anger and acute jealousy she exhibits when she believes that Timias is attracted to Amoret,[45] suggests that her behavior is not as distinct from Mirabella's as subsequent occurrences might intimate.

In addition, the sexual undertones informing the relationship between Timias and Belphoebe indicate their unspoken involvement in an inversion of the sexual situations plaguing Mirabella. While less overt than Scorn and Disdain's sadistic involvement with Mirabella, there are still strong suggestions that the pair are involved in a sadomasochistic dyad, although here the female character is in control.[46] The absence of physical sexual contact does not diminish this possibility; in fact, according to some modern studies of sadomasochistic behavior, sexual activity is not an essential element of such scenes of erotic domination.[47]

Timias's behavior consistently supports this hypothesis. When he chooses to "dye, rather dye and dying do her serue" (III. v. 46. 6), for example, he exhibits a desire for physical sacrifice which closely resembles the martyrdom Benjamin finds in *Story of O*.[48] In O's case, the protagonist offers to die rather than lose her dominator, Sir Stephen (204). According to Benjamin, this preference signifies O's "final gesture of heroism, her last opportunity to express her lover's will" (60). Timias similarly chooses to waste unto death as an ultimate gesture of silent love toward Belphoebe: "Yet neuer he his hart to her reuealed, / But rather chose to dye for sorrow great" (III. v. 49. 7–8).

When making such pronouncements, Timias repeatedly announces his unworthiness and contrasts it to Belphoebe's perceived deific status: "Thou a meane Squire, of meeke and lowly place, / She heauenly borne, and of celestiall hew" (III. v: 47, 3–4). The squire's self-effacement here demonstrates a correlation between the primary component of their relationship and Benjamin's partial definition of domination: "domination is an alienated form of differentiation, [an] effort to recreate tension through distance, idealization, and objectification" (68). When Timias asks whether "Angell, or Goddesse do I call thee right?" (III. v. 35. 5) and moves to "kisse [her] blessed feete" (III. v. 35. 9), he situates Belphoebe outside his rightful realm. Such idealization, which others in the poem also extend toward her, fixes Belphoebe in a position of unquestioned dominance over an increasingly submissive Timias. He devotes himself entirely to abject adoration of the hunter, continually announcing his unworthiness and beginning his conscious journey toward death, while keeping Belphoebe firmly situated upon her pedestal of domination.

Timias's behavior toward Belphoebe concurrently suggests that gender categories also blur under the strain of asymmetrical "worthiness." The squire, in fact, adopts the tortured role generally reserved for female figures in the epic. Referring to himself as "Vnthankfull wretch" (III. v. 45. 1), he renounces his body and chooses pain in honor of Belphoebe:

> . . . the mighty ill:
> . . . gan ransack fast

His inward parts, and all his entrayles wast,
That neither bloud in face, nor life in hart
It left, but both did quite drye vp, and blast;

(III. v. 48. 3–7)

As Benjamin notes, "current psychoanalytic theory appreciates that pain is a route to pleasure only when it involves submission to an idealized figure" (60–61). Anticipating this conclusion, Timias's surrender to intense pain here suggests that all his physical sensations have been subsumed into his passion for the unobtainable Belphoebe.

The self-abusing emotions which Timias exhibits further his association with the sadomasochism described in *Story of O*. Just as the squire succumbs to guilt and shame when he falls in love with Belphoebe, "O is thus required to confess to desires which become shameful the moment they are annexed to her" (Silverman 1984: 341). In response to these guilty feelings, both characters become "the masochistic subject who not only receives but wants [the punishment]" (Silverman 1984: 337). Like O, Timias chooses to suffer physical and emotional torment in order to prove his devotion to a cruel lover.

At the same time, Belphoebe easily fulfills the role of dominator in this relationship.[49] She initially nurses Timias back to health: "no paines did spare, / To do him ease" (III. v: 50. 1–2), yet she simultaneously refuses him the only certain remedy because she deems him unworthy: "To him, and to all th'vnworthy world forlore / She did enuy that soueraigne salue" (III. v. 50. 8–9). As one of the privileged, Belphoebe assumes the right to determine Timias's future existence—a prerogative she never hesitates to exercise. Hence, she can exclaim "Is this the faith" (IV. vii: 36. 8) to Timias and storm off when she encounters him with the unconscious Amoret, without justifying her restriction of his generally unwanted affections.[50] Here, Belphoebe's control over Timias's behavior again parallels the domination in *Story of O* whereby "This physical territorialization is accompanied by a verbal colonization which brings O's body into alignment with a whole network of rules and prohibitions" (Silverman 1984: 335–36). When Belphoebe determines that Timias has violated these prohibitions, she drives

him away. In keeping with the masochistic aspect of this relationship, however, Timias continues his own punishment even in her
absence: "And wast his wretched daies in wofull plight; / So on
him selfe to wreake his follies own despight" (IV. vii: 39. 8–9).
   The image of Belphoebe as sexual dominator is strengthened
by her remarkable lust for blood, a characteristic which is also
camouflaged by her privileged position. Her bloodthirsty predilections attract little comment, in fact, despite her role as an exemplar
of chastity. Notably, this intense attraction to blood first appears
when the hunter initially encounters Timias. Upon that occasion,
she and her maidens charge through the forest, in eager search of
the carcass they expect to find. Here, the narrator underscores
Belphoebe's voracious appetite for gore:

> She on a day, as she pursewd the chace
>   Of some wild beast, which with her arrowes keene
> She wounded had, the same along did trace
> By tract of bloud, which she had freshly seene,
> To haue besprinckled all the grassy greene;
> By the great persue, which she there perceau'd,
> Well hoped she the beast engor'd had beene,
> And made more hast, the life to haue bereau'd:
> But ah, her expectation greatly was deceau'd.
>
> (III. v: 28)[51]

When she reaches the spot, the narrative's unexpected christolog-
ical allusion marks the anomaly of this virgin's bloodthirsty interest:

> Shortly she came, whereas that woefull Squire
>   With bloud deformed, lay in deadly swownd:
> In whose faire eyes, like lamps of quenched fire,
> The Christall humour stood congealed rownd;
> His locks, like faded leaues fallen to grownd,
> Knotted with bloud, in bounches rudely ran.
>
> (III. v: 29. 1–6)

The tone in this passage and the details offered match Belphoebe's
apparent fascination with such sites. The virgin hunter seems to
relish the sight of blood.

Similarly, in another scene with Timian associations, Belphoebe pauses at the bloody body of a recently killed rapist in rapt fixation. Here again, the narrator provides graphic detail, suffused with sexual imagery:

> She sent an arrow forth with mighty draught,
> That in the very dore him ouercaught,
> And in his nape arriuing, through it thrild
> His greedy throte, therewith in two distraught,
> That all his vitall spirites thereby spild,
> And all his hairy brest with gory bloud was fild.
>
> (IV. vii: 31. 4–9)
>
> Yet ouer him she there long gazing stood,
> And oft admir'd his monstrous shape, and oft
> His mighty limbs, whilest all with filthy bloud
> The place there ouerflowne, seemd like a sodaine flood.
>
> (IV. vii: 32. 6–9)

Belphoebe is drawn by the "hideous noise" of the rape: "whilest thus in battell they embusied were [she] drew thereto, making her eare her guide" (IV. vii: 29. 1; 4), a detail further supporting her characterization as voyeur of blood and lust. Her captivation by the gore clearly overwhelms outrage at the rapist's crimes or concern for his female victims' plight.

The juxtaposition of Belphoebe's appetite for sexually-charged carnage with important encounters between herself and Timias demonstrates how vexed her presentation as paragon of chaste virtue becomes under scrutiny. In allegorical terms, as well as from a psychoanalytic perspective, Belphoebe's insistence upon Timias's sexual repression as a sign of respect for her inviolate chastity becomes increasingly suspect as she transfers her own passion and sexual curiosity into the woods, directing it toward bloodied male corpses rather than upon living, healthy bodies. Virtuous reputations in the epic usually do not withstand such fascination with the forbidden. Once again, however, her metahuman stature keeps her potentially suspect behavior from jeopardizing the respect and love of her admirers in Faeryland. Few other female figures could count on a similar response.

The stories of Mirabella, Pastorella, and Belphoebe draw our attention once again to the gendered dimension of Spenser's *Faerie Queene*. These female figures readily invoke associations with Petrarchism, pastoral, and Neoplatonic theories of love, but they concurrently remind us of the epic's underlying commentary about women. Though fashioned within a framework of literary convention, each character also alerts us to the complexities impeding female journeys towards virtue. As the discussion above emphasizes, the amount of "virtue" available to female figures in the poem is often predetermined by their birth and their appearance. Thus, their respective designations as disdainful Petrarchan beauty; simple, but worthy pastoral maid; or Neoplatonic beauty representative of the spiritual love which transcends physical attraction,[52] follow directly from their birth, and their behavior is interpreted accordingly. And, as we have seen repeatedly, the significance of beauty in the epic cannot be underestimated. As noted in chapter three, when the narrator calls the "female" virtue chastity "That fairest vertue" (III. Proem, 1. 1), he confirms the presence of an inextricable bond between females deemed "fairest" and those found to possess "virtue." Once we add the category of "worth" we have a much clearer picture of Faeryland's demands upon women than the poem ever provides directly.

5

'Like an Enraged Cow'

Britomart among the Chased and the Unchaste

THE IMPORTANCE OF "virtue's" etymology in *The Faerie Queene* is nowhere more striking than in the characterization of Britomart. Even though she serves as the titular knight for the "female" virtue chastity, Britomart can only enact this role from a position of "manliness."[1] Throughout most of the epic she dresses like a man, interacts with women as though she were male, and only rarely acknowledges her sex or gender—most notably when she acquiesces to patriarchal prerogatives by deposing Radigund and then relinquishing her own power as soon as possible.[2] Judith Butler recently defined gender as "the cultural meanings that the sexed body assumes" (6).[3] Britomart takes this figuration a step further by presenting a sexed body of fluctuating gender.[4] Primarily "male," she nevertheless remains "female" as needed.[5] Hence, she interacts as a man in the field, but does not support female rulership.[6] Concurrently, Britomart's characterization insinuates the threatening qualities inherent within conceptualizations of virtuous females.[7] Her revealed beauty, for example, confounds her companions, since it provokes the desire that virtue must resist. Britomart hides her sex,[8] therefore, since "femaleness" thwarts virtue in men and because undisguised women often attract charges of seduction. Discussing a related issue in modern cinema, Elaine Showalter asserts that the cross-dressing in "Tootsie" announces "that feminist ideas are much less threatening when they come from a man" (123). Similarly, Britomart demonstrates that female virtue becomes more palatable when it is personified by a manly woman, particularly one who honors the constrictions limiting her "place" as female.[9] Kaja Silverman suggests that "the subject's pattern of identifica-

tion . . . assumes its meaning and political value in relation to his
or her socially assigned gender" (1988: 148). Britomart's "meaning"
and "political value" reflect this premise, as her "assigned" gender
shifts when necessary. She thus avoids many of the problems associated with more rigid gender identifications.[10]

As a behavioral model for women seeking to live chastely, however, Britomart leaves much to be desired.[11] Like the queen she
partially figures, Britomart symbolizes many qualities which she
only tangentially manifests and which defy realization by ordinary
women.[12] Any female "noble person" hoping to fashion herself in
the "vertuous and gentle discipline" of chastity based upon Britomart's representation would find herself in quite a quandary.[13]

The chaste knight's portrayal, for instance, contradicts much
of the advice contained in early modern treatises on her virtue.
Wandering the countryside in male attire and engaging in activities
marked as male would lead to charges of unchasteness in "real life"
as easily as it often does for other women in the poem.[14] Thomas
Gataker, for example, insists in *Marriage Duties* (1620) that women
who travel outside the home are unlikely to be chaste: "*Chastitie*
and *home keeping* together, as the one a meanes of preseruing the
other: so (Proverbs 7, 12) the wise man maketh such *gadding abroad*
a note of such a light and lewd housewife" (sig. D3v).[15] George
Whetstone, in his 1582 *An Heptameron of Civill Discourses*, similarly
chastises women who leave the domestic realm: "The uncontrouled
wife desireth to walke at lybertie, and to be visited of many: of
which the ruling Husband, would barre her" (sig. Qiii). Britomart
also speaks freely and interacts with a wide range of people, activities which the treatises on chastity often denounce.[16] With few
exceptions, most of the other female figures who defy such stric-
tures are portrayed as malevolent or wanton; or, like Amoret and
Florimell, they become implicated as agents in whatever perils
threaten them.

At the allegorical level, women might find more to emulate,
but even there, Spenser's conceptualization of "chastity" remains
oblique.[17] Like Elizabeth, Britomart is an improbable woman il-
lustrating an improbable role.[18] Few other women in the epic—and
probably in society—could transgress gender roles with such impunity. Although she serves as an exemplary female, Britomart

occupies a male subject position through most of the epic, thereby further complicating an already complex equation between gender and virtue.[19] While critics have often commented on the distance which frequently separates male titular knights from their respective virtues, Britomart's similarly conflicted relationship with "chastity" needs further elucidation.

The poem offers a knight of chastity whose characterization remains as ambiguous as her gender. Britomart is portrayed as surprisingly dim-witted and she is plagued by repeated misapprehensions. The warrior maiden's lack of insight and intelligence, however, are essential for her destiny. She understandably displays fearful ignorance when she is overcome by desire at the sight of Artegall's image in her father's mirror, but many of her other confusions cannot so easily be attributed to maidenly naiveté.[20] When she visits Malecasta's castle, for example, the narrative offers a befuddled knight who never considers that the wanton woman's lust might be deflected if the visitor revealed her sex; nor indeed does the knight even notice that her lovestruck hostess thinks she is entertaining an attractive young man.[21] Subsequently, after rescuing Amoret, Britomart overlooks the young maiden's apprehension about her unknown protector/escort, allowing her instead to believe in the female knight's apparent gender. Similarly, she demurs from the pursuit of Florimell because she refuses to enter into "beauties chace," thereby leaving the hapless damsel prey to an array of lustful advances.[22] Paul J. Alpers characterizes the warrior maiden as "triumphally innocent" (379), but given her stature and responsibilities in the poem, this label is overly optimistic. The narrative insists upon Britomart's strictly limited understanding, but in light of the problematic nature of chastity, this maneuver seems more pragmatic than triumphant.

The portrayal of Britomart's behavior in these scenes cannot be explained away as representative of a single-minded devotion to her quest, nor can these incidents be dismissed as amusing but irrelevant details in the epic. Britomart's intellectual dullness performs a unique function in the development and preservation of her particular virtue. In order to uphold the version of chastity lauded in *The Faerie Queene*, Britomart cannot acquire insight or understanding. Titular chastity demands tough, yet beautiful naiveté, and Britomart possesses the looks, the brains, and the ferocity needed to fill the role to perfection. Although male knights are similarly blind at times, there is no other figure whose ignorance is similarly central to her/his virtue.[23] Granted, the messages presented to Britomart in Isis Church and at Busyrane's castle also challenge many viewers' perceptive powers, as countless Spenserians could attest. Still, it is no accident that these inpenetrable visions characterize the quest of this necessarily inpenetrable warrior. Her ignorance must be preserved in order to guarantee the integrity of her maidenhead.

Her presentation may be partly in response to contemporary writings about female chastity. Early modern English constructions of female sexuality present such complicated physical, spiritual, and psychological demands upon women that the goal of chastity often seems beyond the reach of a living female.[24] Not surprisingly, therefore, in *Willoby his Avisa: or the True Picture of a modest maid: and of a chaste and constant Wife* (1594), Henry Willoby insists that his heroine's chastity is possible only because she has "by grace a natiue shield / To lewd assaults that cannot yield" (sig. CIV), not because of human female qualities. Furthermore, as the perils of most virginal women in Spenser's epic indicate, conserving even fictional chastity presents no mean feat. Given such practical and imaginative constraints, Spenser's problematic portrayal of idealized womanhood should not surprise us. Britomart's complex pursuit of her man, if not explicitly of her virtue, responds brilliantly to the convoluted demands of Elizabethan chastity. The chaste knight's luck, her ignorance, and her serious gender confusion enable her to conform to a multitude of complex behavioral requirements, such as modesty, innocence, and neutralized sexuality. Her exemplary status, however, coheres only at a transcendent, allegorical level. At the literal level, her narrative generates contradictions, not a clear paradigm of chastity.

For example, while Britomart's story does not contain unequivocally lesbian undercurrents, she often manifests behavior and responses to women which imply that her martial disguise muddles everyone's understanding of her gender and her heterosexuality, including her own.[25] She would compromise her chastity, of course, if she demonstrated lustful interest in the women around her; thus,

her sexual naiveté serves her well. Nevertheless, Britomart's interaction with Amoret and her refusal to help Florimell suggest a
narrative presumption that the titular knight can retain her chastity
only if she does not behave as a woman or implicate herself in
female activities, themselves inherently suspect. Her relations with
these two imperiled virgins help emphasize that her role as exemplar of female chastity very rarely includes the protection of other
women's integrity. Instead, Britomart remains indifferent to Florimell's fate, exposing the ever-fleeing maiden to the lust of one and
all, and she shows no compassion for Amoret's understandable and
obvious terror, purposefully keeping the young woman in fear because it better suits her own ends:

> Thereto her [Amoret] feare was made so much the greater
> Through fine abusion of that Briton mayd:
> *Who for to hide her fained sex the better,*
> *And maske her wounded mind, both did and sayd*
> *Full many things doubtfull to be wayd,*
> That well she wist not what by them to gesse,
> For other whiles to her she purpos made,
> Of loue, and otherwhiles of lustfulnesse,
> That much she feard his mind would grow to some excesse.
> *His will she feard; for him she surely thought*
> *To be a man,* such as indeed he seemed,
> And much the more, by that he lately wrought,
> When her from deadly thraldome he redeemed,
> For which no seruice she too much esteemed,
> Yet dread of shame, and doubt of fowle dishonor
> Made her not yeeld so much, as due she deemed.
> Yet *Britomart* attended duly on her,
>   As well became a knight, and did to her all honor.
>   (IV. i. 7–8; emphasis added)

Britomart reveals her very female coiffure at other moments;
therefore, her failure to allay Amoret's reasonable concern could
make her portrayal appear cruel and selfish without the excuse of
Britomart's murky understanding.[26] Notably, she displays a similar
lack of compassion for women throughout her adventures.

By leaving Amoret in the dark about her rescuer's sex and

intentions, Britomart relegates the frightened woman not only to a potentially perilous space, but to one which often subjects hapless women to narratorial censure. We understand, of course, that Britomart is a reasonably safe companion, but within the poem the frightened virgin receives no information to suggest whether or not she has encountered yet another fraudulent rescuer waiting for an opportune moment to pounce.[27] Numerous other characters, including Britomart, fall victim to such counterfeit samaritans, but the martial maid does nothing to alleviate the tension, and the narrative merely offers a descriptive account of the scene with no commentary on the interchange.

Subsequently, Britomart throws herself into the male role of official champion to the beset maiden and enters Amoret as a contestant in Satyrane's beauty pageant/tournament: "At last the most redoubted *Britonesse*, / Her louely *Amoret* did open shew" (IV. v: 13. 1–2; emphasis added). Britomart's gesture here demonstrates compliance with standard male-female constructs. Once again, the designation of "fairest" transcends stated values—a phenomenon illustrated here when the False Florimell is widely acclaimed as the tournament's belle, despite failing the test for chastity. Even though Britomart refuses to accept the vaporous beauty as her prize, this portrayal reaffirms her male orientation, not moral outrage, because she simply declines to abandon her own lady:

> And she herselfe adiudged to the Knight,
> That bore the Hebene speare, as wonne in fight.
> But *Britomart* would not thereto assent,
> Ne her owne *Amoret* forgoe so light
> For that strange Dame, whose beauties wonderment
> She lesse esteem'd, then th'others vertuous gouernment.
>
> (IV. v: 20. 4–9)

As usual, Britomart's apparent disregard here for "beauties chace" is presented within a framework which undermines presumptions of her moral superiority. There is only a slight suggestion that Britomart disdains the tournament's values. Instead, she expresses satisfaction with the lady by her side. Britomart rejects promiscuity or fickleness, but fails again to soothe Amoret's fears.

Britomart's troublesome response to the perils of Amoret fig-

ures prominently in this vexed study of chastity. Despite several
chances to extend her protection of chastity to other women, Britomart always lets these opportunities pass, suggesting a narrative
belief that the protection of female chastity requires segregation
from the female realm. Although Britomart saves Amoret from
Busyrane, for example, her vigilance does not match her valor and
Amoret is stolen away again while Britomart sleeps. Hamilton
maintains that "Amoret exposes herself to rape under some inner
compulsion" (1977: 473), but it seems equally plausible that the text
may be indicating a need for bladder relief or a stretch when the
poor maiden "walkt through the wood, for pleasure, or for need"
(IV. vii: 4. 2).[28] Since she is with her protector at the time, it
makes sense that she is "of nought affeard" (IV. vii: 4. 1). Unfortunately, Britomart is not alert enough to Amoret's presence and
potential peril and she "heard not the shrilling sound, / There
where through weary trauel she lay sleeping sound" (IV. vii: 4.
8–9). Hamilton, however, again places blame on the victim—
" 'Feebly': suggests that she does not want to, or cannot, arouse
Britomart's virtue" (1977: 473)—instead of chastising Britomart for
falling asleep at her post.

Such deflections of responsibility are not convincing. It ought
to be clear to everyone in Faeryland by this stage that attractive,
virgin women are always at risk, but Britomart is shown to be too
intent upon her own goals to notice and take proper precautions.
Consequently, Amoret is whisked back into captivity while Britomart dozes and while critics confer about women's fear of sex and
Amoret's inner compulsion toward bondage.[29]

The narrative's insistence upon Britomart's inertia regarding
other women's threatened or suspect chastity asserts itself also in
the martial maid's encounters with the two Florimells.[30] The description of the true Florimell being pursued by the foster presents
a picture of abject terror:

> Still, as she fled, her eye she backward threw,
>   As fearing euill, that pursewd her fast;
> And her faire yellow locks behind her flew,
>   Loosely disperst with puffe of euery blast:
> All as a blazing starre doth farre outcast

His hearie beames, and flaming locks dispred,
At sight wherof the people stand aghast:
But the sage wisard telles, as he has red,
That it importunes death and dolefull drerihed.

(III. i: 16)

While Arthur and Guyon stand by with unmoving interest: "So as they gazed after her a while" (III. i: 17. 1), the source of her danger comes rushing into view "Breathing out beastly lust her to defile" (III. i: 17. 3). Only then does the pair spring into action, but as I discuss in chapter 1, their intentions seem dubious at best. After the dust of their rapid departure settles, the narrative returns to the bemused Britomart who remains behind:

The whiles faire *Britomart*, whose constant mind,
Would not so lightly follow beauties chace,
Ne reckt of Ladies Loue, did stay behind,
And them awayted there a certain space,
To weet if they would turne backe to that place:
But when she saw them gone, she forward went,
As lay her iourney, through that perlous Pace,
With stedfast courage and stout hardiment;
Ne euill thing she fear'd, ne euill thing she ment.

(III. i: 19)

Although the narrator tries to defuse adverse interpretations of Britomart's actions by reference to her "constant mind," this stanza reaffirms both her slow-wittedness and its implications for beleaguered virgins who could really use the assistance of a strong, sympathetic female warrior. Hamilton again offers support for Britomart, this time at the expense of the hapless Florimell: "The contrast with Florimell is clear: Britomart is pure in thought while Florimell fears even Arthur who 'ment / To her no euill thought, nor euill deed' (iv 50. 2–3)" (1977: 308).[31]

What Arthur "ment" is clearly not so straightforward. More to the point here, however, is the narrative's consistent presentation of a knight of chastity who refuses to concern herself with the problems facing other women, even when they directly relate to the virtue she champions. Her demonstrated reluctance to intervene against such a virulent and obvious threat against chastity as the foster and her willingness to allow "beauties chace" rather than rescuing the targets of male lust evinces the underlying ignorance and/or selfishness informing her quest. Britomart's overt goal consistently centers around her efforts to find and marry Artegall, an aim which requires her to retain her own chastity. Her abandonment of other sexually besieged women implies that her chastity demands a strict self-interestedness. Since she remains in disguise through much of the epic, she is not even providing lessons through example; instead, after leaving her father's house, she abstains from the female world.

Staying at home and acting like a woman, of course, would not have brought Britomart into contact with her fated mate. Accordingly, as Glauce and her charge anxiously attend to Britomart's awakening sexual interest, their actions highlight characteristics needing development or deflection prior to the sheltered maid's transformation into a chaste and loyal dynastic wife. At the same time, the future knight and her nurse support the poem's implied message that neither an unaided nor "womanly" woman would be able to represent or defend this important female virtue.[32]

Britomart's minimal interpretive powers predominate here, setting the tone for her subsequent series of misreadings and nonreadings. Britomart's first sighting of Artegall initially brings her great consternation, although her encounter with the vision is one she has actively sought:

> One day it fortuned, faire *Britomart*
>   Into her fathers closet to repayre;
>   For nothing he from her reseru'd apart,
>   Being his onely daughter and his hayre:
>   Where when she had espyde that mirrhour fayre,
>   Her selfe a while therein she vewd in vaine;
>   Tho her auizing of the vertues rare,
>   Which thereof spoken were, she gan againe
> Her to bethinke of, that mote to her selfe pertaine.
>
> (III. ii: 22)[33]

Britomart, however, cannot discern anything from the mirror's image—"her selfe a while therein she vewd in vaine." When the young woman tries to contend with the mirror's message, she displays her complete inability to read it correctly: "Sad, solemne, sowre, and full of fancies fraile / She woxe; yet wist she neither how, nor why, / She wist not" (III. ii: 27. 5–7). The narrator mocks her efforts—"silly Mayd" (III. ii: 27. 7)—without noting that the confused young woman's "sad sighes, and sorrowes deepe" (III. ii: 28. 6) result from the ignorance which characterizes most of her actions in the epic.

Initially, Britomart and Glauce attempt to deal with the situation through ineffective female maneuvers. The image of Artegall disturbs Britomart greatly and her cloudy understanding of its implications furthers her discomfiture. Once she is wounded by love, it becomes clear that she can have no rest before some remedy is discovered:

> And if that any drop of slombring rest
>   Did chaunce to still into her wearie spright,
>   When feeble nature felt her selfe opprest,
>   Streight way with dreames, and with fantasticke sight
>   Of dreadfull things the same was put to flight,
>   That oft out of her bed she did astart,
>   As one with vew of ghastly feends affright:
>   Tho gan she to renew her former smart,
> And thinke of that faire visage, written in her hart.
>
> (III. ii: 29)

This tossing and turning proves useless and Britomart begins to despair that she will ever find relief. She remains so convinced that the torments afflicting her possess deadly powers that she resists Glauce's ministrations, fearing that her nurse might also succumb to the distress:

> Ah Nurse, what needeth thee to eke my paine?
> Is not enough, that I alone doe dye,
> But it must doubled be with death of twaine?
> For nought for me but death there doth remaine.
>
> (III. ii: 35. 2–5)

Her concern soon turns to frustration, however, when she perceives that her nurse is not immediately as overcome with feelings of hopelessness about the situation as she is: "These idle words (said she) doe nought asswage / My stubborne smart, but more annoyance breed" (III. ii: 37. 1–2). She manifests her fury against Glauce by insisting that "reason" cannot be an agent of her healing and by proclaiming that her pain is unique: "But mine is not (quoth she) like others wound; / For which no reason can find remedy. / Was neuer such, but mote the like be found" (III. ii: 36. 1–3). Although they soon join forces in order to combat Britomart's fiercesome bout with lovesickness, the pair first exhibit the lack of cooperation which often characterizes female-female interactions in the poem.[34] Even once they begin to act together, their efforts reinforce notions of female frailty.

Glauce's and Britomart's sparring here, followed by the nurse's fruitless medicinal cures, illustrates the futility of "female" solutions to Britomart's injuries. The series of events described here suggest that help could only emanate from the male realm. The two women could probably bumble along endlessly in this fashion, but there is no indication that they would have any better success. Fortunately for the dynasty at stake, Glauce recognizes that she has exhausted the remedies at her disposal when the potions she administers prove useless:

Full many wayes within her troubled mind,
  Old *Glauce* cast, to cure this Ladies griefe:
Full many waies she sought, but none could find,
  Nor herbes, nor charmes,

(III. iii: 5. 1–4)

In desperation—and in fear of King Ryence's wrath—the pair seek sage male intervention, here represented by Merlin, the fashioner of the mirror which produced the offending image. Through the rest of Britomart's journey, she will stumble upon the right course often, though without understanding. At the outset, however, when comprehension is needed, she must get help from a man. "Wavering womens' wits" cannot suffice here. Before Britomart can proceed, the narrative implies that she needs to acquire the mystical insights of this male enchanter, then adopt the ways and garments of the male gender. Although she retains her "womanly" inability to understand most of what confronts her,

Britomart is presented as suppressing many of her typically female attributes in order to prepare, paradoxically, for the virtue most associated with women in the epic—as well as in the culture which produced the poem. Subsequently, Britomart remains a perplexing mix of emotions and responses associated alternately with the "female" and "male" realms.

Merlin's response to the fearful women's visit marks the beginning of Britomart's transformation into a warrior of often indeterminate gender, as she apparently intuits that before she can bring her quest to completion, she will need to become more male than female. The enchanter's solemn recounting of Britomart's dynastic destiny, however, lacks any immediate connection with the confused and hurt girl's questions. The reader can supply the intermediary steps which indicate that Merlin is assuring Britomart of her love's nobility, but there is a great distance to be covered between this interpretation and the needs of the "doubtfull Mayd" (III. iii: 20. 1) frightened by the onset of incomprehensible love and by her "bleeding bowels" (III. ii: 39. 2), which probably indicates the beginning of menstruation. Merlin's response does, however, initiate a model that will pertain throughout Britomart's adventures. For the rest of her presentation in the poem, her understanding does not matter, so long as she behaves in accordance with her destiny.

Initially, therefore, Britomart needs to change her affect. As the tales of Florimell and Amoret suggest, troubled virgins don't fare too well in Faeryland. Thus, in order to meet the challenges ahead, Britomart must transform quickly. The lengthy and detailed history provided by Merlin, which even alludes to the precipitous loss of the love she now seeks, shifts her focus away from her own troubles toward her role in the grander scheme of things. The woman who leaves Merlin's hideaway goes out to fulfill her destiny. Ironically, but necessarily, this move demands that she now emphasize her male sensibilities, honing the martial skills she learned as a child (III. ii: 6–7). The knight of chastity, though genitally female, dons more than male clothing when she begins her quest.

Critics occasionally comment upon the "maleness" of Britomart's presentation in the epic, but generally without closely considering its implications for female chastity.[35] The high expectations placed upon women in the culture were replicated for female figures in *The Faerie Queene* and exacerbated by the overwhelming disregard even the most exalted male knights display for chaste women. Cut off from the protection offered a few iconic women such as Mercilla and old women such as Glauce, no young and nubile female has a prayer of retaining her virginity without an excessive struggle. The fiction of the epic generally has more room than the "non-fictive" writings of the culture to shield women such as Florimell and Priscilla whose maidenheads are lost or suspect, but the perils of the poem make it impossible for the vast majority of female characters to survive without continual assault and consequent suspicion.

The female knight representing chastity therefore faces a particularly thorny task.[36] Since mental agility can compromise this virtue as significantly as actions can, an overly intelligent or crafty woman would be unacceptable in this role.[37] Faeryland could not easily accommodate a Viola or a Portia as its dominant exemplar of virtuous female sexuality.[38] Standard critical responses to Amoret and Florimell also make it clear that a swift pair of feet is not a sufficient safeguard against accusations of unconscious sexual incontinence, even if running away does successfully protect some women's virginity. The knight of chastity, therefore, must rely on something other than cunning or speed.

Britomart's apparently "unconscious" response to this potentially serious dilemma transforms her into one of the few character types suited for the task; namely, a woman reacting more than she acts, relying upon instinct rather than intellect, and operating predominantly as a male within a male-oriented environment, though ready to relinquish power and decision-making to the anatomical males. Among all the women depicted in the poem, Britomart is best able to represent unassailable femininity, but only because she remains free from many of the impediments afflicting more traditionally sketched female figures. Ultimately, only this woman who keeps forgetting whether she is male or female and who never understands much about what she is doing is capable of embodying exemplary womanhood; only she can simultaneously manifest the conflicting demands that destiny exerts.

Britomart's ability to reconcile these conflicts accomplishes what " . . . liuing art may not least part expresse, / Nor life-resembling pencill it can paint" (III. Proem, 2. 1–2). The narrator overcomes his professed hesitancy about creating an image of "rare chastitee" (III. Proem, 5. 9) worthy enough to present to his "dred Soueraine" (III. Proem, 3. 5) by fashioning a champion for the virtue as multiply fictive as the Elizabeth he honors. Neither image represents anything close to the reality of a living woman, but the portraits of Britomart and of "*Cynthia*, his heauens fairest light" (III. Proem, 4. 6) each further other goals. That real women could not emulate Britomart any more than they could model themselves after Elizabeth does not matter in the long run.

Accordingly, Britomart begins her transformation from girl into unique heroine. Although the armor Britomart puts on before commencing her quest has previously shielded another female warrior, "Faire *Angela*" (III. iii: 56. 2), "the strange disguise" (III. iii: 51. 9) provided by Glauce represses many of Britomart's female characteristics.[39] The new warrior also betrays no explicit debt to the female warrior tradition which the narrator claims to miss: "Where is the Antique glory now become / That whilome wont in women to appeare?" (III. iv: 1. 1–2) Once she determines "her Maides attire / To turn into a massy habergeon" (III. iii: 57. 7–8), Britomart enters a world where her hidden sex enhances her ability to remain chaste. The "mayd Martiall" (III. iii: 53. 9) who sneaks away "Couered with secret cloud of silent night" (III. iii: 61. 8) is not the same damsel who crept into her father's closet to view the magic mirror. Instead, she begins to enact her part as "Most noble Virgin" (III. iii: 21. 6), exemplar of "Chastity, / That fairest vertue, farre aboue the rest" (III. Proem, 1. 1–2). Her place within the lost tradition of warrior women remains obscure, however. Despite Angela's armor, Palladine's cameo appearance, and the narrator's invocation of "Penthesilee," "Debora," and "Camill" (III. iv: 2), the only female connection which resonates with Britomart's presentation in the poem is that linking her with "thee, O Queene" (III. iv: 3. 8). As readers, we note Britomart's resemblance to Bradamante and others, but within the poem, she stands alone.

Regardless, once she is properly accoutered, nothing can keep Britomart from pursuing her man. Her opening appearance in the poem reflects her epic stature: "the famous *Britomart*" (III. i: 8.

6) while her previous "female" life remains ensconced within retro-spective accounts. During the period of the epic's completion, Henry Smith remarked in *A Preparative for Marriage* (1591) that "Chastitie careth to please but one" (sig. F6). Britomart's single-mindedness indicates her implicit regard for this "female" dictum, even though she predominantly follows the example of her fellow male knights. As Marinell could testify, she fights first and asks questions later; she exchanges tales (both false and true) with con-genial knights she meets along the way; she rescues and protects appealing young ladies; and she beats to a pulp anyone blocking her progress. Artegall becomes the sole focus of her boundless energies, and she undertakes this task with such ferocity that she comically doesn't initially recognize the Salvage Knight as her fated mate.

At first glance, this presentation of Britomart seems innocuous and to the point, but it readily becomes clear that personifying chastity demands more than grace and aplomb. Faeryland compli-cates the pursuits of all its inhabitants, and neither Britomart's gender nor her naiveté completely distances her from this envi-ronment's perils. In modern terms, however, Britomart remains a "Teflon heroine," whose mistakes generally provoke amusement, not censure, thereby protecting her fragile virtue. The humor evinced through the narrator's epithet "silly maid" reverberates during the innocent maiden's ill-conceived sojourn with the lustful Malecasta. This air of amusement circulating throughout Brito-mart's adventures helps deflect the possibility that readers might suspect the maid's motives and hence her virtue. Such a delicate virtue could not withstand any serious questioning of its integrity; hence, its champion remains enclosed in a protective covering of patronizing humor such as Merlin displays when the girl and her nurse seek his guidance. So long as Britomart prompts gentle laugh-ter, unwanted suspicion can be kept at bay, a distance the epic consistently provides.

Nevertheless, the laughter chastity evokes in *The Faerie Queene* is never confronted by the narrator or the characters in the epic. As I argue with regard to Satyrane, the Squire of Dames and others, humorous responses to chastity work subtly but effectively to undermine the female characters' opportunities to achieve recognized virtue. The amusement imbuing discussions about the seeming lack of chaste women, the blatant disregard for the magic girdle's exposure of the False Florimell, and the jocular chivalric gathering which unflinchingly includes knights with dubious moral histories suggest that none of these characters take chastity—the only "female" virtue—very seriously. Furthermore, critics' propensity to blame virgin women for their troubles fortifies the message that virtue and women are largely considered incompatible. Women prompt humor, lust, and suspicion, but rarely admiration for virtue closely and successfully guarded.

The reader's appreciation for the importance of this virtue is further eroded by Britomart's own lack of concern for her companions' moral or ethical histories. For example, her association with Sir Satyrane both at his tournament and during the pursuit of Ollyphant, combined with the juxtaposition of this second episode with the female knight's entry into Busyrane's den of iniquity, highlights the disjunctures evident in her embodiment of purportedly "ideal" female chastity.[40]

Britomart's participation in this skewed tournament indicates her co-option into "male" value systems which judge men and women respectively on their camaraderie or appearance, not their virtue. Sir Satyrane, for instance, hardly stands out as a champion of female virtue, despite his early intervention on Una's behalf and the narratorial appellation of "good." He greets the Squire of Dames' tale with raucous laughter, then initiates a tournament honoring superficial female beauty rather than substantive female virtue. In addition, although he is briefly reunited with his mother (I. vi: 28) after his youthful abduction, he never shows any compassion, remorse, or desire for revenge over her rape and captivity at the hands of his father, who:

> So long in secret cabin there he held
> Her captiue to his sensuall desire,
> Till that with timely fruit her belly sweld,
> And bore a boy vnto that saluage sire:
> Then home he suffred her for to retire,
> For ransome leauing him the late borne childe;
>
> (I. vi: 23. 1–6)

Critics tend to treat Satyrane as a well-meaning bungler, under whose "amiable but short-sighted" (Kane 97) management, "the contest dwindles rapidly to farce" (Heale 110). Such indulgent responses are only partly warranted, however. Granted, Satyrane does attempt to protect the true Florimell from the hyena, but his congeniality with the Squire of Dames and his sponsorship of such a dubious tournament indicates that he upholds female virtue only when he is confronted immediately with an attractive damsel in distress. In general, Satyrane evinces more desire for collegiality than for moral righteousness.

As usual, Britomart remains impervious to her companion's questionable character, focusing instead upon the adventures confronting her. Similar apathy is manifest when she joins forces with Satyrane in the chase after Ollyphant. The narrator's commentary underscores Satyrane's distance from chastity here, but Britomart ignores his failings:

> It was not *Satyrane*, whom he did feare,
>   But *Britomart* the flowre of chastity;
>   For he the powre of chast hands might not beare,
>   But alwayes did their dread encounter fly:
>
>   (III. xi: 6. 1–4)

She also fails to notice when Ollyphant fades from the narrative. Continually caught up in the instant, the maiden warrior repeatedly misses the implications of her actions and of her companion's shortcomings. Male characters respond this way with impunity, however, and the poem often presents us with a Britomart who unreflectively follows suit.

Still, the narrative keeps the alert reader aware of chastity's enemies here, even if Britomart misses their implications. Once Ollyphant vanishes from the text, he is quickly replaced, first by the forlorn Scudamour, then by Busyrane's Ovidian tapestry replete with ornate images noting the vexed plight of virtuous women (III. xi: 29–49). Scudamour's appearance briefly reminds readers of this intrepid knight's audacious capture of Amoret away from the lap of womanhood (IV. x), but this disturbing memory is quickly superseded by the tales introduced through Busyrane's tapestry, which remain more available for interpretation by readers than for comprehension by Britomart.[41]

Images featuring deific deception and domination over unprotected human women predominate in Busyrane's decor. Again and again, the panels confront Britomart with reminders of such familiar tales (to the reader at least) as the stories of Leda and Alcmene. Despite these stories of unrespected chastity, however, Britomart is depicted as responding to her environment with her typical lack of comprehension. Her "greedy eyes" absorb as much as possible of the tapestry and the masque presented to her in the enchanter's house, but she declines interpretation of these scenes of violation against women.[42] Britomart wants to see more, and she eagerly awaits whatever adventures await her there, but she shows little inclination or ability to assimilate the information provided.[43] Without the assistance of a seer such as Merlin, Britomart's powers of discernment remain severely restricted.

Nonetheless, these limitations enhance Britomart's ability to represent her virtue, as the final cantos in Book Three exemplify by foregrounding the essence of her role as female knight personifying female chastity. She continues to react rather than to choose her actions with insight, and by doing so she fulfills her duties admirably. Just as her mistaken interpretation of Talus's news in Book Five brings her to a needed confrontation with Radigund, here it is not necessary that she correctly understand the images before her so long as she frees Amoret without compromising her own sexual purity. Indeed, the extent of her ignorance is so great that the frightened captive virgin needs to intervene and point out the best way to deal with Busyrane. Left to her own devices, Britomart in her fervor would have eliminated the forlorn object of her quest as well as the evil magician.[44]

This scene adds credence to the suggestion that the strength of Britomart's commitment is unconnected with the level of her understanding. The maiden warrior prepares to die in order to save Amoret, even though she is rescuing the captive largely for Scudamour: Britomart no longer claims Amoret for herself. Her knightly valor, in other words, transcends any particular personal gain in this instance. When Ollyphant evaporates into Scudamour, Britomart recognizes an opportunity to act nobly. There is no indication that she perceives the House of Busyrane and its particular horrors as an amplification of the challenges recently and earlier met. Memory is no more Britomart's strong suit than perception is. The only image remaining continuously in her mind is Artegall's. Luckily for endangered souls such as Amoret, Britomart generally remains on track when the peril is immediate. Fortunately for Britomart, she never encounters a snowy Artegall or any other significant obstacle to her virtue. She would never be up for the challenge.

She remains safe, moreover, because of external protection. Repeatedly, Britomart's armor—notably a "male" accoutrement—enables her to maneuver successfully within the world as a woman. Substituting for the confines of home commonly recommended for women, her armor makes genital penetration unlikely. Though accompanied by the constant phallic threat of sword wounds, Britomart is surrounded by, yet protected from the dangers male knights pose to other women. More mobile than most of the lauded women in the epic, she still symbolically carries the walls which ensconce them protectively. One of the boys, though beautiful as needed, Britomart remains safely behind her metaphoric hymen. The martial maid must remain martial in order to protect her maidenhood.

Similarly, the other few non-iconographical women who successfully represent chastity in the epic also remain armed or armored. Britomart is unusual among this small company of female warriors for receiving extended narrative treatment, however.[45] Nothing significant is told us about Angela, whose armor protects chastity's heroine throughout the epic, and we are only offered enough to confuse us when Palladine briefly visits the text. According to the source in Chaucer, Palladine's quest belongs to a man, but Spenser chooses a woman for the role, though the reason for his choice is never articulated:

> But that bold knight, whom ye pursuing saw
>   That Geauntesse, is not such, as she seemed,
> But a faire virgin, that in martiall law,
> And deedes of armes aboue all Dames is deemed,
> And aboue many knights is eke esteemed,
> For her great worth; She *Palladine* is hight:
> She you from death, you me from dread redeemed.

Ne any may that Monster match in fight,
But she, or such as she, that is so chaste a wight.

(III. vii. 52)

Sir Satyrane and the Squire of Dames have need of chaste hands
here, since this scene appears in the midst of their encounter with
Ollyphant, but the appearance of this other chaste warrior woman
remains perplexing. She doesn't stay in the area long enough to
teach or assist Britomart, nor does she provide much more than
background activity which accords with the general topic of the
book. It seems possible that she is introduced in order to allay
readers' fears that Britomart pays insufficient attention to Ollyphant's threatening presence and mysterious disappearance, but
there is so little evidence that such conjectures remain highly
speculative.[46]

Palladine, in fact, has received little critical mention. Although
this absence accords with the lack of narratorial interest displayed
when she appears in the poem, the implications for Britomart of
the existence and intervention of this other chaste woman in armor
need further elaboration, especially since Britomart apparently
shares the marginalizing consensus view which relegates Palladine
to infrequent parenthetical references and to occasional cases of
possible gender confusion where she is referred to as "Sir" (Heale
91).

Given Palladine's remarkably close affiliation with Britomart's
modus operandi and quest, this relegation to the textual sidelines
raises fascinating interpretive possibilities. Her presence certainly
relieves Britomart of any cause for remorse should the titular knight
ever notice that her prey vanished without a trace while she was
in hot pursuit. Palladine has apparently seriously taken on the task
of finding and subduing Argante and Ollyphant; therefore, the
quest is presumably not abandoned when Britomart precipitously
turns her attention first to Scudamour, then to the rescue of
Amoret.

We are, however, given little direct information about Palladine
in the two isolated stanzas in which she appears—though identified
only once (III. vii: 37; 52. 6). The narrative suggests that Palladine

is chasing the incestuous pair without regard to Argante's or Olly-phant's particular quarry. The Squire of Dames and Sir Satyrane certainly profit from her industry, but there is no indication that she undertakes the chase specifically for their benefit. In fact, she makes no effort to establish personal contact with the pair; instead, she simply disappears from the text as rapidly and as unceremoni-ously as she entered it. "Her well beseemes that Quest (quoth *Satyrane*)" (III. vii: 53. 1), but that is as far as his interest and our elucidation gets. Similarly, the beast's subsequent escape receives only perfunctory notice: "Where late he left the Beast, he ouer-came, / He found him not; for he had broke his band, / And was return'd againe vnto his Dame" (III. vii: 61. 6–8). We can only assume that Palladine will resume or continue her chase. The nar-rator joins the characters in changing the subject without much ado and the pair conclude the canto with a lighthearted discussion about the dearth of chaste women available in the world.

This ready dismissal of the chaste woman who has just saved the skins of two less than exemplary male knights takes place while they are humorously noting how few chaste women exist. This juxtaposition reinforces the reader's awareness that chastity is not really honored very highly in this realm. Palladine provides a vivid contrast to the unchaste women under discussion, but neither crit-ics nor interlocutors note the irony of her active participation in a scene which requires her unsullied chastity. The Squire of Dames and Satyrane could easily be dead if the chaste warrior had not intervened on their behalf, but they still fail to factor her in when they count chaste women. Like Britomart, her armor distances her from sexual interest, thereby removing her from the arena most likely to attract male conversation. Consequently, she fades quickly from notice.

As Palladine's treatment indicates, Britomart's environment re-mains relatively hostile to her virtue. Thus, her function within it needs more problematization than it often receives. There is no obvious reason why Palladine could not have acted as titular heroine of this book, nor any non-dynastic explanation why Britomart is not ignored as completely as this other chaste female knight. It seems probable, therefore, that Britomart's chastity serves chiefly as a secondary though necessary characteristic to further her primary role as partner in Artegall's destiny. Artegall's spouse and the mother of his children must be chaste without question; therefore, Britomart personifies this virtue. Her narrow focus remains her strongest quality.

Britomart's limited vision figures prominently in Book Five. Her eager, yet uncomprehending eyes figure prominently when she visits Isis's Church (V. vii). Once again, the warrior maiden receives a dynastic vision which she cannot interpret without male assistance. On her own, moreover, Britomart is ever ready for bad news. She readily suspects prophecies concerning her fate and quickly doubts or misinterprets news about Artegall. Since Britomart will leave the epic shortly after upholding women's inability to govern properly (without special divine dispensation), the narrative's presentation of her muddled perceptions helps confirm a female need for male wisdom.

Isis's priests thus draw particular interest here because they not only provide counsel, they also introduce a description of male chastity, something receiving little attention in the epic:

> For other beds the Priest there vsed none,
>   But on their mother Earths deare lap did lie,
>   And bake their sides vppon the cold hard stone,
>   T'enure them selues to sufferaunce thereby
>   And proud rebellious flesh to mortify.
> For by the vow of their religion
>   They tied were to stedfast chastity,
>   And continence of life, that all forgon,
> They mote the better tend to their deuotion.
> Therefore they mote not taste of fleshly food,
>   Ne feed on ought, the which doth bloud containe,
>
>   (V. vii: 9–10. 2)

The priests' chastity obviously differs substantially from Britomart's, and their astute reading of the warrior maiden's mood and dream indicates that they do not share her chaste ignorance. Britomart's chastity, in contrast, does not rely upon the injunctions overseeing the priests' "proud rebellious flesh"; nor does her virtue seem related to either a vow or to any religious convictions. Britomart's virtue appears to be innate, not something assumed. By attaching the overt representation of male chastity to priests physically cut off from temptations of the flesh while female chastity remains embodied within a woman protected largely by ignorance, the text further underscores the gender distinctions accompanying the concept of chastity. The baffling digression about the relationship between blood and wine which interrupts this depiction of male chastity further heightens the confusion. Hamilton notes that "Spenser follows Plutarch 6 closely" (1977: 575), but this information does little to alleviate the haze obscuring the passage. Neither reader nor titular knight receive much help in interpreting this scene.

Nevertheless, the conspicuous dearth of overtly virginal male knights in *The Faerie Queene* intensifies the interest provoked here. Just as the introduction of the female knight Palladine in place of Chaucer's male virgin Sir Thopas helps emphasize the *female* character of this virtue in Spenser's epic, so the transference of male chastity from members of the chivalric order to vowed priests implies that all women, but only some men, need resolutely aspire to chastity. Chivalric literature includes several suitable male knights who could fill virginal roles, but this substitution suggests that chastity in Faeryland is more properly the domain of others. Certainly, the sexual behavior and attitudes expressed with impunity by male characters in the poem indicate that "male chastity" remains an oxymoronic concept for men outside religious orders.

Britomart's own version of chastity also does not accord with that expressed through Isis's priests, although there are moments during her quest when she might benefit from similar constraints. For example, she appears to accept readily Malecasta's culinary hospitality, which the lewdly-minded hostess clearly intends as an aid toward seduction:

> And aye between the cups, she did prepare
> Way to her loue, and secret darts did throw;
> But *Britomart* would not such guilfull message know.
>
> (III. i: 51. 7–9)

> So when they slaked had the feruent heat
> Of appetite with meates of euery sort,
> The Lady did faire *Britomart* entreat,
> Her to disarme, and with delightfull sport
> To loose her warlike limbs and strong effort.
>
> (III. i: 52. 1–5)

Britomart quickly accepts Malecasta's largesse with the same naive courtesy with which she greets her host's seductive gestures. Her chastity remains intact, however, only slightly grazed by Gardante's arrow. She receives no punishment for misreading the obvious signs of Malecasta's intentions, even though she is wounded in recognition of her always active, though uncomprehending eyes. Clearly, the maiden warrior is not being held to the standards imposed upon Isis's priests. The onus remains upon her only to remain marriageable; as a woman, she is not expected to implement her virtue actively and consciously. Hence, she demonstrates ample conscious and active knightly behavior, but continues to rely upon luck and fate in the sexual realm.

Regardless of the praise they receive periodically, none of the other virgin women could respond adequately to the challenges facing Britomart. Florimell, Amoret, and Belphoebe incite too much unlawful male lust for them to appear "safe" to either character or critic. Furthermore, the regular silence, interrupted by the fearful (sometimes even assertive) speech the first two evince during their perpetual flight and periods of captivity, suggests that their minds are not easily read or controlled. Florimell's readiness to ignore male offers of assistance when Arthur implores her to stop, as well as her decisive, however misguided insistence that the fisherman intervene in her plight (III. viii: 23–24), implicates her as a woman not prepared to align herself unquestioningly with male demands. Similarly, Amoret's open resistance to Scudamour's attempt to claim her as bride marks her as suspect in the male realm (IV. x: 57). By trying to choose continued female companionship rather than matrimony, Amoret manifests a subversive allegiance which undermines the social order celebrated in the poem. Celibacy is not one of the approved choices available to attractive female virgins in the poem, and both critics and characters tend to express displeasure at her preference. Belphoebe occupies a special category within the poem which traditionally has tended to protect her from undue criticism, but it simultaneously restricts her usefulness as an exemplar of chastity. After the fall of Roman Catholicism in England, vowed virginity loses its centrality as an exalted female virtue. Thus, Belphoebe can bear homage to Elizabeth's professed virginity, but alone she cannot serve to illustrate or honor the varied forms of chastity promulgated in the Legend of Chastity. Timias's frustrated devotion to this sylvan champion exemplifies the unacceptable restrictions Belphoebean chastity presents to the masculine world. Womankind as a whole is clearly not being urged to take Belphoebe as their role model. Instead, the most highly honored mode of female chastity incorporates marital sexuality—not coincidentally, a mode which accommodates male sexual desires more readily than celibacy. The overwhelming irony depicted by the need for a woman who dresses and behaves primarily as a man to represent this virtue, receives no acknowledgement in the culture or in the epic. Britomart, though, is a comfortable champion who can soothe troubled male psyches, however uncharacteristic she may be of her gender.

Nevertheless, Britomart's presentation is not as obviously exemplary as it might seem. Without the narrator's regular assurances that she models virtue, readers would not always be able to deduce her status. As noted, characters in the epic designated as "good" or "evil" often behave remarkably similarly, though the narrator greets their actions with widely variant responses. Britomart, for example, displays as conflicted a relationship with virtuous behavior as she does with her gender. Given *The Faerie Queene*'s purported aim to "fashion a gentleman or noble person in vertuous and gentle discipline," one might anticipate lessons in differentiating between valued and derided modes of conduct. Surprisingly, readers frequently need to accept such distinctions on trust rather than logic, as variant readings of the Bower of Bliss episode suggest, for example.[47] In Britomart's case, many of her actions deemed "virtuous" closely resemble behaviors derided in other characters.

Britomart's position is problematized, for example, by her place within an extremely small coterie connected without fanfare in the epic. The members of this "elite" gathering are only occasionally explicitly linked, except through an initially surprising metaphoric code which envelopes each of them. I refer to this grouping in "the enraged cow" of this chapter's title, a label the narrator uses to describe Adicia's fury upon realizing that Samient is still alive and under knightly protection:

> Streight downe she ranne, like an enraged cow,
>   That is berobbed of her youngling dere,
>   With knife in hand, and fatally did vow,
>   To wreake her on that mayden messengere,
>   Whom she had causd be kept as prisonere,
>   By *Artegall*, misween'd for her owne Knight,
>   That brought her backe. And comming present there,
>   She at her ran with all her force and might,
> All flaming with reuenge and furious despight.
>
>   (V. viii: 46)

Adicia's bovine fury here evokes a metaphor which appears rarely in the poem. Malbecco, Radigund, and Britomart are each once described as "chewing cud," an activity shared by no one else in *The Faerie Queene*. The relevant passages are memorable, especially for their intersections:

> Long thus he chawd the cud of inward griefe,
>   And did consume his gall with anguish sore,
>
>   (III. x: 18. 1–2)

> She chaw'd the cud of louers carefull plight;
> Yet could it not so thoroughly digest,
> Being fast fixed in her wounded spright,
> But it tormented her both day and night:
>
>   (V. v: 27. 2–5)

> So as she thus melancholicke did ride,
>   Chawing the cud of griefe and inward paine,
>
>   (V. vi: 19. 1–2)

These passages are remarkably similar, despite these characters' purportedly variant relationships to virtue. In a poem so centrally devoted to characters' and readers' competence in distinguishing between the good guys and the bad guys, such blurrings should not be ignored. In fact, the confederacy of cows here presented seriously threatens our efforts to keep these figures separate. The obsessive qualities of cud-chewing seem most significant here. The three figures wish to be left in isolation, so that they can endlessly reiterate the desperateness of their situations. Only when pressing circumstances intervene do they emerge from their solitary circles of regurgitation, however reluctantly, as Britomart's initial resistance to Dolon illustrates:

> For little lust had she to talke of ought,
>   Or ought to heare, that mote delightfull bee;
>   Her minde was whole possessed of one thought,
>   That gaue none other place.

$$\text{(V. vi: 21. 1–4)}$$

As she demonstrates often, Britomart enjoys wallowing in her own grief and pain. Since she always snaps out of it in time to keep pace with her destiny, this predilection seems harmless, but the infrequency of bovine allusions in the epic and the nature of those who share this metaphoric affinity may give readers pause.

Obviously, arguing seriously about the importance of cow imagery and cud-chewing in *The Faerie Queene* provides the stuff academic satire is made of; still, this superficially minor detail offers an illuminating glimpse at the underlying moral structure of the epic and much of its criticism. Britomart and Radigund parallel each other in too many ways for this further link to be accidental or incidental. In addition, the absence of similar allusions except for those cited in reference to Malbecco and less directly to Adicia heightens the interest of the metaphor.[48] Consider, in contrast, the number of "fairest maids alive" we meet as we traverse Spenser's poetic landscape. Being included among that company seems fairly automatic for characters of the right age and gender. "Those chewing cud" constitute a much more selective gathering.

Leaving Malbecco aside for the moment, the grouping of Britomart, Radigund, and Adicia presents a knotty problem for those attempting to map the intersections between behavior and virtue. Instinct suggests that morosely ruminating about the real or imagined hurts should violate the theological rubric denouncing despair, while rushing in rage to save an endangered spouse might easily attract praise for wifely devotion. Action almost invariably appears in a more favorable light than obsessive thinking; thus, we might conclude that Britomart and Radigund deserve censure, while Adicia represents appropriate spousal dedication. Given what the narrator encourages us to believe about the characters in question, however, that equation does not work.

The confusion increases when the rest of the Malbecco stanza is compared to a stanza appearing shortly prior to Britomart's cud-chewing, where she ends her temper tantrum only after it proves fruitless:

> Then still the smart thereof increased more,
> And seem'd more grieuous, then it was before:
> At last when sorrow he saw booted nought,
> Ne griefe might not his loue to him restore,
> He gan deuise, how her he reskew mought,
> Ten thousand wayes he cast in his confused thought.
>
> (III. x: 18. 4–9)

> But when she had with such vnquiet fits
> Her selfe there close afflicted long in vaine,
> Yet found no easement in her troubled wits,
> She vnto *Talus* forth return'd againe,
> By change of place seeking to ease her paine;
> And gan enquire of him.
>
> (V. vi: 15. 1–6)

Although Malbecco hardly ranks as a role model in virtuous living, Britomart's behavior closely resembles his. Both figures (and Radigund after she falls for Artegall) immerse themselves in despair and self-pity until they finally recognize the futility of their grief and seek more productive, alternate forms of expression. Britomart, of course, ultimately succeeds, while Malbecco fails so dismally that he "Is woxen so deform'd, that he has quight / Forgot he was a man, and *Gealosie* is hight" (III. x: 60. 8–9).

At the beginning of the stanza following Malbecco's transformation into Jealousy, the narrator denounces this mode of emo-

tional expression and offers Britomart as an exemplar of love for
women to follow instead of Malbecco:

> O let him far be banished away,
>   And in his stead let Loue for euer dwell,
>   Sweet Loue, that doth his golden wings embay
>   In blessed Nectar, and pure Pleasures well,
>   Vntroubled of vile feare, or bitter fell.
> And ye faire Ladies, that your kingdomes make
>   In th'harts of men, them gouerne wisely well,
>   And of faire *Britomart* ensample take,
> That was as trew in loue, as Turtle to her make.
>
> (III. xi: 2)

The narrator has not yet presented a convincing case, however. At
this point, there is little to distinguish the two characters. Harry
Berger also notes this resemblance between Britomart and Malbecco, but asserts that "For Britomart, who remains briefly on the
edge of the "Continent" (iv. 10), this is a moment of weakness
during which she luxuriates in her helplessness and "sweet consuming woe" (xi. 45); for Malbecco it is the chosen way of life"
(1988: 162). While it is true that Britomart successfully emerges
from her sojourns in the realm of despair, she does so largely
because she discovers her mistakes. Artegall has not forgotten her
or taken up with another woman; therefore, she drops her grudge
against him and frees him from Radigund's captivity. Malbecco,
on the other hand, discovers that Hellenore revels promiscuously
among the satyrs. Consequently, Malbecco first turns voyeur,
then personifies the emotion consuming him. It remains plausible,
however, that Britomart would have followed in his footsteps had
her fears proven well-founded.

Berger's intriguing essay offers a fascinating account of many
of the complicated relationships presented in *The Faerie Queene*
(1988: 154–71),[49] but his hasty dismissal of Britomart's emotional
kinship with Malbecco denies her ever-problematic status as Knight
of Chastity. Dropping the issue too readily leaves the reader prey
to interpretations emanating from the distinctions "we know" exist
between the virtuous characters and the villains or fools in the

epic. Berger is unquestionably a learned and sensitive reader of Spenser's text; nonetheless, while his response here tells us much about Malbecco, it does not adequately explain Britomart's role in the paradigm being portrayed.

An equally striking juxtaposition can be found in the bovine facet of Radigund's and Britomart's often noted resemblance.[50] With so many qualities and actions already recognized in common, it seems unlikely that this further communal description should be coincidence. As they both chew the cud of despair in love, they evince significant identical features, despite their distinctive personalities and functions in the poem.

Radigund's continual abuse of men and her degradation of Artegall presumably exempt her from consideration as a model for a virtuous life. At the same time, this linkage between the Amazon leader and the Knight of Chastity suggests that individual actions do not always provide the best means for differentiating between characters eliciting censure and those deserving emulation. Britomart's obsessive anguish seems no more worthy than Malbecco's or Radigund's. In origin and intent, in fact, it appears comparable at every turn.

In addition, the virgin knight often responds in a manner resembling Adicia's bovine fury. Her ferocious struggle with Radigund, for instance, is told in animalistic terms:

> As when a Tygre and a Lionesse
>   Are met at spoyling of some hungry pray,
>   Both challenge it with equall greedinesse:
>
> (V. vii: 30. 1–3)
>
> So long they fought, that all the grassie flore
> Was fild with bloud, which from their sides did flow,
> And gushed through their armes, that all in gore
> They trode.
>
> (V. vii: 31. 5–7)

Most notably in this battle, the animal rages they display lead the pair to renounce any care for the physical markings of their sex:

> But through great fury both their skill forgot,
>   And practicke vse in armes: ne spared not

Their dainty parts, which nature had created
So faire and tender, without staine or spot,
For other vses, then they them translated;
Which they now hackt and hewd, as if such vse they hated.

(V. vii: 29. 4–9)

Hamilton refers to this last passage cited as a "playful allusion
to the etymology of Amazon" (1977: 578), though there is nothing lighthearted evident in the scene. The combatants appear
ready to fight until death, putting aside both their humanity and
their sex in order to vent all of their emotional and physical force
into the fray.[51] Lions and tigers provide a more noble analogy
than do "enraged cows," but the images invoked do not diverge
significantly. At the height of their respective battles, Adicia,
Radigund, and Britomart present virtually indistinguishable portraits of women in anger.

Britomart's single-mindedness keeps her on the track of righteousness, but this quality does not adequately justify her reputed
difference from these other women. Adicia and Radigund also display unwavering concentration toward their central concerns. Ironically, Britomart shares more prominent personality traits with
these two critically abjured women than she does with her fellow
virtuous virgins, such as Florimell and Amoret. Throughout the
epic, Britomart remains more combatant than lady. Consequently,
Britomart's story suggests that the ends often count more than the
means when virtue is decided.

The multiple interstices between Britomart and these "unde-
sirables" evaporate, however, during the titular knight's final appearance. After she frees Artegall from Radigund's prison, Britomart ensures that female rule will not continue in that kingdom:

So there a while they afterwards remained,
    Him to refresh, and her late wounds to heale;
    During which space she there as Princess rained,
    And changing all that forme of common weale,
    The liberty of women did repeale,
    Which they had long vsurpt; and them restoring
    To mens subiection, did true Iustice deale:

> That all they as a Goddesse her adoring,
> Her wisedome did admire, and hearkned to her loring.
>
> (V: vii. 42)

Britomart disappears from the poem after she reaffirms male hierarchy, but we are told that her movement does not stop. Instead, she reportedly remains on the road in an attempt to alleviate the frustration of her continued separation from Artegall. Significantly, this choice does not draw the narratorial criticism which is commonly directed against other women alone: "Then hoping that the change of aire and place / Would change her paine, and sorrow somewhat ease, / She parted thence, her anguish to appease" (V. vii: 45. 3–5). She has perhaps learned that chewing the cud of despair does not work: "That womanish complaints she did represse, / And tempred for the time her present heauinesse" (V. vii: 44. 8–9). Since we never hear where her "change of aire and place" takes her or what adventures ensue, her participation in the epic never truly reaches completion, although the poem presents the illusion that Britomart has achieved her destination and her destiny when she is reunited with Artegall, however briefly. Whether she would ever have reappeared in the unwritten later books of *The Faerie Queene* can, of course, never be known.

The allusion to Britomart's further movements reminds us that there are many loose ends to her characterization. None of the knights in the epic take to the road with impunity; therefore, there is no reason to assume that her future wanderings would be uneventful. Since it would have been easy to leave her settled or en route back to a specific destination, unanswerable questions follow in the wake of her departure. We know Britomart's future from Merlin's tales, just as we know Arthur's destiny from countless legends, but we still cannot know how she gets there.

Although speculation about Britomart's unwritten adventures remains futile, it highlights the loose ends remaining for the reader about this heroine. As the discussion above suggests, the conclusions provided often do not correlate very well with the evidence. Reading Britomart as a high-minded heroine who demonstrates the epitome of chaste womanhood, for instance, demands numerous leaps of faith. Casting this warrior maiden as an ideal woman mainly indicates widespread discomfort with those emulating the more traditional traits of "her contrary sex" (III. i: 47. 2). Like the other titular knights, Britomart displays a conflicted relationship with her assigned virtue.

Britomart is a "safe" choice, but she nevertheless presents further evidence that the so-called "virtue" of chastity is largely an intricate and surreptitious mode of female subordination. By offering Britomart as the reputed heroine and central exemplar of this virtue, the text implicitly supports the culture's systematic denial of women. If she lived as a female in Faeryland, Britomart's virtue could never survive. If Britomart were portrayed as insightful or even intelligent, her chastity would be compromised. Like her modern counterparts, who go on the lecture circuit in order to tell other women to stay at home,[52] this Knight of Chastity fulfills largely male roles in a sharply gendered society as she purportedly models a predominantly female virtue. Women who lived as Britomart lived either in Faeryland or in early modern England would be unlikely to gain comparable kudos.

Still, Britomart's complicated and contradictory behavior merely reflects the impossible nature of the virtue she represents. As I have argued throughout this book, the poem's and the culture's conflicted responses toward women and their sexuality encourage an emphasis on "vir-tue," which fundamentally restricts female access to virtue. Female characters are constrained from achieving the "manliness" of vir-tue, while "their" virtue also hovers outside their grasp.

Furthermore, the complex, but consistent representation of women as illusory, fleeting, dangerous, deceptively beautiful, treacherous, yet valuable commodities alerts us to the many issues regarding sexuality and gender in the poem still needing exploration. Topics such as rape, procreation, and attitudes towards postmenopausal female figures have only been touched upon in this study, but figure significantly in the poem. Tensions displayed between male and female characters are often deflected through homoerotic encounters, but our understanding of these permutations remains limited. In addition, the role of sexual exploits and exploitation in the representation of male characters has not been theorized sufficiently. Neither has the poem's frequent displacement of sexual concerns onto figures displaying multiple sexualities. Although Dame Nature's warning that "thy decay thou seekst by thy desire" (VII. vii: 59. 3) may seek to deflect such studies, as readers of *The Faerie Queene*, we have only just begun to explore the configurations of sexuality and desire in the epic. This poem, whose knight of chastity is only one of several characters displaying genders "more then one," offers a much more complex sexual tapestry than we have previously acknowledged.

Notes

Introduction

1. For a useful reading of the Proem's complexities see Jonathan Goldberg (1981: 12–24).

2. As Merritt Hughes notes, although "today we are sure [these lines] were not written by Virgil," in the sixteenth century they "were accepted as genuine and as supremely significant" (318).

3. Here, I clearly disagree with Harry Berger, Jr., who calls the narrator "an *it*, not a *he*" (1991: 10).

4. See the series of essays cited by Nancy Vickers for important discussions regarding the gendered strategies informing Petrarchan conventions. Gordon Coggins provides a guide to sexual topics and incidents in *The Faerie Queene*.

5. "Ideology" is certainly not a term to be used lightly in current critical discourse. As Meaghan Morris notes, "Eleven entries [for 'discourse'] is probably not bad going if you consider what a dictionary of marxisms would have to do with *ideology*" (35). Jean E. Howard and Marion F. O'Connor offer the following definition in the introduction to their collection of essays: "ideology being understood as that inescapable network of beliefs and practices by which variously positioned and historically constituted subjects imagine their relationship to the real and through which they render intelligible the world around them" (3); similarly, Catherine Belsey and Jane Moore define it as "the beliefs, meanings, and practices which shape our thoughts and actions" (245). While recognizing that the term is as fraught as Morris suggests, I am using "ideology" and "ideological" to suggest the fabric of beliefs, presumptions, and perspectives about issues of sex and gender which underlie the structure and philosophical positionings of *The Faerie Queene*, even though it is rarely, if ever, openly acknowledged or noted in the text.

6. Throughout this text, I am presuming that "sex" is an anatomical term and that "gender" is culturally constructed. The disjuncture between these terms becomes particularly important when discussing Britomart. Her actions and others' responses to her often reflect a character of multiple gender(s) regardless of her female anatomy. Numerous feminist critics have discussed the rationale and problemization of such terminological distinctions. See, for example, Jane Flax (particularly 143–50); and Judith Butler (especially 1–34). For an astute account of the sex/gender split specifically in the Renaissance, see Constance Jordan (especially chapter 3).

I am also using terms such as "female characters" and "women" to denote those figures in *The Faerie Queene* which are constructed with female genitalia or attributes gendered as "female," despite my recognition of the difficulties raised by any such categorizations. For discussions of the complexities accompanying such designations, see Denise Riley and Toril Moi.

7. My argument is intended to expand, not replace the many learned theories of allegory and poetics available. See, for example, Rosamund Tuve; Maureen Quilligan (1979); and Arthur F. Kinney.

8. Pamela Benson argues that "the feminine is an essential principle in the grand scheme of *The Faerie Queene*; it represents an alternate order" (1992: 253). While it is true that there is much about the "feminine" which is valued in the poem, this "alternate order" is generally feared.

9. Interestingly, Paglia does not mention whether Una's simulacrum also derives from a "lack of sexual complexity."

10. Stevie Davies also argues that Florimell attracts rapists "magnetically" because she represents something "feminine which by its very nature has no defence, but in order to maintain its particular virtue must lie open to every act of brutality" (70). In a similar critical judgment, Hamilton posits an analogy between Amoret's fear during the attack of Lust and "a creature who would display a similar horror of sex" (1977: 476). It seems that the actions of these female characters invariably receive negative interpretations. First the maidens are blamed for attracting male sexual brutality, then their terror at the prospect of rape becomes transmuted into a "horror of sex," instead of being read as a legitimate or honorable fear in response to imminent sexual violation.

11. In contrast, for a brilliant, subtle analysis of the political implications of Amoret's imprisonment and sexual torture by Busyrane, see Susan Frye's chapter entitled "Engendered Violence: Elizabeth, Spenser, and the Definitions of Chastity (1590)." I am grateful to Professor Frye for sharing the page proofs of this chapter prior to publication.

12. The feminist implications of scenes in *The Faerie Queene* have only recently begun to be addressed by critics such as Lauren Silberman, Susanne Wofford, Mihoko Suzuki, Maureen Quilligan, and Dorothy Stephens.

13. Susanne Wofford (1988) makes a similar point. While our conclusions often differ, Quilligan's discussions in *Milton's Spenser: The Politics of Reading* are extremely thought-provoking. See especially her chapter "The Gender of the Reader and the Problem of Sexuality." See Frye (chapter 3) for a provocative discussion of Elizabeth I's role in complicating the gendered subject positions of Petrarchan discourse.

14. See Louis Montrose ("Shaping Fantasies" [1986a] and "The Elizabethan Subject" [1986b]) and Susan Frye for valuable discussions of the epic's reflection of conflicting attitudes toward Elizabeth Tudor.

15. In the introduction to her recent study, Mihoko Suzuki discusses this issue and describes her project as "read[ing] the epic tradition 'as a woman' " (1). Her work is both intriguing and complementary to my own. Similarly, Simon Shepherd acknowledges this male audience, although he confesses that he did not recognize it until enlightened by a female colleague (1989: 58).

16. See Laura Mulvey (14–26).

17. Frye also briefly alludes to the pornographic resonances of this scene (chapter 3, n. 70).

18. See, for example, Paglia (190).

19. Several other critics have recently discussed related issues. Susanne Lindgren Wofford, for example, brilliantly critiques the role of "gendered symbolization" in the modes of writing and reading explored in the epic (1988: 3). David Lee Miller considers the relationship between male and female psychic interactions and allegory (217). Although I do not agree that "Spenser may well approach the ethical concerns of feminism as nearly as is possible for a male writer in a nondemocratic, patriarchal tradition and social order" (217), I find Miller's account fascinating and insightful. Berry's study also takes a very different direction from mine, but she looks at Petrarchism and Neoplatonism in this period through a feminist perspective. Theresa M. Krier astutely examines many allegorical incidents involving women, but her project emphasizes Spenser's classical forebears, not the epic's ideology of gender. Similarly, Margaret Olofson Thickstun situates *The Faerie Queene*'s representations of women in relation to Puritan doctrine.

20. Quoted in Quilligan (1979: 220).

21. For a complicated and trenchant account of the gendering of allegory in *Piers Plowman*, see Clare A. Lees. I am grateful to Professor Lees for providing a copy of her essay prior to publication.

22. See chapter 3 in particular for a discussion of this fetishization.

23. The portraits of deceptive male characters are presented quite differently. Dolon, for instance, disguises his intentions, not his physical body, and Busyrane's identity as an enchanter is never hidden. Archimago, of course, is an overpowering male personification of evil. As I note in chapter 3, his presence as dominant figure of malevolence helps contain the threat of female evil.

24. Both published in English in 1985, *Speculum of the Other Woman* and *This Sex Which Is Not One* will be referred to as 1985a and 1985b respectively.

25. For a brief, but valuable discussion of the complexity of the literal level of allegory see Quilligan (1979, especially 67–69). Lauren Silberman offers an insightful discussion of "The (Gendered) Body in Allegory" (1994: chapter 7).

26. Louis Montrose discusses the reader's identification with such a male position in relation to the Bower of Bliss (1986b: 329–30).

27. Ian Maclean discusses the Aristotelian influences upon Renaissance considerations of women's relationship to "virtue" (49–59). Warner Berthoff is certainly correct when he points out that "Virtue" is "feminine in gender in Latin and the Romance languages" and that individual virtues are often given female allegorical forms (53); nevertheless, *The Faerie Queene* and many other works still separate the concept of virtue from the possibility of female realization. See Marina Warner for a useful discussion of the evolution and disjunctures of the links between grammatical gender and allegorical representations of females (1985: 63–87).

28. All *Faerie Queene* references are from *The Faerie Queene*, edited by

A. C. Hamilton (London: Longmans, 1977). Hamilton's editorial comments and glosses are cited as Hamilton 1977.

29. Philippa Berry suggests that Spenser was in doubt "whether his epic was concerned with the representation of a masculine or feminine courtly subject" (155). Granted, there is a lot of gendered tension around this area in the poem, but a male subject position is always presumed, even when a female monarch may be the primary reader addressed. Regardless, Berry's book provides an extremely useful account of the interconnections between Petrarchan and Neoplatonic conventions and representations of Elizabeth.

30. See Katherine Usher Henderson and Barbara F. McManus for an account of this controversy.

31. See Wofford for a valuable discussion of the tension between "the text's self-conscious self-interrogation on the one hand and its unacknowledged and partially submerged discursive self-positioning on the other" (1992: 233). I am grateful to Professor Wofford and to Ellen F. Smith of Stanford UP for access to some of this work's page proofs prior to publication.

32. Rubin, of course, was following Emma Goldman, whose essay "The Traffic in Women" is included in *Anarchism and Other Essays* (New York: Mother Earth, 1911).

33. See Sarah Stanbury (on medieval lyric) and George E. Rowe and Patricia Parker (1987: 64–65) on Spenser for adept analyses using feminist film theory.

34. Feminist studies in Shakespeare first came to many scholars' attention with the collection of essays under this title edited by Carolyn Ruth Swift Lenz, Gayle Greene, and Carol Thomas Neely. For more recent accounts of feminist scholarship in Renaissance Studies, see Carol Thomas Neely (1988) and Lynda E. Boose.

1. 'Beauties Chace'

1. An earlier, shorter version of this chapter appears under the title " 'Beauties Chace': Arthur and Women in *The Faerie Queene*," in *The Passing of Arthur: Loss and Renewal in the Arthurian Tradition*, edited by Christopher Baswell and William Sharpe (New York: Garland, 1988) 207–20. I am grateful to Garland for permission to reprint this essay in revised form.

2. Many critics have not been too concerned, however. The dream is often not mentioned in critical studies of the poem. Roche only notes without comment "Arthur's vision of the Faery Queen" (1964: 35). Freeman simply refers in passing to Arthur's "personal contact with Gloriana" (106). In notable contrast, Miller provides an insightful psychoanalytical and historical reading (120–63) and Elizabeth J. Bellamy offers an extremely useful psychoanalytic reading of the dream (1992: 212–21).

3. See C. S. Lewis (1966: 158–59) for an earlier elaboration upon this question.

4. Suzuki also finds Arthur's chase after Florimell "problematic" (174). Berger notes that this chase is "weird," but decides that "the 'goodly meede' they aspire to is not sexual" (1989: 212; 224). Patrick Cheney describes the scene as part of a conflict between "Ovidian desire" and "Neoplatonic love" (1989: 316–18). Although she does not discuss Spenser's poem, Clare A. Lees offers some valuable insights into the concept of "meede."

5. In contrast, Davies believes that Arthur departs from his usual pattern because Book III represents a world of "feminine powers" (56).

6. Most critics have not been unduly troubled by the implications. Davies, for example, remarks that "the instinct to follow Florimell is experienced as in itself good" (72). Hankins comments merely that "The three men immediately spur their horses after her, Timias in pursuit of the forester, Arthur and Guyon desiring Florimell herself" (164). He then drops the issue. Roche maintains that "we cannot suppose that Spenser intends the reader to think ill of Arthur and Guyon" (1964: 14), but he offers no praiseworthy explanation for the scene. Tonkin shows the most creativity in his energetic, if unconvincing account: "There is at least the suggestion that Arthur sees in Florimell a glimmering of Gloriana's beauty (III. iv: 54), but that hardly accounts for the enthusiasm of his pursuit. Perhaps she is like the form of beauty itself, yet such a reading seems little congruent with narrative probability. The answer, surely, if there is an answer, is that Arthur recognizes in Florimell the spirit of the generative cycle—that his pursuit represents a kind of disinterested pity for the vicissitudes and deprivations which are sadly a part of the natural process" (1972: 72–73). Kathleen Williams argues that Arthur and Guyon chase Florimell as they would "a hind or hare or dove" (113), but that she "is always pursued because always in flight" (113). Anderson finds the two knights " 'Full of great enuie and fell gealosy' if not of her pursuer then of themselves or each other" (99).

7. For a more extensive reading of *The Faerie Queene* from a post-structuralist perspective, see Jonathan Goldberg (1981).

8. Although Spenser, true to his Protestant background, presents the concept of married sex positively, the epic generally situates these relationships in the future. With few exceptions, sanctioned sex is deferred, a tendency which supports the hesitancy about sex discussed here. As Bellamy notes, "only the nondynastic Florimell and Marinell and the English rivers the Thames and the Medway succeed in actually getting married" (1992: 193 n. 8).

9. For accounts of this controversy, see John Bugge, especially 20–29, and James Grantham Turner, especially chapters 1 and 2. Turner offers an extensive discussion of the implications of these issues for Milton's work, drawing from a theological history that would have been available to both writers.

10. At the end of Book One, the Red Crosse Knight is described as "swimming in that sea of blisfull ioy" (I. xii: 41. 5) after his betrothal to Una, which may be a reference to the consummation of their relationship. If it is, such licit sexuality is transient, as the next lines confirm: "He nought forgot,

how whilome he had sworne . . . Vnto his Farie Queene backe to returne" (I. xii: 41. 6, 8). I am grateful to Maureen Quilligan for reminding me of this moment.

11. Arthur's reliance on "narrative sex" here reflects a common practice in the poem. Although the prince is separated from his love involuntarily here, male knights display a consistent preference for talking about their ladies rather than being with them. For discussions of related topics, see Nancy J. Vickers, "The Mistress in the Masterpiece" (1986a) and particularly "This Heraldry in Lucrece's Face" (1986b).

12. Both having been published in translation in 1965, *The Interpretation of Dreams* and "Femininity" will be cited as 1965b and 1965a respectively.

13. The complexity of Gloriana's portrait parallels contradictory responses to Elizabeth which Louis Montrose locates both within Spenser's poem and in the Elizabethan court (1986b).

14. See Vickers for a discussion of the harm produced for female characters by the "product of men talking to men about women" (1985: 96).

15. For a discussion of the concept of the trace, see Jacques Derrida (1976: 46–48).

16. Freeman suggests that "Florimell in her refusal of salvation from any knight who tries to help her, stands as an extreme reflection of the Chastity at the core of the Book" (186).

17. Turner notes the "legal and colloquial" conflation of sexual intercourse with "conversation" during the early modern period (205).

18. As noted elsewhere, critics sometimes blame Florimell for the chase, but since she remains at a distance, any interpretation of her actions relies upon supposition.

19. This interrogation marks another important moment of critical silence. For example, Roche mentions the rescue, but without elaboration (1964: 207–208); Tonkin simply remarks that Arthur's action here "seems almost to make him the hero" (1972: 73); Kathleen Williams (128) and Hankins (160) quickly skim past the episode; DeNeef focuses on Sclaunder (121); and Freeman briefly comments that Arthur is "present, as any other knight could have been, to care for Aemylia and Amoret" (239).

20. As Freeman observes, "It will be long before the knight realises the real identity of Duessa in spite of all that he has heard from Fradubio" (29).

21. In her forthcoming book, Lauren Silberman rightly draws attention to the description of Lust as a male example of this "enthusiasm for the carnivalesque body" (1994: chapter 3). Such suggestions of monstrous sexuality among evil male figures certainly exist, but there is a conflation of monstrosity and nearly all female sexuality which is not replicated in the male realm. I am grateful to Professor Silberman for sharing her manuscript with me prior to publication.

22. See Hankins for an allegorical account of Duessa's exposure (101–105). Lockerd provides a Jungian analysis (100–101).

23. Even though, as Freeman comments, "Duessa is constantly associated

with false appearances and with darkness . . . Deception is what Duessa represents through all her dealings with the Red Crosse Knight" (93).

24. In these scenes, Spenser is not duplicating emblem books; rather, he adapts some of their features to help shape these heavily iconic representations of women in the poem. Examples from the emblem books can be found in a range of sources, most notably including Henkel and Schone; Geoffrey Whitney, *A Choice of Emblems* (1586); Henry Hawkins, *The Devout Hart* (1634) and *Parthenia Sacra* (1633); Henry Peacham, *Minerva Britanna* (1612).

25. For an important discussion of related issues in the blazon tradition, see Nancy Vickers (1981).

26. Contemporary emblems occasionally present naked male figures in a similar fashion, but Spenser tends not to replicate these images in his poem. The emblematic figures in the epic are nearly always female.

27. See Patricia Parker for a valuable discussion of the related "verbal display" of a woman (1987: 154) in a variety of early modern texts (1987: 126–54). Parker details the gendering and representation of "forms of economic, sexual, and epistemological possession" of "women and other strange things" (1987: 154).

28. The sisters rarely receive critical mention, except for brief accounts of their allegorical significance, such as Freeman (119–20), Kathleen Williams (28–29), and Lockerd (108–10) offer. One significant exception to this tendency can be found in Miller's discussion of Fidelia (88–92).

29. Hamilton notes that "Faith and Hope are not fulfilled in this world" (1977: 130).

30. See Gail Paster for a fascinating comparison between Charissa's "good" breasts and Duessa's "bad" breasts (206–207).

31. Una fulfills a similar function for the Red Crosse Knight when he confronts Despair.

32. This description also recalls Busyrane's chambers, but the magician's role as active agent in Amoret's torture distinguishes him from the emblematic females discussed here. Emblematic figures "show" or "tell"; they rarely "do."

33. The original citation may be found in Alain Corbin, "La Relation intime ou les plaisirs de l'échange," in *Histoire de la vie privée*, vol. 4, ed. Michelle Perrot (Paris: Seuil, 1987), 559. Apter also includes Laure Adler's description of the growing appeal of such set scenes: "Certainly voyeurism has always been an essential component of desire, but the house of ill-fame began systematically to offer tableaux vivants" (42). The original citation is found in Adler (Paris: Hachette, 1990) 130.

34. Krier offers an account of the classical allusions and implications of Spenser's portrayal of voyeurism and vision. Her work provides a complementary view of similar, though generally distinct topics.

35. See Hankins (56–60) and Kathleen Williams (64–65) for allegorical readings of the body imagery in this episode.

36. For a fascinating account of "Alma's nought," see Miller (164–214).

37. See, for example, Hamilton (1977: 251). Miller suggests that we see "an explicit image of the higher unity of man and woman in a single body" (182).

38. Aptekar's book discusses the iconography of Book Five in great detail. For other analyses of Mercilla's portrayal, see also Angus Fletcher (1971: 168–69), Kathleen Williams (176–77), and Freeman (287–90).

39. Significantly, the description of Duessa's stripping, with its emphasis upon the witch as "old" with "dried dugs" (I. viii) suggests that she is being represented as post-menopausal. As the undisguised hags which I discuss in chapter 2 demonstrate, presumed reproductive availability seems to be an important facet of "evil" women's surreptitious power.

40. Again, I refer interested readers to Miller's discussion of the related absence of genitalia in Alma's Castle. See "How to 'Avoid' the Genitals" (Miller 169–83). See also Vickers (1981) for a discussion of fears about female nudity in relation to the Diana and Actaeon story.

41. Obviously, even the metaphoric inclusion of female genitals would require great skill on the part of the poet in order to avoid offense—a talent he displays in the Garden of Adonis (III. vi: 43). Given his amply demonstrated facility with metaphor and allusion, the omissions and deferrals in these instances are particularly noteworthy. The silence about these absences which is maintained by narrator and characters increases the uneasiness these scenes generate. Notably, as Clare Kinney points out, the most visible representation of female sexual anatomy is never visited by the titular knights: "no quester visits the Garden of Adonis; for the first time an important locus of instruction is reserved for the poet and the reader alone" (77). Quilligan makes a similar point (1979: 231).

In addition, the "wilde Bore" which Venus has trapped in a cave beneath "that Mount" (III. vi: 48) implies that this site of female sexual pleasure may concurrently figure forth anxieties about both the threat of castration and the possibility that women control that threat, even while this locus presents "eternall blis" (III. vi: 48. 1). This possibility, linked with Greenblatt's assessment that the Garden of Adonis "has almost no erotic appeal" (171), suggests that while the knights in the poem are being shielded once again from the sight of female genitalia, the readers are being presented with a view which furthers the interpretation of such genitals as unsatisfying and dangerous.

Although she is making a very different point, Quilligan supports this reading by her argument that "the most comfortable and unthreatened viewpoint for reading the events of the garden is female" (1983: 196). The perceived need here for a "female" audience underscores the threat implicit in the scene for those reading from a "male" position.

See Pamela Benson for a "profeminist" reading of the boar's entrapment (1992: 256) which is at odds with my interpretation.

42. The narrative suggests that Calidore *might* have had a clear view of female genitals when it shows Calidore "Beholding all" (IV. x: 11. 5) "That euen

he him selfe his eyes enuyed" (VI. x: 11. 7), but the character's uncertainty about the vision leaves the question unanswered.

43. For a particularly useful description of the Garden of Adonis, see Bellamy (1992: 239–47).

44. As Bellamy's remark about "Book 3's recurring 'wombs' " (1992: 209) suggests, wombs receive ample mention elsewhere, but in the instances cited here, the characters and the reader are left to wonder whether the elision of external signs of sex corresponds to the characters' internal circumstances.

45. For a discussion of the representations of female genitalia in Ariosto, see Valeria Finucci (166–67). I discovered this book late in the process of revising my own and found that we discuss similar topics, although she focuses on other authors.

46. Since the magnetically attractive False Florimell presumably also possesses male genitals (III. viii: 8) and since unknowing knights could easily attribute them to Britomart also, a reader might conclude that the most desirable or least threatening female genital is a penis.

2. Nightmares of Desire

1. A shorter version of this chapter appears in *Studies in Philology* under the title "Nightmares of Desire: Evil Women in *The Faerie Queene*." At the time of this writing, it is scheduled to appear in the Summer 1994 issue. I am grateful to the editors of *Studies in Philology* for permission to republish this piece in an expanded version.

2. Ernest Jones's theory of dreams in *On the Nightmare* suggests an important correlation between the succubitic dreams discussed here and Britomart's dream in Isis Temple. Jones compares the belief in incubi with a practice known as "Incubation or Temple-sleep." Claiming that this predominantly Egyptian custom most commonly involves "the union of a person with a god or goddess during sleep in the sacellum of the temple," Jones contends that since this dream substitutes a divine figure for the incubus, it represents "the most perfect manifestation of the erotic wishes that have been most fully brought into harmony with the standards of the ego" (92–93). Britomart's erotic longings accompany her search for her destined mate; hence, her sexual dreams constitute an "incubation" in contrast with the succubitic illicit fantasies of male knights.

3. *Aristotle on Sleep and Dreams*, edited and translated by David Gallop (Lewiston, New York: Broadview, 1990).

4. *A Discovrse of the Damned Art of Witchcraft*, 1610. Reginald Scot exemplifies another contemporary theory of dreams when he attributes "diabolicall" dreams to "the heavie and blacke humor of melancholie" (104).

5. This materiality corresponds to some contemporary theories of demonic spirits. Robert Burton, for instance, discusses a lengthy controversy over the alleged "corporeality" of devils (157–76).

6. As Quilligan observes, such "literalization of etymology" is "characteristic of allegorical narrative" (1979: 135).

7. Much of the material on witches and succubi in this chapter has been culled from the following sources: Lambert Daneau, *A Dialogue of Witches*, 1575; George Gifford, *A Discourse of the Subtill Practice of Devils*, 1587; Henry Holland, *A Treatise Against Witchcraft*, 1590; William Perkins, *A Discovrse of the Damned Art of Witchcraft*, 1610; Reginald Scot, *The Discoverie of Witchcraft*, 1584; Montague Summers, ed. *Malleus Maleficarum* (1608 edition); Walter Bruel [Gualterus Bruele], *The Physician's Practice*, 1639; and Philip Barrough, *The Method of Physick*, 1590. For our purposes here, the variations between the witchcraft treatises of this period are less important than their intersections. Spenser drew from demonic folklore for his portrayals of malevolent women, but he did not follow the tradition very closely.

8. The terms witches, hags, succubi, and nightmares were often used interchangeably or to describe different aspects of the same phenomenon. Walter Bruel, for example, explains that the "INCUBVS or NIGHTMARE . . . is not, as some suppose, caused by an old Hagge riding us" (sig. H1v-H2). "Witch" and "succubus" are often synonymous in contemporary treatises, though there are also variations. In addition, succubi are often labeled as "succubi witches." I am calling the females involved in enervating sexual activities "succubi," while those designated as "witches" may or may not participate in sexual deeds and are regularly termed "witches" in Spenser's text. "Witches" in the poem are often involved in the creation or manifestation of "forged beauties." As I note later, the designation "succubus" does not appear in *The Faerie Queene*, but many of the malevolent females display succubitic qualities. Concurrently, there are many elements concerning witches in sixteenth- and seventeenth-century documents which do not factor into the portraits of witches in Spenser's poem. Hence, much of the current scholarship on witches in the early modern period appears to bear only indirect interest for readers of *The Faerie Queene*.

9. Robert Burton offers the following description: "in such as are troubled with Incubus, or witch-ridden (as we call it); if they lie on their backs, they suppose an old woman rides, & sits so hard upon them, that they are almost stifled for want of breath, when there is nothing offends but a concourse of bad humours" (220).

10. Not all of these characters are "women," although their female genitalia regularly draw specific mention. The female aspects of these figures receive significant attention. Although they cannot all be grouped as "women," they are closely linked by their anatomical sex.

11. Though not mentioning the sexual element that Jones finds in nightmares, Freud makes a similar claim about dreams in general in *The Interpretation of Dreams*: "psychical material that has been suppressed comes to light in dreams" (113).

12. *The Faerie Queene* diverges from many contemporary writings when knights escape serious censure after sleeping with succubi. Although Protestant

England was no longer bound by the anti-witchcraft bull of Pope Innocent VIII (December, 1484), its condemnation of those consorting with witches remained consistent with Elizabethan anti-witchcraft legislation and treatises. Numerous critics are currently working on issues concerned with witchcraft during this period. See, for example, Karen Newman (1991: 51–70); Kathleen McLuskie (57–86); and Nancy Gutierrez.

13. Spenser adheres to this pattern by fashioning the powerful male figure of sorcery, Archimago, whose evil generally overshadows that of the female emissaries from the devil.

14. The mermaids in Book Two are unusual for their homicidal tendencies. A personified "Murder" is brought as evidence against Duessa at her trial (V. ix: 48. 1–4), but by this point in the epic, Duessa figures less as a nightmarish female and more directly as Mary, Queen of Scots. Murder is not part of Duessa's standard modus operandi in the earlier books.

15. Reginald Scot, for example, reports in 1584 that witches are old women "in whose drousie minds the divill hath goten a fine seat" (4).

16. Unlike *The Faerie Queene*, the witchcraft treatises emphasize witches' humanity, as Nancy Gutierrez notes: "[witchcraft] is a human activity, encouraged, if not initiated by the devil that aims to thwart God" (4).

17. Duessa's affiliation with male figures of evil corresponds with this tendency.

18. The same kind of story is often repeated whether the treatises argue that witches and succubi are real or imagined. Theological considerations loom large in these determinations. The Catholic *Malleus Maleficarum*, for example, proclaims that "to deny the existence of witches is contrary to the obvious sense of the Canon is shown by ecclesiastical law" (4). Johannes Weir attributes "the illusions and spells of demons" (3) to the devil—"with God's permission" (283), while Reginald Scot maintains that "it is neither a witch, nor divell, but a glorious God" (2) who is responsible for supposed witchcraft.

19. These treatises tend to discuss incubi and succubi simultaneously and in fairly identical terms. Both groups of spirits appear to fulfill similar functions; that is, "heterosexual" sexual intercourse with humans. The differences between the two demonic groups thus result from the physiological variations between their male and female human partners. In *The Faerie Queene*, however, there is no male counterpart for the succubi presented, presumably since "good" women could not be visited by such a spirit and remain virtuous.

20. Edward Topsell reports that wine with the "tongue or gall of a dragon" can relieve men from "the spirits of the night, called Incubi and succubi, or else Night-mares" (sig. Ppp4).

21. Nohrnberg also discusses Duessa's succubitic qualities, linking her to the Lilith legend (228–46).

22. For a discussion of Acrasia's threat in the context of Elizabethan politics, see Greenblatt (182–85). Ian Sowton offers an interpretation which is complementary to mine. He argues that Acrasia represents "a woman's pleasure where she takes that pleasure on her own terms" (410) and suggests that this

intersection of female power and pleasure "can only appear in the male lexicon as enchantment and witchery" (410).

23. For a fascinating account of the threat of castration here and of the Bower of Bliss as a site of female danger, see Parker (1987: 54–66).

24. For further information concerning early modern concepts of sexual physiology see Ian Maclean (28–46) and Audrey Eccles.

25. In *Malleus Maleficarum*, there is a lengthy section discussing such reports. See, for example, 117–22.

26. Weaver is summarizing Rosemary Reuther here.

27. Harriet Hawkins summarizes and critiques the lengthy critical debate over the ferocity of Guyon's destruction of the Bower (55–77). See also Greenblatt (157–92). Lloyd A. Wright attempts to divert readers' attention from Guyon's violence to his "heroism." Madelon [Sprengnether] Gohlke discusses the issue in light of allegory's declining appeal among literary critics.

28. For an account of the role of Acrasia and concupiscence in the Legend of Temperance, see Zailig Pollock. Greenblatt discusses why this aspect of the Bower cannot be eradicated completely (177).

29. C. S. Lewis (1936: 331).

30. Here, I disagree with Arlene N. Okerlund, among others, who argues that the reader is tempted by the maidens and the Bower, but that Guyon never is.

31. In *Essential Articles for the Study of Edmund Spenser* (Hamden, Ct.: Archon, 1972), A. C. Hamilton reprints two of the classic articles concerned with the relationship between art and nature in Book Two; namely, A. S. P. Woodhouse, "Nature and Grace in *The Faerie Queene*," and C. S. Lewis, "*The Faerie Queene*." Several other articles in this collection also discuss the Bower of Bliss.

32. For an account of the critical controversy over the role of Christianity in the Legend of Temperance, see Peter D. Stambler and Anthea Hume (especially 59–71).

33. *Thelma and Louise*, directed by Ridley Scott, 1991.

34. See J. S. P. Tatlock (171).

35. Examples of this type of liaison are often included subtly—in the tapestry at Busyrane's enclave, for instance.

36. Notably, witches were often associated with Catholicism. Scot, for example, claims that witches were commonly "papists or such as knowe no religion" (4).

37. For discussions of Duessa's association with Catholicism and apostasy, see Douglas Waters and Nohrnberg (223–28).

38. Hamilton notes the progression here from *insomnium* to *phantasma* which recalls Macrobius, *Commentary on the Dream of Scipio*: I. iii: 2–8 (Hamilton 1977: 41).

39. For general accounts of Neoplatonism in Spenser, see Mohinimohan Bhattacherje and Elizabeth Bieman.

40. In chapter 3, I discuss the hyena-monster who figures in this episode.

Not only does the Snowy Florimell substitute successfully for Florimell, but the hyena conflates the true maiden with her palfrey in III. vii.

41. Although Ate generally figures as a hag in the epic, she also displays "witchlike" transformations; therefore, I am discussing her in both sections.

42. As noted in the previous chapter, given the vexed portrayal of female sexuality in the poem, it is not surprising that many of the "evil" female characters presented who are past childbearing years appear as hags, not succubi.

43. Munera's economic transgressions qualify her also for crimes against "worth" as discussed in chapter 5.

44. The mutilation of Munera's body also connects her with "good" women, however, such as Amoret. I briefly discuss such butcheries later, but it is important to note that this type of treatment cannot be used as a guide to determine women's good or evil qualities.

45. While exceptions to this pattern are rare, they do exist. The "old woman" (IV. vii: 13. 7) who protects Æmylia from the ravages of Lust is described as a hag when the captive pair finally emerges from the cave (IV. vii: 34. 3).

46. Interestingly, David Hufford has published a volume studying this same concept in modern Newfoundland.

47. Suzuki claims that "Spenser consistently figures linguistic duplicity through female monsters, who seduce by concealing their hideous deformity under an attractive appearance" (196). Much of Suzuki's argument in this section is convincing, but conflating all female "monsters" together misses the important nuances accompanying their differences.

48. Since female characters so often represent sexual threats in the poem, the use of a post-menopausal hag here representing "impotence" is particularly interesting.

49. Given the predominance of literal bondage in *The Faerie Queene*, it is interesting to note that in her discussion of Occasion, Wofford suggests that in this episode "the allegory indeed requires a gesture of binding and containing" (1992: 312).

50. Occasion exemplifies a nightmarish inversion of the "maternal world" Jonathan Goldberg finds glorified in the Legend of Chastity (1975).

51. Ate's purported taste for blood (IV. i: 26. 5) is not apparently directed toward infants.

52. Archbishop Herman of Wied (sig. A5v).

53. From *The Araignment of Lewde, idle, froward, vertuous and honest Women* (1615), quoted in Katherine Usher Henderson and Barbara F. McManus (215).

54. For discussions of Spenser's use of iconography here, see John Manning and Alastair Fowler (1976), and David W. Burchmore (1981).

55. Suzuki notes that it is unusual for a creature such as the Blatant Beast to be depicted in male form (204).

56. There are notable exceptions to this tendency. Silberman, for example,

memorably labels Orgoglio as "an ambulatory erection" (1987: 213). In addition, see John W. Schroeder (149–53; 158). Similarly, Wofford describes Lust as "a giant version of the male genitals" (1992: 315). Ironically, however, male figures of evil in the poem may also possess *female* sexual organs, as indicated by a reference to the male dragon's "womb" in Book One (I. xii: 10. 5).

57. For a discussion of the concept of "excess" in the Elizabethan sumptuary laws, see Marjorie Garber (27–28). Garber reads "excess" in this context as the site of the transvestite.

58. Although they are writing about other texts here, Derrida and Irigaray could easily be describing most of the female characters in Spenser's epic.

59. For a masterly account of related issues in Shakespeare, see Janet Adelman.

60. I discuss Mirabella at considerable length in chapter 4.

61. According to the text (V. ix: 40), Duessa is technically on trial for treason, but since her sexual transgressions play such a large part in the poem, it is difficult to imagine that they do not also figure into her conviction. Otherwise, as Richard S. McCabe notes, modern readers are likely to agree with Kerby Neill that "there seems to be practically no connection between Duessa's appearance in the first and second parts of *The Faerie Queene*" (quoted in McCabe, 226).

3. The Importance of Being Fairest

1. Of course, as John Charles Nelson notes, even the Platonic "picture of divine love is shattered by the unexpected appearance of love in the flesh" (68).

2. See Bieman's discussion of *The Fowre Hymnes* (153–62) for a useful interpretation of Spenser's presentation of Neoplatonism's "divisions between earthly love and beauty and heavenly love and beauty" (156).

3. Elizabeth Cropper discusses a related phenomenon in Renaissance portraiture. She argues that "Many portraits of unknown beautiful women are now characterized as representations of ideal beauty in which the question of identity is immaterial" (178).

4. See Parker (1987: 126–54) and the series of essays by Vickers for important discussions of the role of Petrarchism and the blazon tradition in fashioning such structures.

5. For an insightful reading of the similar Petrarchan strategies operating in Shakespeare's "Rape of Lucrece," see Vickers (1985). As Vickers notes in this essay, "The canonical legacy of description in praise of beauty is, after all, a legacy shaped predominantly by the male imagination for the male imagination; it is, in large part, the product of men talking to men about women" (1985: 96).

6. Critics also tend to read female characters according to their beauty. Berger, for example, asserts that "Florimell's beauty expresses her desire, announces the readiness of woman for love" (1989: 222).

7. For a now classic account of homosocial coding in later literature see Eve Kosofsky Sedgwick.

8. Judith Anderson argues that "the poet creates this myth about the three brothers, their sister Cambina, Cambel, and his sister Canacee to realize the fluidity that 'infusion' implies" (119); Roche reads them as "the forces of concord" (1964: 164). Tonkin suggests that "Cambina's arrival makes possible the establishment of friendship, the mutual respect and affection which is the ground of all love and which leads to concord" (1972: 73). Goldberg focuses on questions of narrative (1981: 31–44). These emphases provide valuable insights into the text, but tend to elide the gendered implications of the episode.

9. Roche provides an allegorical reading of this episode (1964: 17–31) which is more complementary than contradictory to the interpretation I offer here.

10. I discuss Mirabella's story in detail in chapter 4. Unlike Canacee, Mirabella does not have a male relative with interests in her match; therefore, she is required to choose a man, any man, whereas Canacee is allowed to be pickier. Without narratorial intervention, it would be difficult for a reader to differentiate between Mirabella's refusal of her suitors and Canacee's similar rejections in IV. ii: 36–37.

11. In his discussion of the Neoplatonic aspects of this episode, Kane labels Cambell's involvement as a "struggle for purification" (117).

12. Patrick Cheney (1985) offers a useful account of magic in this episode.

13. Although Nohrnberg argues that "another paradoxical form of chastity is brother-sister love" (432), the emphasis here lies more with eroticism than with chastity.

14. For Neoplatonic readings of the three brothers, see David W. Burchmore (1984) and Nohrnberg (608–19). Silberman suggests that the brothers do not have "sexual desire [as] a primary motivation" (1994: chapter 5)—an observation which supports a "homosocial" reading of the episode.

15. The epic's subtle devaluation of female chastity is also quietly played out in this episode. Like Satyrane's mother, the mother of the three champions became pregnant through rape (IV. ii: 45), but the narrative merely notes this event without comment.

16. Kathleen Williams also comments on the "ritual-like" aura of the battle (123).

17. Rubin argues that "the aim of preventing the occurrence of genetically close matings" does not expain the universality of incest taboos. Instead, she claims that by "forbidding unions within a group [the incest taboo] enjoins marital exchange between groups" (173), as we see demonstrated in this episode.

18. As Hamilton notes, Cambina's name comes from the Italian *cambiare* or "exchange" (1977: 439).

19. Roche calls Cambina "not so much a character as an aggregate of iconographical details" (1964: 22–23). Her function within the Lévi-Strauss model supports this reading.

20. Berger describes a similar situation in *The Shepheardes Calender*: "Women at best serve instrumental functions in the YMPA [Young Men's Pastoral Association]. Whether they are idealized or monsterized, worshiped or chased, whether they are sources of artistic inspiration, entertainment, or manly honor, their job is to contribute to the male bonding which poetry celebrates" (1988: 359).

21. When Arthur and others "mend" virginities by fiat, their actions recall similar maneuvers by the Spanish bawd Celestina, who was rumored to have "made and vnmade 100000 virginityes in this Citye" in Fernando de Roja's *La Celestina* [c. 1499] (Lacalle 130). Celestina's "restorations" of virginity are not presented as exemplary, however, in contrast to the similar acts performed by knights in *The Faerie Queene*. This text was not translated into English until 1631, but Guadalupe Martinez Lacalle notes that it was introduced to England at the beginning of the sixteenth century. See *Celestine or the Tragick-Comedie of Calisto and Melibea*, translated by James Mabbe, edited by Guadalupe Martinez Lacalle (London: Tamesis, 1972) 2.

22. Freeman argues that the reconciliation between Pœana and Placidas "demonstrates the need for forgiveness in the conduct of personal relationships" (236).

23. Tonkin claims that Calidore's falsehood is merely a "white lie" (1972: 223), but this view ignores the considerable consequences accompanying societal beliefs about female chastity both in the literature and in the culture.

24. For an interesting alternate reading of this episode, see Debra Belt.

25. The scene has caused some critical discomfort, but little serious distress. For example, see Tonkin (1972: 45–48). Kathleen Williams seems more concerned with what she perceives as Priscilla's "venial, fussy inability to love or serve freely because she cannot look beyond her own social standing and good name" (220) than she is with Calidore's actions.

26. Tonkin believes that "In meting out justice to Crudor and Briana, Calidore takes the lessons of Artegall a stage further. Not only does he punish: he also saves" (1972: 40); Freeman argues that the theme of education is central to this episode (306); Hankins maintains that the "unexpected requital of her disdain by the granting of her dearest wish so transforms Briana that she becomes gracious, generous, and happy" (186).

27. Once again, it is difficult not to think of Mirabella here. Haughtiness is ordinarily not accepted in unattached women, but Crudor's presence shields Briana from serious consequences.

28. Kathleen Williams maintains that "Calidore converts Briana by being good to her" (193).

29. In Britomart's case, as in others, there is no immediate perpetrator of her pain. Nonetheless, the prevalence of these "darts" helps illuminate the attitudes toward women being supported in the text. Champagne offers an interesting Lacanian reading of Britomart's wounding (99–100).

30. Since Busyrane is portrayed as a poet/writer, his use of the dart most openly conflates the literal and figurative meanings of such "piercings."

31. See chapter 4 for a discussion of some of the sadomasochistic practices represented in the poem.

32. The presence of "satire" in Satyrane's name and the widely known character flaws among many present at the tourney clearly alert the reader to remain suspicious of the event and to question the kind of discourse about beauty being honored. Nevertheless, the implied critique of this system is consistently more subtle than the elements which support it.

33. Many critics find no difficulty with this inversion which they attribute to an uncomplicated use of convention. Krier, for example, terms the episode "a relatively perfunctory adaptation of romance competitions" (132).

34. The girdle is briefly called "Cestus," thereby alerting readers to its place in mythology. Freeman, among other critics, gives a short account of the girdle's history (233–34). Wofford discusses the episode of the girdle and other "yron chaines" of love in terms of "the violence of Elizabethan power" (1992: 326). See Goldberg for a useful account of the girdle's interpretive complexities (1981: 128n, 149–50). Silberman provides a fascinating Freudian and linguistic reading of the girdle episode (1994: chapter 6).

35. Although this tourney probably represents one site where the poem calls into question the values being upheld, it still helps reinforce the patterns of female diminishment already established.

36. In his discussion of the implications of this episode, Nohrnberg suggests that "Spenser's treatment [of the False Florimell] implies that a good deal of the sentiment expressed in Petrarchan form is only superficially chaste" (575).

37. As many critics have noted, Spenser's poem presents an active engagement in the historic debate on the relationship between truth and beauty. Mark Rose and Robert Ellrodt, for instance, each offer interpretations of the issue's role in Spenser's poetry, while John Charles Nelson provides a more general account of Neoplatonism and love treatises. While such studies illuminate conventional presentations of the beauty/virtue split, they do not consider the female perspective adequately, nor do their conclusions eliminate the questions raised regarding male motivation and behavior represented in *The Faerie Queene*. As Berger notes, "Florimell is no less a male invention than the False Florimell. Both equally project and reflect male desires, and their effects sometimes converge, just as Neoplatonist fantasies equally slide into Petrarchan fantasies" (1989: 220–21).

38. Since I am completing my revisions of this chapter shortly after the appearance of the film "The Crying Game," it is particularly difficult not to read the epic's presentation of this false beauty's complicated gender as commentary on the construction of heterosexual desire.

39. Roche suggests that the motley crew present at the tournament defuses the occasion's danger for virtue (1964: 163–67), but the harm done to women during this tournament and at similar events is not eradicated later. Female characters and the representations of women are affected negatively, no matter what the eventual outcome. Nevertheless, critics frequently minimize or ignore

the significance of the girdle's misuse. For example, see Freeman (234) and Hankins (146–47). Kathleen Williams, with rather charming optimism, suggests that even the rowdy knights at the tournament "if they had known of her [Florimell's] sufferings her knights would, in their burning fury, have ruined towers, cities, and kingdoms" (115).

40. The narrator's lack of comment here warrants notice. Narratorial silences deserve the same attention accorded to narratorial interjections. There is often a fertile space for individual interpretation left between incidents presented in the epic, the knights' responses to them, and any narrative commentary. Additionally, however, the narrator often helps guide the reader toward specific conclusions by falling silent in the midst of stories about women or changing the topic, leaving female characters in peril. Although there is much in this episode to suggest that the poem is raising questions about the values being honored, there are still moments of apparent support for the actions depicted.

41. Given the importance of homosocial relationships among male characters in the poem, it is not surprising that the beauty deemed too beautiful to be Florimell is actually a male spright in drag (III. viii: 8). Since chaste women are considered a scarce commodity among those at the tourney, the Snowy Florimell's refusal of the witch's son's advances (III. viii: 10) may further indicate that the most desirable woman—and the only woman likely to be chaste—is actually male.

42. Britomart's discernment here is not necessarily, however, the product of "chastity's" ability to distinguish between "true" and "false" female beauty. The "strange"-ness and "wonderment" of the scene result at least in part from the multiply-doubled genders being presented here. Britomart=female/male. Snowy Florimell=male spright/deceptive female beauty. Each character figures exceptional indeterminacy; hence, Britomart's refusal to be dazzled could represent her dismissal of the marvelous, not simply of false beauty.

43. Nelson discusses Ficino's considerations of this problematic relationship between beauty and "vulgar love" (75–84).

44. Roche finds the laughter less charged, arguing that "the seeds of eventual victory are evident in the unity of the good characters" (1964: 167). Future reconciliation is not sufficient, however, to make this frivolity benign.

45. Roche, however, contends that "Satyrane represents the best elements of nature and society combined, the honesty and integrity of the naturally unified man" (1964: 157), and claims that "his one shortcoming is his inability to rise above the natural reason" (1964: 163). Hankins sees Satyrane as "the irascible faculty within the soul" (146).

46. For an account of "the squire group," see Reed Way Dasenbrock. Most Spenserians spend little time on the Squire of Dames. Freeman, for example, focuses upon the Chaucerian elements of the tale, then concludes that "In the narrative of the Squire of Dames, the Book reaches a witty social situation focussed upon human beings" (211).

47. Freeman also notes the male bonding evident throughout the scene

(232). She concentrates upon Aristotelian doctrines of friendship, however, not upon the implications for women.

48. Finucci offers a discussion of smutty jokes, Freud, and Castiglione (75–103), which I discovered after completing this section.

49. Some critics attempt to justify the humor presented during these disturbing sequences. Benson, for instance, describes the "benign comic tone" of the fisherman's attempted rape of Florimell, maintaining that although Florimell is terrified, "[the experience] is delightful for the reader" (1986: 89). Without denying the humorous tone, I suggest that the evident humor presented in this scene should unsettle rather than amuse the reader.

50. Critics often try to neutralize such problematic portrayals of women by emphasizing the poem's allegory. Marie H. Buncombe, for instance, contends that "if one substitutes 'gentlewoman' for 'gentleman,' then Florimell serves the author's stated intention as the allegorical symbol of a combination of the Neo-Platonic concept of love and the Christian virtues of the chaste, unmarried noblewoman at court" (165). Such arguments remain unconvincing, since the literal action of the poem regularly provides a concurrent message which contradicts and supplements the allegorical message. Remarking that "Spenser's sensitivity toward his female characters has been noted many times by his critics" (175), Buncombe asserts that "nowhere is this trait more evident than in his treatment of the various women, especially Florimell, in *The Faerie Queene*" (175). However appealing it might be to fashion a feminist Spenser, the text generally suggests that he was an Elizabethan male holding fairly typical attitudes toward women.

51. Readers interested in the Roche/Hieatt debate regarding relations between Amoret and Scudamour will find Roche's early summary of the interchange useful (1964: 129). In addition, see his update in "Britomart at Busyrane's Again, or Brideshead Revisited."

52. Critics frequently fail to find fault with Scudamour; indeed, he often receives praise for his exploits, while Amoret is often criticized. For examples of both responses to Scudamour, see Freeman (244–45); Tonkin (1972: 199, 216); Hankins (159–60); Roche (1964: 128–33); Kathleen Williams (105–107); Greenblatt (175); and Davies (47–48). Silberman offers an intriguing reading based in part on Renaissance concepts of mathematics (1994: chapter 4).

53. As Berger notes, Amoret is punished both for what she does and what she does not do. He observes that "as an object of hate and revenge, it is irrelevant to the logic of the masque that she [Amoret] refuses love *because* she will not deny Scudamour; the refusal itself is all that matters" (1988: 185). Similarly, her consent or resistance to either man does not affect her treatment in the two scenes.

There is also an unsettling parallel between this incident and what Vickers finds in Shakespeare's "Rape of Lucrece." It would be easy to substitute "Amoret" for "Lucrece" in Vickers's analysis: "Although virtue is always at issue, it soon competes with beauty for the distinction of being Lucrece's most appreciable quality" (1985: 102).

54. We get most of our information about Amoret from the narrator or from other characters; therefore, it is generally very difficult to discern what "feelings" we might associate accurately with the maiden. Silberman argues that Amoret offers "both female resistance and female compliance in one figure" and thus "introduces genuine uncertainty into Petrarchan discourse" (1994: chapter 3). Since Amoret rarely speaks, her purported motivations remain ambiguous.

55. Spenser critics often find more fault with Amoret than with Scudamour. Tonkin, for example, sees in Amoret a fear of sex (1972: 108) and agrees with critics who interpret "this episode as symbolic of Amoret's growth into womanhood" (1972: 216). He maintains that any "regret" associated with the incident results from "the trials and dangers and misgivings" associated with "attaining womanhood" (1972: 304). Tonkin also alludes to "Spenser's skill in female psychology" (1972: 223), but such readings seem to emanate more from sympathy with Spenser than from any "realistic" female psychology portrayed in Amoret. Joanne Craig, in contrast, notes that "Amoret is either tormented or terrified; but how could either be otherwise in a culture that regularly represents men as hunters and women as prey?" (16). See Wofford (1992: 471 n. 22) for a brief overview of the variant critical responses to this interpretive problem.

56. Venus's initial abduction of Amoret also receives surprisingly little critical attention. Alpers suggests that readers may find the incident painful because of our humanity, but contends that Chrysogone "is a model of human fertility . . . not a model of human experience" (391). Similarly, Krier stresses the "romance wonder" of the scene (141) and Miller frames it as a "fable" (235). Other critics ignore the possible implications of the incident completely, just as no one expresses discomfort with the abuse inflicted upon Sir Satyrane's mother. Such justifications on the basis of allegory do not take sufficient account of the cultural coding underlying such allegory, however. Even though Chrysogone and other similar characters are not "real" women, their fates exemplify typical attitudes expressed throughout the epic and in other texts in the period.

57. The Venus depicted here also reflects the ambivalence about women and their sexuality which regularly receives attention in the poem. Though she is called "the Queene of beautie" (IV. x: 29. 6) and repeatedly referred to as "she," her gender is classified as uncertain: "she hath both kinds in one, / Both male and female, both vnder one name" (IV. x: 41. 6–7). Such ambiguity heightens the questions raised about female sexuality in the epic, particularly in this episode, where a woman's fight for continued virginity is overcome with the aid of this "female" deity.

58. Here, I clearly disagree with Pamela Benson, who announces that Scudamour "is right, of course" (1992: 280) when he proclaims that Amoret's virginity should not be devoted to Venus.

59. As Kathleen Williams observes, "Scudamour is a devotee of the de-

structive Cupid of the world, who changes his aspect so completely in the simple and happy Garden of Adonis" (106).

60. As I noted in "'The Prison of Sad Paine': Amoret in 1590" (MLA 1992), Amoret's story is a compilation of others' tales; she does not tell it herself.

61. Craig claims that connections between the two men are accidental. Noting that there is a "slight hint in Book III that Scudamour and Busyrane have something in common," she maintains that "Surely the establishment of such a connection cannot have been Spenser's conscious design in either book" (19). We can never know what Spenser intended, of course, but it seems unlikely that the connections are coincidental or ideologically neutral.

62. "Bad" men are not averse to rape, as Florimell discovers during her encounter with the fisherman (III. viii), but they often first try to woo their captives, as the same maid learns with both Proteus and the witch's son (III. vii). This propensity for wooing often makes it more difficult to distinguish "good" knights from these miscreants. Arthur's libidinal excitement, for instance, suggests little experience with similar restraint. Since the women he pursues tend to escape, it is impossible to know how he would respond to their unimpeded presence.

63. See chapter 1 for a discussion of Florimell's continuous flight, even from Arthur. Many critics find fault with the virgin's perpetual motion. Benson, for example, contends that "[Florimell's] fear has overwhelmed her reason; she is not making a rational defense of her chastity—as she shows when she runs not only from every trembling leaf, but also from Arthur" (1986: 85). Kathleen Williams makes a similar point, asserting that "If [Florimell] is always in flight because always pursued, it is equally true that she is always pursued because always in flight, bringing about the chase it is her intention to escape" (113). Such arguments remain unconvincing, although blaming the women may help protect the image of a sympathetic Spenser.

64. As Hamilton notes, the loss of the girdle may suggest the loss of Florimell's maidenhead, but this is never made explicit (1977: 370).

65. For a discussion of the "trace," see Jacques Derrida (1976: 46–48).

66. As the tales of Amoret and Florimell suggest, the existence of a male suitor tends not to provide the same protection. In fact, Amoret's abduction from her wedding implies that a woman may not be perceived as "claimed property" until after consummation.

67. Although not noted in the text, Sansloy's initial reluctance to rape Una and the similar hesitation exhibited by the brigand with Pastorella in Book Six may result from a recognition of the substantial benefits to be gained by winning rather than raping a woman with known or suspected familial links to another man.

68. I am grateful to Susan Snyder for drawing my attention to this connection.

69. Vickers (1985) discusses the dangers women face when they become

the object of such narratives. In addition, see Gayle Rubin for an analysis of Lévi-Strauss's conflation of the exchange of women and the exchange of words (201).

4. 'Fayre of face . . . though meane her lot'

1. As the OED indicates, "worth" and "valor" are closely linked linguistically.

2. In the essays cited, Vickers demonstrates how readily female beauty and value become conflated in Petrarchism and the blazon tradition. Vickers's essays brilliantly illuminate the Petrarchan tradition from a feminist perspective.

3. For an account of contemporary England's changing economic conditions and the accompanying effect upon issues concerned with status and gender relations, see Susan Cahn. For a discussion of related topics, see Susan Dwyer Amussen.

4. Although "metahuman" is not an ideal term, it expresses an important distinction of rank. Characters such as Belphoebe, who operate in the human realm despite their celestial origins, cannot be accommodated by ordinary determinations of social or economic status. "Metahuman" indicates that such figures interact on a human plane, but also evince deific characteristics. Unlike goddesses such as Venus and Diana, who affect, but do not usually directly involve themselves with humanity, Belphoebe fulfills a special place in the human/deific realms illustrated.

5. In her series of articles, Vickers offers important readings of the interplay of gender and Petrarchism in literature from this period. See also Susan Frye, who rightly notes that Spenser was "just as likely to point out Petrarchism's defects as he was to use such codes in all seriousness" (135).

6. Wofford briefly discusses the relationship between marriage and social role in Elizabethan England and Spenser's epic (1992: 318–20). For useful discussions on related topics, see Ann Rosalind Jones and Peter Stallybrass; Louis Adrian Montrose (1977); and Richard C. McCoy.

7. Some Spenserians also believe that Mirabella's punishment is appropriate, despite its violence. Tonkin, for example, states that "Mirabella is only getting what she deserves" (1972: 90); similarly, Freeman announces that Mirabella "is heartless and deserves her punishment" (320). See also Hankins (182–83). Ian Sowton offers a very brief remark in opposition to such readings, reading Mirabella's representation as an instance of female desires coming into conflict with the social order (414).

8. DeNeef explains Mirabella's presence in the poem as an exemplar of the need for Christian charity (137). Ironically, little critical charity is displayed toward Mirabella.

9. Kathleen Williams focuses upon Mirabella's obligation to honor the "grace" which her beauty bestows upon her (212).

10. Notably, the obligation to recognize the relative worthiness of potential suitors works both ways for women. Æmylia ends up the captive of Lust

because she ignores her status as "Daughter vnto a Lord of high degree" (IV. vii: 15. 2) and falls in love with "a Squire of low degree" (IV. vii: 15. 7).

11. Tonkin also raises the question of parody in his discussion of the Petrarchan elements of Mirabella's story (1972: 93).

12. The narrative appropriation of Mirabella's voice here accords with Vickers's observation that "bodies fetishized by a poetic voice logically do not have a voice of their own; the world of making words, of making texts, is not theirs" (1981: 277). Vickers's writings on Petrarchism help bring new light on this entire episode.

13. For a lengthy account of the case against Mirabella see Tonkin (1972: 87–100).

14. Kenneth Gross refers to "Mirabella, the vengeful, self-isolated lady of Petrarchan poetry, surrounded by dead or dying suitors" (213). This view echoes that expressed by numerous critics. Kane also reads Mirabella from this perspective, but does not find her chastened at the end, claiming instead that "Mirabella even through self-humiliation is still trying to control her destiny" (196).

15. Anne Shaver also notes this parallel. Professor Shaver and I were initially working out our theories about Mirabella at the same time and I am very appreciative of her insights. Our views about this episode are often complementary.

16. See chapter 3 for a discussion of the humor in this episode.

17. Notably, although the poem flirts with the possibility of female/female relationships with regard to Britomart, this further threat is not considered during Mirabella's story. Nonetheless, as Rubin notes, in this system, the only thing worse than a woman refusing a marriage partner is two women refusing in order to choose each other (183).

18. Still, Anderson argues that Arthur's "effort to rescue Mirabella is a vital step in the development of a central theme, the relationship of fortune to human responsibility and to human freedom" (174).

19. See, for example, Hankins (186) and Kathleen Williams (219–20).

20. Critics often seem unconcerned by this aspect of the episode. Heale, for instance, states that the Mirabella segment is designed "to lighten the mood" (163).

21. Vickers argues that "Rape is the price Lucrece pays for having been described" (1985: 102). Here, it appears that rape is the price Mirabella pays for having been honored. See Vickers (1986) for a discussion of the relationship between female representation and violence against women.

22. See the following for discussions of related issues: Paula J. Caplan; Michelle A. Massé; Jan Cohn; Sandra Lee Bartky; Kaja Silverman (1984); Gini Graham Scott; Jessica Benjamin; Susan Griffin (1981); Marianne Hester; Linda Williams; Robin Ruth Linden et al.; Maria Marcus; and Elaine Scarry.

23. O, as Michelle A. Massé notes, undergoes repeated beatings and sadistic sexual acts as contrition for "having acted willfully or believing that she had a self" (125). O's body is kept continually available for beating or sexual

violation from a variety of men. Her central lesson, Massé asserts, is to learn that "anyone with a penis has the right to the uninhibited exercise of authority, while anyone with a vagina is receptive, passive, and unquestioningly obedient" (123). In Susan Griffin's terms, O "gradually unlearns all the knowledge of her body" (219) through an extended period of deprivation and abuse. In each of these arguments, "Mirabella" could easily substitute for "O."

24. Given the problematic nature of female speech in texts from this period, it is particularly noteworthy that Mirabella is presented as so exceptionally articulate in this scene.

25. Although Mirabella's blessings have the strongest obligations attached, the narrative emphasizes that all three women have received "gifts" of beauty and chastity. See VI. viii: 1. 5; III. vi: 2. 5–6; and VI. x: 25. 4–5.

26. The issues of social standing presented through Pastorella's story are often ignored in favor of a focus upon the elements of romance present. See Freeman (322–28), for example. Kathleen Williams emphasizes the mythic aspects of Pastorella's tale (189), while claiming that the story indicates "the importance of natural gifts, not of social rank" (196).

27. In contrast, Lucifera is subjected to scorn because "she did thinke her peareless worth to pas / That parentage" (I. iv: 11. 3–4). Apparently, being the offspring of Pluto and Proserpina does not allow such reevaluations of one's "worth."

28. Anderson, among others, underscores Pastorella's "rebirth" upon her return to the status of her birth (181).

29. Hankins argues, however, that Calidore's behavior "resulted from a genuine respect for the feelings of others" (192).

30. See Tonkin (1972: 290–91) for a discussion of the differences he perceives between Mirabella and Pastorella. In general, my treatment of these characters is at odds with his.

31. Krier usefully discusses the complexities of Belphoebe's presentation, noting that "the language used to describe Belphoebe's bodily life raises conflicts between Ovidian virginity and erotic Petrarchan rose, and conflicts between Queen Elizabeth's politic self-presentation as adored mistress and as virgin" (164). Berry perceives Elizabeth's role in similar terms: "it was as the unattainable *object* of masculine desire that Elizabeth was represented, in an assimilation of Petrarchan and Neoplatonic attitudes" (62), while Montrose emphasizes the Petrarchan displacement of Elizabeth onto Belphoebe (1986b: 325–28). Berry also highlights the "ambiguous" portrayal of Belphoebe in the poem (93).

32. Miller, however, considers the complexities of the episode, including its historical and allegorical elements, in his discussion of the scene as a site of castration (224–35). Berger, on the other hand, argues that in this episode "the critique is directed only at the Petrarchan ideology, not the characters. Their ardors and innocence are merely amusing" (1989: 232). He does grant that "one could argue that [Spenser's] treatment of Belphoebe is only superficially benign

and actually insidious" (1989: 234), but then retreats from that reading. Although we often disagree in our interpretations of this episode, I find Berger's Petrarchan reading of it quite useful (1989: 226–35).

33. It often seems, in fact, that Belphoebe "forgives" Timias before Spenserians do.

34. See Elizabeth J. Bellamy (1991) for a fascinating psychoanalytic reading of the relationship between Timias and Belphoebe.

35. Nonetheless, Silberman describes this episode as "bittersweet comedy" (1994: chapter 1).

36. Still, Freeman claims that the story of Timias and Belphoebe "demonstrates the need for forgiveness in the conduct of personal relationships" (236). See Kathleen Williams for a discussion of Belphoebe which allows some criticism of the interaction with Timias, but which still finds her "admirable and delightful" (100 ff). Hankins maintains that "the love of Belphoebe and Timias represents the association of virginity with grace and honour" (149), while DeNeef suggests that "Belphoebe is, in effect, too good" (116).

37. Tonkin finds Timias culpable, however, because of the squire's "old impetuous ways" (1972: 76).

38. The historical parallel of Timias and Belphoebe with Raleigh and Elizabeth has figured prominently in readings of the episode. For accounts of this analogy, see Roche (1964: 142–43); Krier (200–204); Bieman (200–206); Berry (160–61); Wofford (1992: 320–23); and James P. Bednarz. As many critics have suggested, Belphoebe's position as an image of Elizabeth is an important aspect of her characterization, and the hunter's sovereign aspect contributes to the pattern I am describing, even though I am most interested in her deific origins.

39. This response fits with Berger's argument that "Whatever power Belphoebe has over men is a power ceded to her by the men who have power over her in the sense that she is their fantasy" (1989: 233).

40. Critics often uphold Belphoebe's "special" nature and subsequent immunity. See, for example, Richard Berleth.

41. Alpers considers Belphoebe "the exemplar of heroic virginity" (387), but he notes that her position makes her "an unsatisfactory image of human erotic desire" (390). Nohrnberg discusses her as a figure of both Venus and Diana (453–54).

42. Many critics also see Belphoebe in a special light. Paglia, for instance, views her as "a work of sculpture embedded in the text" (179).

43. Roche terms her "the Neoplatonic heavenly Venus" (1964: 137) and describes her birth as "a Platonic Idea, the embodiment of which on earth acts as example of its special virtue to man" (1964: 107).

44. As noted in chapter 3, "darts" frequently assail female characters. Timias's similar affliction marks one of the many instances of his story which parallel the treatment of women. Belphoebe's stature prompts these cases of gender inversion.

45. Spenserians frequently also find Timias blameworthy here. Hamilton,

for example, states that "with Amoret wounded, Lust overcomes Timias" (1961: 162). This encounter is often presented as justification for what follows in the narrative.

46. Clearly, the story of Timias and Belphoebe is as multi-faceted as any of Spenser's tales. By emphasizing the undercurrents of erotic domination, I do not mean to discount the historical or allegorical aspects of the episode. In fact, it is quite possible that the text provides a sadomasochistic presentation of Timias and Belphoebe as commentary on the eroticized, yet strongly hierarchical relationship between Elizabeth and Ralegh.

47. For example, see Gini Graham Scott (212–15). Scott restricts "sex" in this context to "intercourse, fellatio, cunnilingus, or hand manipulation to orgasm" (212). She argues that while participants may find sadomasochistic activities sexually arousing, such directly sexual contact is not necessarily present.

48. Krier, who reads Belphoebe as a Petrarchan figure (164–65), interprets Timias's submission as the "Petrarchan lover's way of sustaining the elevation of the loved woman" (207). Kane also interprets Belphoebe from a Petrarchan standpoint (120–21).

49. Paglia notes a "recurrent motif of sadomasochistic sexual bondage" in the epic (189). I agree with her assessment and find this episode a prime example.

50. Roche claims that the "concept of honor" explicates her reaction here (1964: 144–47).

51. This scene tends not to trouble critics. Krier, for instance, maintains that "we find her attractive because of such poise," which she reads as "a kind of obliviousness, a virginal immersion in her own being, which is challenged when she finds Timias" (163).

52. For extended discussions of these conventions, see Leonard Forster; Paul N. Siegel; Jerome Mazzaro; David Kalstone; William Keach; John Smith Harrison; Ernst Cassirer; Lu Emily Pearson; Richard B. Young; Hallett Smith; Daniel Javitch; G. M. Matthews; Carol Thomas Neely (1978); and Arthur F. Marroti.

5. 'Like an Enraged Cow'

1. As Simon Shepherd reminds us, in the Renaissance "Masculinity and femininity of mind or soul were thought capable of existing in people irrespective of their biological definition" (1981: 35). Lillian Robinson maintains that Spenser "knows what he means by the concept [femininity]" (316), but he offers no such certainty to the reader.

2. For other readings of Britomart's multiple sexualities, see Shirley F. Staton (1987); Gary Grund; Claudia M. Champagne; and Lesley W. Brill. Nohrnberg refers to the heroine as "her own man" (444). In a brief essay, John Z. Zhang reads Britomart in terms drawn from Lacan's "mirror stage," claiming that "Britomart would never be Spenser's symbol of chastity or ideal

love in the book if she did not have such qualities as valor, courage, and power that enable her to bring about noble deeds" (2). Zhang's argument that Britomart's "masculinity is achieved through a narcissistic process in which she identifies herself with her lover, Arthegall" (2), is interesting, but needs more elaboration than such a short format provides. Mary R. Bowman explains Britomart's relinquishing of authority as part of Spenser's critique of Elizabeth.

3. Teresa de Lauretis also discusses gender as a "representation subject to social and ideological coding" (1987: 96). De Lauretis elaborates upon the implications of this representation for both character and spectator.

4. Josephine Waters Bennett suggests that textual references to Britomart as "he" in Book III result from the poet's inattention (151). Perhaps the poet occasionally confuses Britomart's gender as much as the knight herself does.

5. Ian Sowton argues that when Britomart turns her rule over to Artegall, her action illustrates "the Spenserian text's androcentric ideology at work, still dominant and reasserting itself" (413). He further notes succinctly that "it is a pretty complex series of gender representations that can suggest such a variety of subject positions for Britomart yet finally bring her to where, at the moment of her greatest political power, she authorizes her own (and other women's) subjection" (413).

6. Here, I disagree with many astute readers of this poem. Berger, for example, terms Britomart "the Ideal Woman," and suggests that chastity "is fundamental not merely because it is essential, but also because it is rudimentary" (1988: 94). The poem often asserts such ideas, but they are simultaneously though generally silently undermined.

7. Suzuki offers a compelling alternate reading, which interprets Britomart as filling "a heroic role usually reserved for men" which "thus claims to portray woman for the first time as a subject from her own perspective and not as an object from a male perspective" (153). As attractive as this Britomart may be, it is hard to sustain a view of the heroine's subjectivity through the portrayal of her ignorance. See also Montrose (1986a) for an important discussion of the complexities of "chastity" as represented through Elizabeth and contemporary literature.

8. Bellamy discusses Britomart's "noncomplicity with the laws of gender signification" (1992: 202) from a psychoanalytical perspective (1992: 202–11). Similarly, in her analysis of Ariosto, she comments upon Bradamante's "combative androgyny" (1992: 112).

9. The "womanish man" and "mannish woman" controversy which raged around the time of the poem's composition heightens the interest around the question of Britomart's male attire. For useful accounts of this dispute, see Linda Woodbridge, and Katherine Usher Henderson and Barbara F. McManus.

10. Quilligan offers an insightful discussion of the gendered readership of Book Three (1983: 185–99).

11. Ironically, readers have often found Britomart the "most real" of the characters in the poem. In 1896, Mary E. Litchfield labeled Britomart "the most charming of Spenser's heroines" with the strongest "human interest" of any

character in the poem (iii), while more recently, Stevie Davies claimed that "Britomart is distinctly felt by most readers to exist as a person rather than a walking concept" (58).

12. Numerous critics have discussed the complex representations of Elizabeth I's gender. See, for example, Philippa Berry and Leah S. Marcus (51–105). Suzanne Hull provides a useful account of the typical books available for women during this period, writings which often dictate behavior at odds with Britomart's representation.

13. For discussions of Elizabeth's figurations in The Legend of Chastity and in related texts see Susanne Woods (1985); Bruce Thomas Boehrer; Louis Adrian Montrose (1980; 1986a and 1986b); Gary Grund; Elizabeth Jane Bellamy (1987); Philippa Berry (134–65); Pamela Benson (1985); Benjamin Lockerd (64–67); and Susan Frye (chapter 3).

14. As Maureen Quilligan pointed out to me, the story of Nereana in Lady Mary Wroth's *Urania* offers an example of the scorn a woman receives when she travels undisguised to seek her beloved.

15. Of course, Spenser's literary predecessor Ariosto presented mobile female knights; nevertheless, noting the contrast between Britomart's behavior and the activities recommended for women in Elizabethan England helps us recognize the tensions and contradictions apparent in the martial maid's presentation.

16. See, for example, Philip Stubbes, *A Christal Glass for Christian Women* (1592), sig. A2v-A3; Henry Smith, *A Preparative to Marriage* (1591), sig. F6; Thomas Salter, *A Mirror Mete for all Mothers, Matrones, and Maidens* (1579), 85; and Thomas Gataker, *The Marriage Duties* (1620), sig. D2v and sig. E2v.

17. As Graham Hough notes: "If it were not for the title of the book and the expectations established by the two earlier ones, one would hardly have suspected Britomart of being the champion of chastity" (1962: 168).

18. There are numerous studies which, in contrast to mine, read Britomart's potrayal in the context of Italian Romance or Neoplatonism. See, for example, Stephen A. Barney; Josephine Waters Bennett; Graham Hough; and Elizabeth Bieman.

19. Marina Warner describes "female allegory" and discusses the difficulties of tracing in society either benefits or detriments to women resulting from "the common relation of abstract nouns of virtue to feminine gender in Indo-European languages" (1985: xxi). My understanding of Britomart raises similar questions; i.e., just because Britomart is technically female and chastity is presented as a female virtue, this does not mean that there is necessarily an unassailable link between either Britomart or chastity and the category "woman."

20. Bieman focuses on the Petrarchan elements of Britomart's lovesickness (see especially 157 and 160). Recognition of such aspects does not, however, exonerate Britomart from charges of intellectual dullness.

21. This scene is predominantly comic, as several critics note. See, for example, Paul J. Alpers (379). Nevertheless, such recognition does not preclude

acknowledgment of the ideological implications of the incident. Nohrnberg reads the episode as romance (434–35).

22. Carolynn Van Dyke asserts that Britomart displays "coolness" when she encounters Malecasta and that she does not assist Florimell because the warrior knight is also female (1985: 263). Britomart's shifting gender makes these scenes much more complex than this reading suggests. Berger notes that Britomart's decision not to follow Florimell raises many interpretive questions for the reader (1989: 213–14). He also discusses the importance of Ovidian and Ariostan allusions in this incident (1989: 214–17).

23. Wofford rightly reminds us that characters in *The Faerie Queene* repeatedly miss the lessons available to readers (1992: 220–22). Such blindness is an *essential* quality of Britomart's virtue, however, while this kind of ignorance works very differently for the male titular heroes. The Red Crosse Knight, for example, often misreads, makes mistakes, and needs Una's assistance, but "holiness" is not *dependent* upon his ignorance. In contrast, the easy slippage which occurs between the carnal sense of "to know" and its other meanings underscores the centrality of "un-knowing" to the virtue of chastity. Too much knowledge of any kind would bring Britomart's virtue into question, while only particular types of knowledge would compromise the male knights. The Red Crosse Knight's lack of insight leads to his seduction; a similar lapse is not available to the Knight of Chastity.

24. Many of the treatises on chastity implicitly support this presumption. Thomas Salter's *A Mirror Mete for all Mothers, Matrones, and Maidens* (1579); John Larke's *The Boke of Wisdome, otherwise called the Flower of Vertue* (1565); Philip Stubbes's *A Christal Glass for Christian Women* (1592); and Thomas Bentley's *The Monument of Matrones: Containing the Seven Lampes of Virginitie* (1582) represent just a few of the texts which draw many of their examples of virtuous women either from the dead or the fictive.

25. In a compelling argument, Paglia terms Britomart's relationship with Glauce "proto-lesbian" (181) and focuses on the "lesbian suggestiveness" of her encounter with Malecasta (182). Silberman, in contrast, argues that Spenser suppresses the "undercurrent of lesbianism" found in *Orlando Furioso* (25. 4–70), his source for this episode (1994: chapter 1). Dorothy Stephens offers a brilliant and complex consideration of this issue in the unpublished essay cited (1993). It seems likely that the poem uses such scenes to introduce the dangers perceived as accompanying this kind of erotic encounter, but the narrative never confronts these issues directly. This silencing accords with Gayle Rubin's assertion that traditionally "the social organization of sex rests upon gender, obligatory heterosexuality, and the constraint of female sexuality" (179). Although Rubin is not discussing early modern England, her remarks describe the sexual landscape of *The Faerie Queene*.

26. Stephens argues convincingly that Britomart here "feigns only in order to flirt," thereby raising "the dialogue to a higher erotic pitch" (1991: 531).

27. The confusing complexity of Britomart's interactions with Amoret

suggests that Robinson is being overly optimistic in her claim that "the reader knows just what connections to make" (288) when Britomart, unlike Scudamour, is able to gain access to Busyrane's fortress.

28. As Silberman notes, "there is little doubt about what need would induce someone to visit the bushes in the middle of the night" (1994: chapter 7). More traditonal critical responses to this scene may illustrate Gail Paster's contention that "sex [is] easier to discuss than excretion" (23). This brief moment in *The Faerie Queene* can be illuminated by Paster's discussion of "Leaky Vessels: The Incontinent Women of City Comedy" (23–63).

29. Numerous critics discuss Amoret's perils as externalizations of her inner fears. For example, Helen Cheney Gilde agrees with and summarizes this trend in Spenserian criticism (1971: 63–74). Gilde also accuses Amoret of "frigidity" (68). For related arguments, see Berger (1988: 184); Horton (107–10); Robinson (317); and Kane (102).

30. Britomart's apparent gender confusion also remains central in these encounters.

31. As noted, Florimell is often blamed for attracting male aggression or for fleeing needlessly. See, for example, Kane (118); Horton (147); Alpers (395); and Isabel G. MacCaffrey (297). Robinson goes so far as to claim that Florimell's fear of sexual assault "deranges her mind" (318).

32. As I argue in chapter 1, the women in the epic generally presented for virtuous emulation are those situated iconically within houses or castles. In notable contrast, even though Britomart stays at home until puberty, she was raised "to tossen speare and shield" (III. ii: 6. 4).

33. For a psychological reading of this episode, see Lockerd, especially 67–69. Berger also examines the events in Book Three from a psychological perspective (1988: 89–117).

34. Krier claims that women form enviable intimate "communities" in the epic (146–47). The groupings she describes, however, tend to include women we meet only briefly—and generally, from a male point of view, as objects of sexual desire. The women we see repeatedly in the epic remain alone or with a single confederate, most often a servant.

35. Richard Lanham offers a notable exception to this pattern. Lanham argues that "the relationship of the martial Britomart to the diseased-with-love one is logical on a narrative level only if we think of both as a *man*" (436). He goes on to complicate Britomart's ostensible relationship with both married and virginal chastity.

36. Michael Leslie also notes the problematic nature of her quest which "involves not only chastity but an aggressiveness and combativeness inappropriate to the traditional role of a wife" (83).

37. Thomas Salter, for example, warns parents to be careful with their daughters' learning (71–81). He is particularly worried that they might be too early "made to understande the evelles immynente too humaine life" (15). The anonymous *A Discourse of the Married and Single Life* (1621) finds both female literacy and illiteracy dangerous (sig. D3-D3v). As we know, education for

women was controversial during this period. Consequently, Britomart's "chaste" ignorance may represent one proposed solution to the dilemma.

38. Davies also distinguishes Britomart from Viola, but maintains that "Spenser's transvestite woman is not deliberately feigning a role as alien to her true nature as, say, Shakespeare's Viola" (59). Though I demur from claiming to know Britomart's "true nature," I believe the main difference here is found instead in the degree of self-consciousness the two female characters display. Viola recognizes her doubly-gendered role, while Britomart keeps forgetting hers.

39. For a Jungian reading of Britomart's armor, see Lockerd (145–47). Leslie argues that only "the removal of her helmet allows her sexual feelings expression" (70).

40. As Quilligan notes, Britomart at times also "seems to be downright mean-spirited, unheroically vengeful, and not at all the romantic exemplar of chastity" (1979: 81).

41. In contrast, Tonkin believes that Amoret is the "naive reader of this elaborate pageant," while Britomart displays "greater sophistication" in her interpretation (1989: 131). Wofford attributes Britomart's incomprehension to "her distance from the conventions being displayed around her" (1992: 308).

42. Joanne Craig argues that the house of Busyrane "may be obscure because the suggestion, implicit in the story of Amoret and Scudamour, that sexual dominance and constraint are inevitable is too distressing to confront directly" (16).

43. Berger argues that the masque "reveals itself to Britomart as having been created within the mind" (1988: 181). Whatever may be revealed, however, is presented to the reader, not the protagonist. Lanham takes this suggestion a step further, arguing that "In the House of Busyrane, Britomart really has no character at all, male or female, and another name could be substituted for hers without embarrassing the narrative" (439).

44. Since I received Professor Frye's page proofs just as I was completing my revisions, I was unable to take her reading fully into account here, but note that in her third chapter, she provides a fascinating analysis of the sexual issues represented in this episode.

45. As I discussed in chapter 4, Belphoebe's non-human status places her into another category.

46. Freeman speculates that Palladine "is probably an early version of Britomart" (211). Although not speaking specifically about Palladine, Bennett also suggests that many of the textual questions in Book Three result from Spenser's revisions (142–53).

47. There are many interpretations of this controversial episode. See, for example, Lloyd A. Wright (1974) and several articles in A. C. Hamilton (1972), including N. S. Brooke, R. Nevo, and James Carscallen.

48. Suzuki offers a Virgilian and Ovidian reading of Britomart's encounters with Malbecco which presents the heroine in a very different light (159–73).

49. In this essay, Berger discusses "boundary figures" (such as Amoret

and Belphoebe), whom he defines as "temporary externalizations, or personifications, whose fixed exemplary purposes are directly responsible for the dramatic and psychological dilemmas they cause and suffer." (1988: 169). He "suspect[s] that Spenser's final aim, at least in one stage of his planning, was to discard not only the decadent forms—Malbecco, Paridell, Hellenore, et al.—but also the boundary figures, and perhaps even the antique Britons" (1988: 171).

50. For an insightful reading of the Britomart-Radigund episode, see Suzuki (177–95). See also Woods (1985; 1991) and Elizabeth D. Harvey (32–46). Professor Harvey's book became available as I was completing my revisions, so I was unable to use it extensively.

51. Here, I disagree with Bieman's contention that "Clearly the female sexuality of the combatants is indicated as far less tainted by sin than is the warlike fury which they are visiting upon each other" (159).

52. For a discussion of this phenomenon in modern times, see Susan Faludi (229–67).

Works Cited

Primary Sources

Barrough, Philip. *The Method of Physick.* 1590.

Becon, Thomas. *The Demaundes of Holy Scriptures.* 1577.

Bruel, Walter [Gualterus Bruele]. *Praxis Medicinae or the Physician's Practice.* 1639.

Buoni, Tommaso. *Problems of Beautie.* 1606.

Burton, Robert. *The Anatomy of Melancholy.* Ed. Floyd Dell and Paul Jordan-Smith. New York: Tudor, 1927.

Castiglione, Baldesar. *The Book of the Courtier.* Trans. George Bull. Baltimore: Penguin, 1967.

Celestine or the Tragick-Comedie of Calisto and Melibea. Trans. James Mabbe. Ed. Guadalupe Martinez Lacalle. London: Temesis, 1972.

Daneau, Lambert. *A Dialogue of Witches.* 1575.

A Discourse of the Married and Single Life. 1621.

Gataker, Thomas. *Marriage Duties.* 1620.

Gifford, George. *A Discourse of the Subtill Practice of Devils.* 1587.

Guillemeau, James. *Child-birth or the Happy Deliverie of Women.* 1612. Amsterdam: Theatrvm Orbus Terrarvm, 1972.

Hawkins, Henry. *The Devout Hart.* 1634. Ed. John Horden. English Emblem Book Series 11. Scolar, 1975.

———. *Parthenia Sacra.* 1633. Ed. John Horden. English Emblem Book Series 10. Scolar, 1975.

Herman, Archbishop of Wied. *A brefe and playne declaratyon of the dewty of maried folkes.* 1533[?].

Holland, Henry. *A Treatise Against Witchcraft.* 1590.

Jones, John. *The Arte and Science of Preseruing Bodie and Soule in al Health, Wisdome, and Catholicke Religion.* 1579.

Larke, John. *The Boke of Wisdome, otherwise called the Flower of Vertue.* 1565.

Macrobius. *Commentary on the Dream of Scipio.* Trans. William Harris Stahl. New York: Columbia University Press, 1952.

Malleus Maleficarum. Ed. Montague Summers. New York: Benjamin Blom, 1928. Reprint, 1970.

Niccholes, Alexander. *A Discourse of Marriage and Wiving.* 1615.

Peacham, Henry. *Minerva Britanna.* 1612. Ed. John Horden. English Emblem Book Series 5. Scolar, 1969.

Perkins, William. *A Discovrse of the Damned Art of Witchcraft.* 1610.

Pico della Mirandola, Giovanni. *Commentary on a Poem of Platonic Love.* Trans. Douglas Carmichael. Lanham: University Press of America, 1986.

Sadler, John. *The Sicke Womans Private Looking-Glasse.* 1636. Norwood: Walter Johnson, 1977.

Salter, Thomas. *A Mirror Mete for all Mothers, Matrones, and Maidens.* 1579. Ed. Janis Butler Holm. New York: Garland, 1987.

Scot, Reginald. *The Discoverie of Witchcraft.* 1584. Ed. Montague Summer. London: John Rodker, 1930.

Smith, Henry. *A Preparative to Marriage.* 1591.

Spenser, Edmund. *The Faerie Queene.* Ed. A. C. Hamilton. London: Longmans, 1977.

Stubbes, Philip. *A Christal Glass for Christian Women.* 1592.

Tasso, Hercule. *Of Mariage and Wiuing.* 1599.

Topsell, Edward. *History of Four-footed Beasts, Serpents and Insects.* London, 1607.

Vicary, Thomas. *The Profitable Treatise of the Anatomy of Mans Body.* 1577. English Experience Series 629. Amsterdam: Da Capo, 1973.

Webster, John. *The Displaying of Supposed Witchcraft.* 1677.

Weir, Johannes. *Witches, Devils, and Doctors in the Renaissance: Johann Weyer, 'De praestigiis daemonum'. Medieval & Renaissance Texts & Studies* 73. Ed. George Mora. Trans. John Shea. Binghamton, NY: 1991.

Whateley, William. *A Bride-Bush or a Wedding Sermon.* 1617.

———. *A Care-Cloth: or a Treatise of the Cumbers and Troubles of Marriage.* 1624. Norwood: Walter Johnson, 1976.

Whetstone, George. *An Heptameron of Civill Discourses.* 1582.

Whitney, Geoffrey. *A Choice of Emblems.* 1586. Ed. John Horden. English Emblem Book Series 3. Menston: Scolar, 1969.

Willoby, Henry. *Willoby his Avisa: or the True Picture of a modest maid and of a chaste and Constant Wife.* 1594.

Wroth, Mary. *The Countesse of Mountgomeries Urania,* 1621.

Secondary Sources

Adelman, Janet. *Suffocating Mothers: Fantasies of Maternal Origin in Shakespeare's Plays, Hamlet to The Tempest.* New York: Routledge, 1992.

Adler, Laure. *La Vie quotidienne dans les maisons closes, 1830–1930.* Paris: Hachette, 1990.

Alpers, Paul J. *The Poetry of The Faerie Queene.* Princeton: Princeton University Press, 1967.

Amussen, Susan Dwyer. *An Ordered Society: Gender and Class in Early Modern England.* New York: Blackwell, 1988.

Anderson, Judith H. *The Growth of a Personal Voice*. New Haven: Yale University Press, 1976.

Aptekar, Jane. *Icons of Justice: Iconography and Thematic Imagery in The Faerie Queene*. New York: Columbia University Press, 1969.

Apter, Emily. *Feminizing the Fetish: Psychoanalysis and Narrative Obsession in Turn-of-the-Century France*. Ithaca: Cornell University Press, 1991.

Barney, Stephen A. *Allegories of History, Allegories of Love*. Hamden, CT: Shoe String, 1979.

Barthes, Roland. "Striptease." *Literary Theories in Praxis*. Ed. Shirley F. Staton. Philadelphia: University of Pennsylvania Press, 1987. 179–81.

Bartky, Sandra Lee. *Femininity and Domination: Studies in the Phenomenology of Oppression*. New York: Routledge, 1990.

Bednarz, James P. "Ralegh in Spenser's Historical Allegory." *Spenser Studies* 4 (1984): 49–70.

Bellamy Elizabeth J. "Em(body)ments of Power: Versions of the Body in Pain in Spenser." *Literature, Interpretation, Theory* 2.4 (1991) 303–21.

———. *Translations of Power: Narcissism and the Unconscious in Epic History*. Ithaca: Cornell University Press, 1992.

———. "The Vocative and the Vocational: The Unreadability of Elizabeth in *The Faerie Queene*." *English Literary History* 54.1 (1987): 1–30.

Belsey, Catherine, and Jane Moore, eds. *The Feminist Reader: Essays in the Gender and the Politics of Literary Criticism*. New York: Blackwell, 1989.

Belt, Debra. "Hostile Audiences and the Courteous Reader in *The Faerie Queene*, Book VI." *Spenser Studies* 9 (1991): 107–36.

Benjamin, Jessica. *The Bonds of Love: Psychoanalysis, Feminism, and the Problem of Domination*. New York: Pantheon, 1988.

Bennett, Josephine Waters. *The Evolution of The Faerie Queene*. Chicago: University of Chicago Press, 1942.

Benson, Pamela J. "Florimell at Sea: The Action of Grace in *Faerie Queene*, Book III." *Spenser Studies* 6 (1986): 83–94.

———. *The Invention of the Renaissance Woman: The Challenge of Female Independence in the Literature and Thought of Italy and England*. University Park: The Pennsylvania State University Press, 1992.

———. "Rule Virginia: Protestant Theories of Female Regiment." *English Literary Renaissance* 15.3 (1985): 277–92.

Berger, Harry, Jr. " 'Kidnapped Romance': Discourse in *The Faerie Queene*." *Unfolded Tales: Essays on Renaissance Romance*. Ed. George M. Logan and Gordon Teskey. Ithaca: Cornell University Press, 1989. 208–56.

———. "Narrative as Rhetoric in *The Faerie Queene*." *English Literary Renaissance* 21.1 (1991): 3–49.

———. *Revisionary Play: Studies in the Spenserian Dynamics*. Berkeley: University of California Press, 1988.

Berleth, Richard. "Heaven's Favorable and Free: Belphoebe's Nativity in *The Faerie Queene*." *English Literary History* 40 (1973): 479–500.

Berry, Philippa. *Of Chastity and Power: Elizabethan Literature and the Unmarried Queen.* New York: Routledge, 1989.

Berthoff, Warner. *Literature and the Continuances of Virtue.* Princeton: Princeton University Press, 1986.

Bhattacherje, Mohinimohan. *Platonic Ideas in Spenser.* London, 1935. Reprint. Westport, CT: Greenwood, 1970.

Bieman, Elizabeth. *Plato Baptized: Towards the Interpretation of Spenser's Mimetic Fictions.* Toronto: University of Toronto Press, 1988.

Boehrer, Bruce Thomas. " 'Careless Modestee': Chastity as Politics in Book 3 of *The Faerie Queene*." *English Literary History* 55.3 (1988): 555–73.

Boose, Lynda E. "The Family in Shakespeare Studies; or—Studies in the Family of Shakespeareans; or—The Politics of Politics." *Renaissance Quarterly* 40.1 (1987): 707–42.

Bowman, Mary R. " 'she there as princess rained': Spenser's Figure of Elizabeth." *Renaissance Quarterly* 43.3 (1990): 509–28.

Brill, Lesley W. "Chastity as the Ideal Sexuality in the Third Book of *The Faerie Queene*." *Studies in English Literature* 11.1 (1971): 15–26.

Brooke, N. S. "C. S. Lewis and Spenser: Nature, Art, and the Bower of Bliss." *Essential Articles for the Study of Edmund Spenser.* Ed. A. C. Hamilton. Hamden, CT: Shoe String, 1972. 13–28.

Bugge, John. *Virginitas: An Essay in the History of a Medieval Ideal.* The Hague: Martinus Nijhoff, 1975.

Buncombe, Marie H. "Faire Florimell as Faire Game: The Virtuous, Unmarried Woman in *The Faerie Queene* and *The Courtier*." *CLA Journal* 28.2 (1984): 164–75.

Burchmore, David W. "The Medieval Sources of Spenser's Occasion Episode." *Spenser Studies* 2 (1981): 93–120.

———. "Triamond, Agape, and the Fates: Neoplatonic Cosmology in Spenser's Legend of Friendship." *Spenser Studies* 5 (1985): 45–64.

Butler, Judith. *Gender Trouble: Feminism and the Subversion of Identity.* New York: Routledge, 1990.

Cahn, Susan. *Industry of Devotion: The Transformation of Women's Work in England, 1500–1660.* New York: Columbia University Press, 1987.

Caplan, Paula J. *The Myth of Women's Masochism.* New York: Dutton, 1985.

Carscallen, James. "The Goodly Frame of Temperance: The Metaphor of Cosmos in *The Faerie Queene*, Book II." *Essential Articles for the Study of Edmund Spenser.* Ed. A. C. Hamilton. Hamden, CT: Shoe String, 1972. 347–65.

Cassirer, Ernst. *The Platonic Renaissance in England.* Trans. James P. Pettegrove. London: Thomas Nelson, 1953.

Cavanagh, Sheila T. " 'Beauties Chace': Arthur and Women in *The Faerie*

Queene." *The Passing of Arthur: Loss and Renewal in the Arthurian Tradition.* Ed. Christopher Baswell and William Sharpe. New York: Garland, 1988. 207–20.

———. "Nightmares of Desire: Evil Women in *The Faerie Queene.*" *Studies in Philology,* forthcoming, 1994.

———. " 'The Prison of Sad Paine': Amoret in 1590." Unpublished paper, MLA 1992.

Champagne, Claudia M. "Wounding the Body of Woman in Book III of *The Faerie Queene.*" *Literature, Interpretation, Theory* 2.2 (1990) 95–115.

Cheney, Patrick. " 'And Doubted Her to Deeme an Earthly Wight': Male Neoplatonic 'Magic' and the Problem of Female Identity in Spenser's Allegory of the Two Florimells." *Studies in Philology* 86.3 (1989): 310–40.

———. "Spenser's Completion of *The Squire's Tale*: love, magic, and heroic action in the Legend of Cambell and Triamond." *The Journal of Medieval and Renaissance Studies* 15.2 (1985): 135–54.

Cixous, Hélène, and Catherine Clément. *The Newly Born Woman.* Trans. Betsy Wing. Theory and History of Literature Series 24. Minneapolis: University of Minnesota Press, 1986.

Coggins, Gordon. *Queint Device: A Guide to Sexuality in Edmund Spenser.* Huntsville, Ontario: Distek, 1989.

Cohn, Jan. *Romance and the Erotics of Property: Mass-Market Fiction for Women.* Durham: Duke University Press, 1988.

Corbin, Alain. "La Relation intime ou les plaisirs de l'échange." *Histoire de la vie privée* 4. Ed. Michelle Perrot. Paris: Seuil, 1987.

Craig, Joanne. " 'As if but one soule in them all did dwell': Busyrane, Scudamour, and Radigund." *English Studies in Canada* 14.1 (1988): 15–25.

Cropper, Elizabeth. "The Beauty of Woman: Problems in the Rhetoric of Renaissance Portraiture." *Rewriting the Renaissance: The Discourses of Sexual Difference in Early Modern Europe.* Ed. Margaret W. Ferguson, Maureen Quilligan, and Nancy J. Vickers. Chicago: University of Chicago Press, 1986. 175–90.

Dasenbrook, Reed Way. "Escaping the Squires' Double Bind in Books III and IV of *The Faerie Queene.*" *Studies in English Literature* 26.1 (1986): 25–45.

Davies, Stevie. *The Feminine Reclaimed: The Idea of Woman in Spenser, Shakespeare, and Milton.* Lexington: University Press of Kentucky, 1986.

de Lauretis, Teresa. *Technologies of Gender: Essays on Theory, Film, and Fiction.* Bloomington: Indiana University Press, 1987.

DeNeef, A. Leigh. *Spenser and the Motives of Metaphor.* Durham: Duke University Press, 1982.

Derrida, Jacques. *Dissemination*. Trans. Barbara Johnson. Chicago: University of Chicago Press, 1981.

———. *Of Grammatology*. Trans. Gayatri Spivak. Baltimore: Johns Hopkins University Press, 1976.

———. *Spurs: Nietzche's Styles*. Trans. Barbara Harlow. Chicago: University of Chicago Press, 1978.

Doane, Mary Ann. *Femmes Fatales: Feminism, Film Theory, Psychoanalysis*. New York: Routledge, 1991.

Eccles, Audrey. *Obstetrics and Gynaecology in Tudor and Stuart England*. Kent: Kent State University Press, 1982.

Ellrodt, Robert. *Neoplatonism in the Poetry of Spenser*. Geneva: Librairie E. Droz, 1960.

Faludi, Susan. *Backlash: The Undeclared War Against American Women*. New York: Crown, 1991.

Finucci, Valeria. *The Lady Vanishes: Subjectivity and Representation in Castiglione and Ariosto*. Stanford: Stanford University Press, 1992.

Flax, Jane. *Thinking Fragments: Psychoanalysis, Feminism, and Postmodernism in the Contemporary West*. Berkeley: University of California Press, 1990.

Fletcher, Angus. *Allegory: The Theory of a Symbolic Mode*. Ithaca: Cornell University Press, 1964.

———. *The Prophetic Moment: An Essay on Spenser*. Chicago: University of Chicago Press, 1971.

Forster, Leonard. *The Icy Fire: Five Studies in European Petrarchism*. Cambridge: Cambridge University Press, 1969.

Fowler, Alastair. *Triumphal Forms: Structural Patterns in Elizabethan Poetry*. Cambridge: Cambridge University Press, 1970.

Freeman, Rosemary. *The Faerie Queene: A Companion for Readers*. London: Chatto & Windus, 1970.

Freud, Sigmund. "Femininity." *New Introductory Lectures on Psychoanalysis*. Trans. James Strachey, New York: Norton, 1965. 112–35.

———. *The Interpretation of Dreams*. Trans. James Strachey. New York: Avon, 1965.

———. *Jokes and Their Relation to the Unconscious*. Ed. James Strachey. New York: Norton, 1963.

———. "The Taboo of Virginity." *Freud on War, Sex, and Neurosis*. New York: Arts & Science, 1947. 221–44.

Frye, Susan. *Elizabeth I: The Competition for Representation*. New York: Oxford University Press, 1993.

Fuss, Diana. *Essentially Speaking: Feminism, Nature and Difference*. New York: Routledge, 1989.

Gallop, David, ed. and trans. *Aristotle on Sleep and Dreams*. Lewiston, NY: Broadview, 1990.

Gamman, Lorraine, and Margaret Marshment, eds. *The Female Gaze: Women as Viewers of Popular Culture.* Seattle: Real Comet Press, 1989.

Garber, Marjorie. *Vested Interests: Cross-Dressing and Cultural Anxiety.* New York: Routledge, 1992.

Gilde, Helen Cheney. "'The Sweet Lodge of Love and Deare Delight': The Problem of Amoret." *Philological Quarterly* 50.1 (1971): 63–74.

Gohlke, Madelon. "Embattled Allegory: Book II of *The Faerie Queene*." *English Literary Renaissance* 8.2 (1978): 123–40.

Goldberg, Jonathan. *Endlesse Worke: Spenser and the Structures of Discourse.* Baltimore: Johns Hopkins University Press, 1981.

———. "The Mothers in Book III of *The Faerie Queene*." *Texas Studies in Literature and Language* 17.1 (1975): 5–26.

Greenblatt, Stephen. *Renaissance Self-Fashioning from More to Shakespeare.* Chicago: University of Chicago Press, 1980.

Griffin, Susan. *Pornography and Silence: Culture's Revenge against Nature.* New York: Harper & Row, 1981.

Gross, Kenneth. *Spenserian Poetics: Idolatry, Iconoclasm, and Magic.* Ithaca: Cornell University Press, 1985.

Grund, Gary. "The Queen's Two Bodies: Britomart and Spenser's *Faerie Queene*, Book III." *Cahiers Élisabéthains* 20 (1981): 11–33.

Gubar, Susan, and Joan Hoff, eds. *For Adult Users Only: The Dilemma of Violent Pornography.* Bloomington: Indiana University Press, 1989.

Gutierrez, Nancy. "Witchcraft and Adultery in *Othello*: Strategies of Subversion." *Playing with Gender: A Renaissance Pursuit.* Ed. Jean R. Brink et al. Urbana: University of Illinois Press, 1991. 3–19.

Hamilton, A. C., ed. *Essential Articles for the Study of Edmund Spenser.* Hamden, CT: Archon, 1972.

———. *The Structure of Allegory in The Faerie Queene.* Oxford: Clarendon, 1961.

Hankins, John Erskine. *Source and Meaning in Spenser's Allegory.* Oxford: Clarendon, 1971.

Harrison, John Smith. *Platonism in English Poetry of the Sixteenth and Seventeenth Centuries.* New York: Columbia University Press. 1915.

Harvey, Elizabeth D. *Ventriloquized Voices: Feminist Theory and English Renaissance Texts.* New York: Routledge, 1992.

Hawkins, Harriet. *Poetic Freedom and Poetic Truth: Chaucer, Shakespeare, Marlowe, Milton.* Oxford: Clarendon, 1976.

Heale, Elizabeth. *The Faerie Queene: A Reader's Guide,* Cambridge: Cambridge University Press, 1987.

Henderson, Katherine Usher, and Barbara F. McManus. *Half Humankind: Contexts and Texts of the Controversy about Women in England, 1540–1640.* Urbana: University of Illinois Press, 1985.

Henkel, Arthur, and Albrecht Schone, eds. *Emblemata: Handbuch zur Sinn-*

bildkunst des XVI und XVII Jahrhunderts. Stuttgart: J. B. Metzler, 1967.

Herrmann, Claudine. *The Tongue Snatchers.* Trans. Nancy Kline. Lincoln: University of Nebraska Press, 1989.

Hester, Marianne. *Lewd Women and Wicked Witches: A Study of the Dynamics of Male Domination.* New York: Routledge, 1992.

Horton, Ronald Arthur. *The Unity of The Faerie Queene.* Athens: University of Georgia Press, 1978.

Hough, Graham. *A Preface to The Faerie Queene.* London: Duckworth, 1962.

Howard, Jean E., and Marion F. O'Connor, eds. *Shakespeare Reproduced: The Text in History and Ideology.* New York: Methuen, 1987.

Hufford, David. *The Terror that Comes in the Night: An Experience-Centered Study of Supernatural Assault Traditions.* Publications of the American Folklore Society 7. Philadelphia: University of Pennsylvania Press, 1982.

Hughes, Merritt Y. *Virgil and Spenser.* University of California Publications in English 2.3 (263–418). Berkeley: University of California Press, 1929.

Hull, Suzanne W. *Chaste, Silent & Obedient:English Books for Women, 1475–1640.* San Marino: Huntington Library, 1982.

Hume, Anthea. *Edmund Spenser: Protestant Poet.* Cambridge: Cambridge University Press, 1984.

Inton-Peterson, Margaret, and Beverly Roskos-Ewoldson. "Mitigating the Effects of Violent Pornography." *For Adult Users Only: The Dilemma of Violent Pornography.* Ed. Susan Gubar and Joan Hoff. Bloomington: Indiana University Press, 1989. 218–39.

Irigaray, Luce. *Speculum of the Other Woman.* Trans. Gillian Gill. Ithaca: Cornell University Press, 1985.

———. *This Sex Which Is Not One.* Trans. Catherine Porter. Ithaca: Cornell University Press, 1985.

Javitch, Daniel. *Poetry and Courtliness in Renaissance England.* Princeton: Princeton University Press, 1978.

Jones, Ann Rosalind. *The Currency of Eros: Women's Love Lyric in Europe, 1540–1620.* Bloomington: Indiana University Press, 1990.

Jones, Ann Rosalind, and Peter Stallybrass. "The Politics of *Astrophil and Stella.*" *Studies in English Literature* 24.1 (1984): 53–68.

Jones, Ernest. *On the Nightmare.* New York: Liveright, 1951.

Jordan, Constance. *Renaissance Feminism: Literary Texts and Political Models.* Ithaca: Cornell University Press, 1990.

Joyce, James. *Ulysses.* New York: Random House, 1946.

Kalstone, David. *Sidney's Poetry: Contexts and Interpretations.* Cambridge, MA: Harvard University Press, 1965.

Kane, Sean. *Spenser's Moral Allegory.* Toronto: University of Toronto Press, 1989.

Keach, William. *Elizabethan Erotic Narratives.* New Brunswick: Rutgers University Press, 1976.

Kennedy, Judith M., and James A. Reither, eds. *A Theatre for Spenserians.* Toronto: University of Toronto Press, 1973.

Kinney, Arthur F. *Humanist Poetics: Thought, Rhetoric, and Fiction in Sixteenth-Century England.* Amherst: University of Massachusetts Press, 1986.

Kinney, Clare Regan. *Strategies of Poetic Narrative: Chaucer, Spenser, Milton, Eliot.* Cambridge: Cambridge University Press, 1992.

Krier, Theresa M. *Gazing on Secret Sights: Spenser, Classical Imitation and the Decorums of Vision.* Ithaca: Cornell University Press, 1990.

Lacan, Jacques. *Feminine Sexuality.* Trans. Jacqueline Rose. Ed. Juliet Mitchell and Jacqueline Rose. New York: Norton, 1985.

Lanham, Richard. "The Literal Britomart." *Modern Language Quarterly* 28.4 (1967): 426–45.

Lees, Clare A. "Gender and Exchange in *Piers Plowman.*" *Class and Gender in Early Literature: Intersections.* Ed. Britton J. Harwood and Gillian R. Overing. Bloomington: Indiana University Press, 1994.

Lenz, Carolyn Ruth Swift, et al., eds. *The Woman's Part: Feminist Criticism of Shakespeare.* Urbana: University of Illinois Press, 1980.

Leslie, Michael. *Spenser's 'Fierce Warres and Faithfull Loves': Martial and Chivalric Symbolism in The Faerie Queene.* Totowa: Barnes and Noble, 1983.

Lévi-Strauss, Claude. *The Elementary Structures of Kinship.* Trans. James Harle Bell et al. Boston: Beacon, 1969.

Lewis, C. S. *The Allegory of Love.* Oxford: Clarendon, 1936.

———. "Nature and Grace in *The Faerie Queene.*" *Essential Articles for the Study of Edmund Spenser.* Ed. A. C. Hamilton. Hamden, CT: Archon, 1972. 3–12.

———. *Studies in Medieval and Renaissance Literature.* Cambridge: Cambridge University Press, 1966.

Linden, Robin Ruth, et al., eds. *Against Sadomasochism: A Radical Feminist Analysis.* East Palo Alto: Frog in the Well, 1982.

Litchfield, Mary E. *Spenser's Britomart.* Boston: Athenæum, 1896.

Lockerd, Benjamin G., Jr. *The Sacred Marriage: Psychic Integration in The Faerie Queene.* Lewisburg: Bucknell University Press, 1987.

MacCaffrey, Isabel. *Spenser's Allegory: An Anatomy of Imagination.* Princeton: Princeton University Press, 1976.

Maclean, Ian. *The Renaissance Notion of Woman.* New York: Cambridge University Press, 1980.

Manning, John, and Alastair Fowler. "The Iconography of Spenser's Occasion." *Journal of the Warburg and Courtauld Institutes* 39 (1976): 263–66.

Marcus, Leah S. *Puzzling Shakespeare: Local Reading and Its Discontents.* Berkeley: University of California Press, 1988.

Marcus, Maria. *A Taste for Pain: On Masochism and Female Sexuality.* Trans. Joan Tate. New York: St. Martin's, 1981.

Marotti, Arthur F. " 'Love is not Love': Elizabethan Sonnet Sequences and the Social Order." *English Literary History* 49. 2 (1982): 396–428.

Martines, Lauro. *Society and History in English Renaissance Verse.* New York: Blackwell, 1985.

Massé, Michelle A. *In the Name of Love: Women, Masochism, and the Gothic.* Ithaca: Cornell University Press, 1992.

Matthews, G. M. "Sex and the Sonnet." *Essays in Criticism* 2 (1952): 119–37.

Mazzaro, Jerome. *Transformations in the Renaissance English Lyric.* Ithaca: Cornell University Press, 1970.

McCabe, Richard A. "The Masks of Duessa: Spenser, Mary Queen of Scots, and James VI." *English Literary Renaissance* 17.2 (1987): 224–43.

McCoy, Richard C. *Sir Philip Sidney: Rebellion in Arcadia.* New Brunswick: Rutgers University Press, 1979.

McLuskie, Kathleen. *Renaissance Dramatists.* Atlantic Highlands: Humanities Press, 1989.

Miller, David Lee. *The Poem's Two Bodies: The Poetics of the 1590 Faerie Queene.* Princeton: Princeton University Press, 1988.

Moi, Toril. "Feminist, Female, Feminine." *The Feminist Reader.* Ed. Catherine Belsey and Jane Moore. New York: Blackwell, 1989. 117–32.

Montrose, Louis Adrian. *"A Midsummer Night's Dream* and the Shaping Fantasies of Elizabethan Culture: Gender, Power, Form." *Rewriting the Renaissance.* Ed. Margaret W. Ferguson, Maureen Quilligan, and Nancy J. Vickers. Chicago: University of Chicago Press, 1986. 65–87.

———. "Celebration and Insinuation: Sir Philip Sidney and the Motives of Elizabethan Courtship." *Renaissance Drama* n.s. 8 (1977): 3–35.

———. " 'Eliza, Queene of Shepheardes,' and the Pastoral of Power." *English Literary Renaissance* 10.2 (1980): 153–82.

———. "The Elizabethan Subject and the Spenserian Text." *Literary Theory/Renaissance Texts.* Ed. Patricia Parker and David Quint. Baltimore: The Johns Hopkins University Press: 1986. 303–41.

Morris, Meaghan. *The Pirate's Fiancée: Feminism, Reading, Postmodernism.* New York: Verso, 1988.

Mulvey, Laura. *Visual and Other Pleasures.* Bloomington: Indiana University Press, 1989.

Neely, Carol Thomas. "Constructing the Subject: Feminist Practices and the New Renaissance Discourses." *English Literary Renaissance* 18.1 (1988): 5–18.

———. "The Structure of English Renaissance Sonnet Sequences." *English Literary History* 45 (1978): 359–89.

Nelson, John Charles. *Renaissance Theory of Love: The Context of Giordano's Eroici furor.* New York: Columbia University Press, 1958.

Nevo, R. "Spenser's 'Bower of Bliss' and a Key Metaphor from Renaissance Poetic." *Essential Articles for the Study of Edmund Spenser.* Ed. A. C. Hamilton. Hamden, CT: Shoe String, 1972. 29–39.

Newman, Karen. *Fashioning Femininity and English Renaissance Drama.* Chicago: University of Chicago Press, 1991.

Nohrnberg, James. *The Analogy of The Faerie Queene.* Princeton: Princeton University Press, 1976.

Okerlund, Arlene N. "Spenser's Wanton Maidens: Reader Psychology and the Bower of Bliss." *PMLA* 88.1 (1973): 62–68.

Paglia, Camille. *Sexual Personae: Art and Decadence from Nefertiti to Emily Dickinson.* New York: Vintage, 1991.

Parker, Patricia. *Literary Fat Ladies: Rhetoric, Gender, Property.* New York: Methuen, 1987.

Paster, Gail Kern. *The Body Embarrassed: Drama and the Disciplines of Shame in Early Modern England.* Ithaca: Cornell University Press, 1993.

Pearson, Lu Emily. *Elizabethan Love Conventions.* Berkeley: University of California Press, 1933.

Pollock, Zailig. "Concupiscence and Intemperance in the Bower of Bliss." *Studies in English Literature.* 20.1 (1980): 43–58.

Quilligan, Maureen. "The Comedy of Female Authority in *The Faerie Queene.*" *English Literary Renaissance.* 17.2 (1987): 156–72.

———. *The Language of Allegory: Defining the Genre.* Ithaca: Cornell University Press, 1979.

———. *Milton's Spenser: The Politics of Reading.* Ithaca: Cornell University Press, 1983.

Réage, Pauline. *Story of O.* Trans. Sabine d'Estree. New York: Ballantine, 1973.

Riley, Denise. *Am I That Name? Feminism and the Category of 'Women' in History.* Minneapolis: University of Minnesota Press, 1988.

Robinson, Lillian S. *Monstrous Regiment: The Lady Knight in Sixteenth-Century Epic.* New York: Garland, 1985.

Roche, Thomas P., Jr. "Britomart at Busyrane's Again, or Brideshead Revisited." *Spenser at Kalamazoo.* Ed. Francis G. Greco. Clarion: Clarion University Press (1983): 121–42.

———. *The Kindly Flame: A Study of the Third and Fourth Books of Spenser's Faerie Queene.* Princeton: Princeton University Press, 1964.

Rooney, Ellen. *Seductive Reasoning: Pluralism as the Problematic of Contemporary Literary Theory.* Ithaca: Cornell University Press, 1989.

Rose, Mark. *Heroic Love: Studies in Sidney and Spenser.* Cambridge, MA: Harvard University Press, 1968.

Rowe, George E. "Privacy, Vision, and Gender in Spenser's Legend of Courtesy." *Modern Language Quarterly* 50.4 (1989): 309–36.

Rubin, Gayle. "The Traffic in Women: Notes on the 'Political Economy' of Sex." *Toward an Anthropology of Women.* Ed. Rayna R. Reiter. New York: Monthly Review, 1975. 156–210.

Sale, Roger. *Reading Spenser: An Introduction to The Faerie Queene.* New York: Random House, 1968.

Scarry, Elaine. *The Body in Pain: The Making and Unmaking of the World.* New York: Oxford University Press, 1985.

Schroeder, John W. "Spenser's Erotic Drama: The Orgoglio Episode." *English Literary History* 29 (1962): 140–59.

Schwab, Gabriele. "Seduced by Witches: Nathaniel Hawthorne's *The Scarlet Letter* in the Context of New England Witchcraft Fictions." *Seduction and Theory: Readings of Gender, Representation, and Rhetoric.* Ed. Dianne Hunter. Urbana: University of Illinois Press, 1989. 170–91.

Scott, Gini Graham. *Dominant Women Submissive Men: An Exploration in Erotic Dominance and Submission.* New York: Praeger, 1983.

Sedgwick, Eve Kosofsky. *Between Men: English Literature and Male Homosocial Desire.* New York: Columbia University Press, 1985.

Shaver, Anne. "Rereading Mirabella." *Spenser Studies* 9 (1991): 211–26.

Shepherd, Simon. *Amazons and Warrior Women: Varieties of Feminism in Seventeenth-Century Drama.* Brighton, Sussex: Harvester, 1981.

———. *Spenser.* New York: Harvester, 1989.

Showalter, Elaine. "Critical Cross-Dressing; Male Feminists and Woman of the Year." *Men in Feminism.* Ed. Alice Jardine and Paul Smith. New York: Methuen, 1987. 116–33.

Shulman, Sandra. *Nightmare.* New York: Macmillan, 1979.

Siegel, Paul N. "The Petrarchan Sonneteers and Neo-Platonic Love." *Studies in Philology* 42.1 (1945): 164–82.

Silberman, Lauren. "The Hermaphrodite and the Metamorphosis of Spenserian Allegory." *English Literary Renaissance* 17.2 (1987): 207–23.

———. "Singing Unsung Heroines: Androgynous Discourse in Book 3 of *The Faerie Queene*." *Rewriting the Renaissance.* Ed. Margaret W. Ferguson, Maureen Quilligan, and Nancy J. Vickers. Chicago: University of Chicago Press, 1986. 259–72.

———. *Transforming Desire: Erotic Knowledge in Books Three and Four of The Faerie Queene.* Berkeley: University of California Press, forthcoming 1994.

Silverman, Kaja. *The Acoustic Mirror: The Female Voice in Psychoanalysis and Cinema.* Bloomington: Indiana University Press, 1988.

———. "*Histoire d'O*: The Construction of a Female Subject." *Pleasure and Danger: Exploring Female Sexuality.* Ed. Carole S. Vance. Boston: Routledge and Kegan Paul, 1984. 320–49.

Smith, Hallett. *Elizabethan Poetry: A Study in Conventions, Meaning, and Expression.* Cambridge, MA: Harvard University Press, 1952.

Soper, Kate. *Troubled Pleasures: Writings on Politics, Gender, and Hedonism.* New York: Verso, 1990.

Sowton, Ian. "Toward a Male Feminist Reading of Spenser's *Faerie Queene.*" *English Studies in Canada* 15.4 (1989): 398–416.

Stambler, Peter D. "The Development of Guyon's Christian Temperance." *English Literary Renaissance* 7.1 (1977): 51–89.

Stanbury, Sarah. "The Virgin's Gaze: Spectacle and Transgression in Middle English Lyrics of the Passion." *PMLA* 106.5 (1991): 1083–94.

Staton, Shirley F. "Reading Spenser's *Faerie Queene*—In a Different Voice." *Ambiguous Realities: Women in the Middle Ages and Renaissance.* Ed. Carole Levin and Jeannie Watson. Detroit: Wayne State University Press, 1987. 145–62.

Stephens, Dorothy. " 'But if ye saw that which no eyes can see': Conditional Erotics in Spenser's Faerie Land." Unpublished paper, International Medieval Studies Congress, 1993.

———. "Into Other Arms: Amoret's Evasion." *English Literary History* 58.8 (1991): 523–44.

Suzuki, Mihoko. *Metamorphoses of Helen: Authority, Difference, and the Epic.* Ithaca: Cornell University Press, 1989.

Tatlock, J. S. P. *The Legendary History of Britain: Geoffrey of Monmouth's Historia Regum Britanniae and Its Early Vernacular Versions.* Berkeley: University of California Press, 1950.

Thelma and Louise. Dir. Ridley Scott. MGM-Pathé Communications, 1991.

Thickstun, Margaret Olofson. *Fictions of the Feminine: Puritan Doctrine and the Representation of Women.* Ithaca: Cornell University Press, 1988.

Tonkin, Humphrey. *The Faerie Queene.* London: Unwin Hyman, 1989.

———. *Spenser's Courteous Pastoral: Book Six of The Faerie Queene.* Oxford: Clarendon, 1972.

Trinh T. Minh-ha. *Woman, Native, Other: Writing Postcoloniality and Feminism.* Bloomington: Indiana University Press, 1989.

Turner, James Grantham. *One Flesh: Paradisal Marriage and Sexual Relations in the Age of Milton.* Oxford: Clarendon, 1987.

Tuve, Rosamund. *Allegorical Imagery: Some Mediaeval Books and Their Posterity.* Princeton: Princeton University Press, 1966.

Van Dyke, Carolynn. *The Fiction of Truth: Structures of Meaning in Narrative and Dramatic Allegory.* Ithaca: Cornell University Press, 1985.

Vickers, Nancy J. " 'The blazon of sweet beauty's best': Shakespeare's *Lucrece.*" *Shakespeare and the Question of Theory.* Ed. Patricia Parker and Geoffrey Hartman. New York: Methuen, 1985. 95–116.

————. "The Body Re-Membered: Petrarchan Lyric and the Strategies of Description." *Mimesis: From Mirror to Method, Augustine to Descartes.* Ed. John D. Lyons and Stephen G. Nichols, Jr. Hanover: University Press of New England, 1982. 100–109.

————. "Diana Described: Scattered Women and Scattered Rhyme." *Critical Inquiry* 8.2 (1981) 265–79.

————. "The Mistress in the Masterpiece." *The Poetics of Gender.* Ed. Nancy K. Miller. New York: Columbia University Press, 1986. 19–42.

————. "This Heraldry in Lucrece's Face." *The Female Body in Western Culture.* Ed. Susan Rubin Suleiman. Cambridge, MA: Harvard University Press, 1986. 209–22.

Warner, Marina. *Alone of All Her Sex.* New York: Knopf, 1976.

————. *Monuments and Maidens: The Allegory of the Female Form.* London: Weidenfeld and Nicolson, 1985.

Waters, Douglas. *Duessa as Theological Satire.* Columbia, MO: University of Missouri Press, 1970.

Weaver, Mary Jo. "Pornography and the Religious Imagination." *For Adult Users Only: The Dilemma of Violent Pornography.* Ed. Susan Gubar and Joan Hoff. Bloomington: Indiana University Press, 1989. 68–86.

Wells, Robin Headlam. *Spenser's Faerie Queene and the Cult of Elizabeth.* Totowa: Barnes and Noble, 1983.

Whigham, Frank. *Ambition and Privilege: The Social Tropes of Elizabethan Courtesy Theory.* Berkeley: University of California Press, 1984.

Williams, Kathleen. *Spenser's World of Glass: A Reading of The Faerie Queene.* Berkeley: University of California Press, 1966.

Williams, Linda. *Hard Core: Power, Pleasure, and the 'Frenzy of the Visible'.* Berkeley: University of California Press, 1989.

Wofford, Susanne Lindgren. *The Choice of Achilles: The Ideology of Figure in the Epic.* Stanford: Stanford University Press, 1992.

————. "Gendering Allegory: Spenser's Bold Reader and the Emergence of Character in *The Faerie Queene* III." *Criticism* 30.1 (1988): 1–22.

Woodbridge, Linda. *Women and the English Renaissance: Literature and the Nature of Womankind, 1540–1620.* Urbana: University of Illinois Press, 1984.

Woodhouse, A. S. P. "Nature and Grace in *The Faerie Queene.*" *Essential Articles for the Study of Edmund Spenser.* Ed. A. C. Hamilton. Hamden, CT: Archon, 1972. 58–83.

Woods, Susanne. "Amazonian Tyranny: Spenser's Radigund and Diachronic Mimesis." *Playing with Gender: A Renaissance Pursuit.* Ed. Jean R. Brink et al. Urbana: University of Illinois Press, 1991. 52–61.

————. "Spenser and the Problem of Women's Rule." *Huntington Library Quarterly* 48.2 (1985): 141–58.

Wright, Lloyd A. "Guyon's Heroism in the Bower of Bliss." *Texas Studies in Literature and Language* 15.4 (1974): 597–604.

Young, Richard B. "English Petrarke: A Study of Sidney's *Astrophel and Stella.*" *Three Studies in the Renaissance: Sidney, Jonson, Milton.* Yale Studies in English 138 (1958). Yale University Press. Reprint. Hamden, Conn.: Archon, 1969.

Zhang, John Z. *The Explicator* 48.1 (1989): 2–3.

Index

SHEILA T. CAVANAGH is Associate Professor of English, associated faculty in Women's Studies, at Emory University. She is currently working on a study of pornographic representation in Early Modern England.